SYRACUSE UNIVERSITY
P9-AOS-731

Central Authority and Regional Autonomy in Indonesia:

A Study in Local Administration, 1950–1960

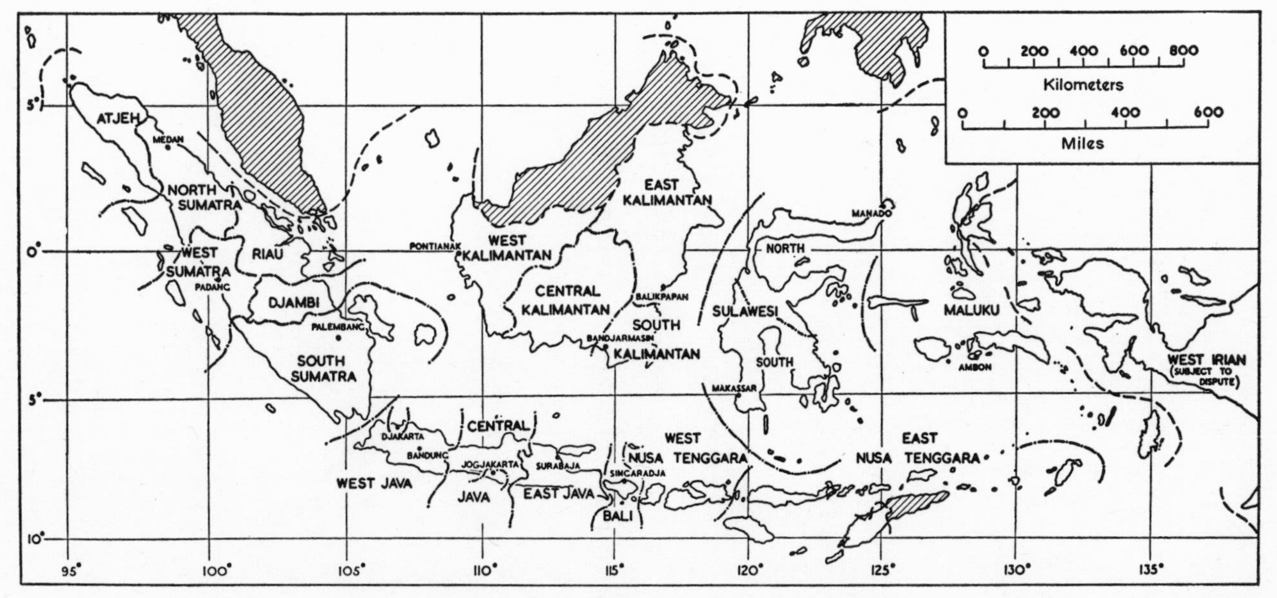

First-level regions of Indonesia, 1960.

Central Authority and Regional Autonomy in Indonesia:

A Study in Local Administration
1950-1960

By J. D. Legge

Professor of History

Monash University, Victoria, Australia

PUBLISHED UNDER THE AUSPICES OF
THE MODERN INDONESIA PROJECT
SOUTHEAST ASIA PROGRAM
CORNELL UNIVERSITY

Cornell University Press

Ithaca, New York

CORNELL UNIVERSITY PRESS

First published 1961
Second printing 1963

This work has been brought to publication with the assistance of a grant from the Ford Foundation.

Library of Congress Catalog Card Number: 61-12043

PRINTED IN THE UNITED STATES OF AMERICA

Preface

ANY state newly emerging from colonial rule is bound to be confronted with difficulties in adjusting its governmental structure to the needs of independence, particularly if it wishes to develop within a democratic framework. One such difficulty is that of fashioning democratic institutions at the local level in a situation, common in agrarian societies, where government has traditionally been the task of a body of professional administrators. Can the firm control from the centre, most recently guaranteed by the colonial power, be reconciled in the new situation with a measure of local self-determination? This problem is complicated where the country in question comprises diverse areas each possessing a developed local consciousness. Indonesia provides an example of both elements in the general problem. Her response to it may in many respects be an individual one, but the problem itself she shares, in some degree at least, both with her Asian neighbors and with the newly emergent states of Africa.

The years 1950–1959 may be regarded as a distinct period in the way in which the problem has been tackled in Indonesia. During that time the Republic attempted, within the framework of a unitary state, to devise a system of local government which would satisfy local self-consciousness and help to counteract tendencies toward regional separatism. By 1959 the bonds of central control, exercised hitherto through the administrative service of the Ministry of Home Affairs, had been severely weakened and machinery had been created for a considerable degree of local autonomy. But in July 1959 the return to the 1945 Constitution foreshadowed a drastic modification of this experiment. Subsequently two presidential edicts (September 1959 and September 1960) reversed the trends of the previous few years, and this study may conveniently end with an account of the initial implementation of these measures.

Some of the material presented in the following pages formed part of an interim study, *Problems of Regional Autonomy in Contemporary Indonesia* (Ithaca, 1957), written just after the basic local government law—Law 1 of 1957—was proclaimed. In that paper observations of local governments were therefore confined to the provisional arrangements which preceded enactment of the new law. Since then the gradual implementation of Law 1, at least until July 1959, enables some judgment to be made about its actual operation. Nevertheless it should be stressed that a study of this whole period must be largely a study of forms rather than of content. Analyses of council constitutions, of the distribution of powers between centre and regions, of financial competence, or of civil service arrangements do not necessarily give an accurate picture of the way institutions actually work—of the finer aspects of decision making or of the way in which paper passes across the desk of a regional head or a regional secretary. But in this case where the machinery of local government has been in process of construction a preoccupation with formal matters is inevitable. This is more especially so since, in Indonesia, the desire to get things into the right conceptual terms appears to be a marked characteristic of all political discussion. It is never enough to devise workable machinery in response to a variety of pressures. The machinery must be an expression of an idea, and there is the feeling that if the concept is right the machinery will be effective. This is perhaps a Javanese rather than an Indonesian characteristic. Involved in the idea of the concept's being right is the Javanese notion of an approximation to a cosmic order on which temporal institutions should be modeled. Certainly something of this extra dimension seems to have marked a good deal of the controversy over local government. It is apparent particularly in the concern with the idea of "dualism"—the combination of central and regional functions in a local government system—and in the efforts to avoid a dualistic system.

In the end the concern with forms does not seem to have provided a sufficient answer to the problem of regionalism. Although the local government plan was in the end applied in as thoroughgoing a fashion as regional pressures had demanded, the centre's acceptance of the principle of fuller autonomy coincided with the peak of regional separatism. In spite of its ultimate failure, however, the experiment is worth examination for the light it may throw on the character of the problem itself.

NOTE ON INDONESIAN PLURALS

The form of Indonesian plurals has presented a slight problem where Indonesian terms have been included in the text. In spoken Indonesian the plural is indicated by repetition of the noun, e.g., *kabupaten-kabupaten.* In the written language this may be indicated either in that form or by the use of a superior figure 2, as in *kabupaten*². Neither of these forms is suitable for an English text, and it has been decided therefore to indicate plurals as in English by the addition of an "s," e.g., *kabupatens.* There is one exception to this rule. In the case of the term *kepala daerah,* where *kepala* is the actual noun, the addition of an "s" would have an odd effect and it has seemed simpler to use the term *kepala daerah* for both singular and plural.

ACKNOWLEDGMENTS

Space does not permit the acknowledgment by name of the many people—officials, members of councils, private individuals—who generously assisted the writer during four visits to Indonesia between 1956 and 1960. The study was made possible by the active co-operation of the Ministry of Home Affairs and by officials of the Ministry in the first-level regions of East Java, Bali, North Sumatra, the former Province of Central Sumatra, the administrative Province of Sulawesi, and the Special Region of Jogjakarta. Particular thanks are due, however, to Mr. Roosdiono, formerly head of the Autonomy and Decentralization Section of the Ministry, for his continuing interest and help, to his successor Mr. Eni Karim, and to Mr. Soemarman, formerly Secretary General of the Ministry. Responsibility for all statements of fact or opinion rests, of course, with the writer alone.

Thanks are due also to the Carnegie Corporation of New York whose financial assistance made possible the initial period of study in Indonesia in 1956, to the Cornell

Modern Indonesia Project and the University of Western Australia for financially providing for three subsequent visits, and in particular to the Director of the Cornell Modern Indonesia Project, Professor George McT. Kahin, for his encouragement throughout the project.

Permission to quote from A. D. A. De Kat Angelino, *Colonial Policy* (1931), has been generously granted by Martinus Nijhoff.

J. D. L.

Melbourne
January 1961

Contents

Maps and Charts

MAPS

CHARTS

Central Authority and Regional Autonomy in Indonesia: A Study in Local Administration, 1950–1960

1

Introduction

TOWARD the end of 1956 the overthrow, by a military commander and a veterans' organization, of the government of the Province of Central Sumatra underlined the precarious character of Indonesian unity. In succeeding months separatist tendencies were to reveal themselves in other areas also and were to culminate in the establishment of the "Revolutionary Government of the Republic of Indonesia" early in 1958. In the eyes of many observers these developments were held to illustrate a chronic weakness of the unitary Republic which had come into existence in 1950—a weakness arising from the diversity of regions and of peoples in Indonesia, from the uneven distribution of population and resources, and from the resultant strength of regional consciousness.

This is too simple an interpretation, and the exact character of regional feeling needs careful analysis before its political significance can be assessed. Yet the explanation is obviously part of the story. Indonesia can hardly be regarded as possessing a natural unity, whether one thinks in ethnic, linguistic, social, or economic terms. It is difficult to define accurately the ethnic groups and subgroups of the country. Well over 100 tribal or subtribal groups have been distinguished in the archipelago,[1] and some of these are imperfectly known. The major societies, however, such as the Atjehnese, the Bataks, the Javanese, the Minangkabau, the Sundanese, stand out clearly, and many of these possess a sense of close unity and a pride in their distinct cultural inheritance which could take precedence over any feeling of national loyalty. To this ingredient of the problem were added others: the concentration of over half the population of the country in the island of Java, the fact that Java was a net consumer while the main export producing areas were to be found in the outer islands, and the traditional interest of the ethnic Javanese in government and administration. Apart from the subtle variations in social organization and outlook from area to area, the sharp differences in the actual physical appearance of the main regions of Indonesia are enough in themselves to suggest the presence of a genuine problem. To observe from the air the closely packed villages of Java and the complex irrigation system on which they depend, the spread of small holders' rubber in the low-lying areas of South Sumatra, the network of estates in the fabulous East Coast Residency of North Sumatra, the broken terrain of West Sumatra, or the pockets of coconut plantation in northern Sulawesi is to see dramatic contrasts of land and economy which underly a variety of regional patriotisms.

The precise force of these factors will need further ex-

[1] See, for example, Raymond Kennedy, *Bibliography of Indonesian Peoples and Cultures* (rev. ed.; New Haven HRAF, 1955), pp. xiii–xx. Unfortunately the list given there does not make clear the principle of classification used, nor does it distinguish clearly between names of social groups and those of individual islands.

amination below, but their presence has for long been recognized in a general way as posing major political difficulties. For the first nine years of postrevolutionary Indonesia's existence the question was considered primarily from an institutional standpoint, and plans for the formation of an adequate local government system have been a serious preoccupation of successive governments. A series of representative and executive councils was constructed as a means of giving to the regions a greater control in the management of their own affairs. The exact form of these councils, the powers they were to exercise, and, in general, the extent to which Indonesia could be regarded as ready for advanced democratic institutions at the local level were matters of considerable difference of opinion. The need to satisfy the regions was countered by that for strong and stable (and therefore, perhaps, authoritarian) government from the centre. But during these years the emphasis was increasingly placed upon fuller powers for local councils as a solution for regional unrest.

This story has to be set against a background of earlier experiment. The outlines of the regional problem were already apparent during the revolutionary period when Holland attempted to mobilize support outside Java for the idea of a federal state to which sovereignty might be transferred rather than to a unitary state dominated by the *de facto* republic which had proclaimed its independence in 1945. The Dutch argued that only a federal constitution would secure justice for the peoples of an independent Indonesia. Only in this way could local consciousness find adequate expression and the more sparsely populated and scattered outer regions be balanced against the weight of metropolitan Java. In July 1946 a conference called at Malino in Celebes and composed of representatives drawn from the areas under Dutch control (a puppet conference in the eyes of the Republic) endorsed the idea of a federal state. The idea was more formally embodied in the ill-fated Linggadjati Agreement of 1946, which provided that "the Netherlands Government and the Government of the Republic shall co-operate in the rapid formation of a sovereign democratic state on a federal basis to be called the United States of Indonesia" (Article II),[2] and it was subsequently applied unilaterally in those parts of the country where the Dutch remained in command. A series of states (*negaras*) was established with a view to their becoming the constituent states of the eventual federation. Indeed, even before the Linggadjati Agreement had been formally initialed, the first of these units—the State of East Indonesia (*Negara Indonesia Timur*) embracing Celebes, the Moluccas, and the Lesser Sundas—had already been created. In the succeeding three years a total of six *negaras* were established (East Sumatra, South Sumatra, Pasundan, Madura, and East Java in addition to East Indonesia) together with a number of "special regions" such as Bangka and West Borneo, which were intended to enjoy a degree of autonomy although they were not of the size or competence to be established as separate states.

In proceeding in this way to the creation of a United States of Indonesia the Dutch claimed that, in their prewar administration of the Indies, they had already laid

[2] Three states were envisaged: the Republic (comprising Java, Sumatra, and Madura), Borneo, and the Great East.

the foundations for a federal solution. One postwar observer has argued that, in spite of the centralized character of Dutch government, "the Indies was slowly but surely evolving into a federal state under the Dutch policy in effect during the twentieth century."[3] This view was based upon the experiments in administrative and political decentralization of 1903 and after. In 1903 an attempt was made to secure a degree of decentralization by the creation of local councils entrusted with some administrative functions. The intention of the reform was twofold. It was intended to modify the extremely high degree of centralization of the existing system, whereby the main burden of government fell upon the shoulders of the central administrative corps, by devolving more duties upon the lower ranks of the service and, secondly, to enlist an element of popular co-operation through the council system.[4] This experiment, however, did not go very far either in content or in geographical extent. Provision was made for the establishment of councils in Residencies or parts of Residencies and in municipalities, and during succeeding years Residency and municipal councils were established in both Java and the Outer Provinces. But except for the municipal councils which were really calculated to serve the interests of Dutch inhabitants of towns, the decentralization was little more than an administrative decentralization, in which the local council was seen more as a means of facilitating the task of the central govern-

[3] A. A. Schiller, *The Formation of Federal Indonesia, 1945–1949* (The Hague, 1955), p. 14.

[4] J. S. Furnivall, *Netherlands India* (Cambridge, Eng., 1939), p. 271.

ment than as a means of enabling a genuine expression of the will of the local population. Council members were at first appointed from among government employees, both European and Indonesian.[5] Effective power lay with the chairmen of councils who were officials of the central government. The council system enabled the chairman to draw on a reservoir of local knowledge and to acquaint himself with local feeling. It was thus designed to offer greater efficiency rather than greater autonomy.

To remedy this defect a new reform measure was enacted in 1922 following the work of a Committee of Revision appointed in 1918 to consider changes in the political organization of the country. The new measure enabled the creation of authorities with a more genuine element of legislative and administrative control of their own affairs. It created a new territorial division—the province—which, together with municipalities and the regencies of Java, was to possess representative institutions. Three provinces were formed in Java—West Java (1925), East Java (1928), and Central Java (1930). The procedure of establishment was gradual. The country was first divided into "governments" under governors, and these regions were converted into provinces by the addition of councils. Outside Java, though Sumatra had also been established as a government, the process was still uncompleted before the outbreak of the Second World War. Similarly, councils were established at the regency level. The majority of council members were elected on a communal basis and by an indirect method, but once again the chairman was an appointed official—the Gov-

[5] A. D. A. De Kat Angelino, *Colonial Policy* (abbr. trans. by G. J. Renier; The Hague, 1931), II, 371.

ernor in the case of a province and the regent in the case of regency councils. These officials also continued to be responsible for the general co-ordination and execution of central government administration in their respective regions, and they thus possessed a double function, an arrangement of which a great deal more will be heard in these pages.

Although these reforms involved a limited devolution of authority from the central government of the Indies to lower regions, there was nothing particularly federal about them. The Governor-General was still ultimately responsible to Holland for the government of the colony, and insofar as there was decentralization it was within the framework of a unitary system par excellence. One could stress equally the close resemblance between the reforms of 1922 and the idea of local autonomy within a unitary state which became the goal of the independent Republic of Indonesia. The comparison covers many points of detail: the organic relation which higher and lower local authorities bear to each other and the method by which the centre surrenders specified powers to the local level are among many important features that are common to both plans.

Thus in developing their proposals for a federal Indonesia after 1945 the Dutch were not building on prewar foundations. They were virtually putting forward a novel proposal toward solving a problem which, though genuine enough, had hardly had occasion to assert itself during the colonial period. Whatever the merits of the proposal it was, from the first, regarded with suspicion by the Republic and was finally to be rejected as being a Dutch-inspired solution. The formal commitment of the Republic to the federal idea in the Linggadjati Agreement did not indicate conversion, and, in any case, the Republic had grounds for objecting to Holland's unilateral action in setting up *negaras* on her own initiative. Such action, it was argued, was a breach of the Linggadjati commitment to "co-operate" in the establishment of a federal state (though, of course, the meaning of the term "co-operate" could well be a matter of dispute). Apart from that technical objection there was reason to believe that the newly created states had not, at least by 1949, developed genuine independence. They remained effectively under the control of Batavia, and even the State of East Indonesia—the first to be created and the most advanced in its political development—was very much under Dutch direction.[6] And there was little rationale for the actual boundaries which were defined. Set up in areas which merely happened to be in Dutch hands, they represented units resulting from the accidents of war rather than from any consideration of the factors which would go to make up a reasonable political entity. It was the belief of the Republic that the whole federal idea represented no more than a tactical move—a policy of divide and rule—by which the Dutch sought to split the nationalist movement and to rally support in the outer islands by capitalizing on the aristocratic fears of Republican leveling and on the general suspicion of Java that existed in the outer islands. In particular it was believed that a federal solution would allow the continuance of Dutch influence after the transfer of sovereignty. For these reasons the idea of a unitary state became an article of nationalist faith. When

[6] G. McT. Kahin, *Nationalism and Revolution in Indonesia* (Ithaca, 1952), pp. 355 ff.

sovereignty was transferred to Indonesia in 1949, it was transferred to a federal state in which the original Republic of Indonesia, much truncated, was merely one member. (See Map 1.) But the unitary ideal remained, and within a few months, partly through the process of merging the individual *negaras* into the Republic and partly through the decision of the federal parliament itself, the federal state was transformed into the unitary "Republic of Indonesia." At the same time the new Republic professed its intention to meet the regional problem by conceding a large measure of local autonomy. The intention was written into the provisional Constitution of 1950:

Article 131

(1) The division of Indonesia into large and small regions possessing the right to control their affairs, and the form of the governmental arrangements of these regions, will be fixed by law having regard to the representative and deliberative system of the state.

(2) To each region will be given the greatest possible degree of autonomy for the management of its own affairs.[7]

Unfortunately for the fulfillment of this promise, the issue was complicated from the beginning by the background which has just been outlined. The federal proposals and the nationalist reaction to them gave a particular slant to all subsequent consideration of the problem of regionalism which was, perhaps, misleading. In the first place, it was a pity that Indonesia's plan for extensive local autonomy within the framework of a unitary state should have been presented simply as the Republic's answer to the Dutch federal proposals. To frame the prob-

[7] Translations from Indonesian documents are the author's.

Map 1. Federal Indonesia. Boundaries shown are of the Republic of the United States of Indonesia on December 27, 1949. (Pasundan is designated here as West Java.) With the exception of Middle Java, whose boundaries date from early March 1949, all approximate the boundaries of fourteen or more months previously. The major exception is West Borneo, whose southwest corner had for a brief period been detached to form the short-lived autonomous area of Kota Waringen. (From *Nationalism and Revolution in Indonesia,* by George McTurnan Kahin; reproduced by permission, Cornell University Press.)

lem merely in terms of alternative constitutional arrangements was to assume that it was essentially capable of solution by these methods—that it was concerned solely or principally with desires for greater local initiative arising from local pride or consciousness of ethnic distinctness or from fears of Javanese predominance. These elements were certainly present, as has been noted, and during the early years of the Republic's existence there was a growing dissatisfaction with the slowness of the central government in preparing and implementing its plans for regional autonomy. At the same time it may be doubted whether the tendency toward regional separatism which displayed itself in dramatic terms at the end of 1956 in Central Sumatra and which found further expression in the following two years can be explained solely in these terms or whether the regional grievances expressed in these movements would be satisfied by the concession of greater powers of local initiative. It will be suggested that at least part of the resistance to Djakarta sprang from sectional dissatisfaction with central government policy in fields (e.g., economic policy and especially currency control) which were clearly of national concern and which, in a federal state, would certainly fall within the province of the federal government rather than that of state governments.

Secondly, to regard decentralization within a unitary state as an alternative to a federal division of powers was to blur distinct elements of the problem. Insofar as alternative constitutional arrangements were really relevant, there still remained the fact that many aspects of local government planning fall quite outside the federal state–unitary state controversy. Either a federal or a decentralized unitary structure must be based upon units of reasonable size and competence which could serve as constituent states or as autonomous provinces. In Indonesia such units must necessarily be artificial. Although there are broad differences from area to area in terms of language, social organization, religious belief, and material culture, it is also the case that, outside the cities and lesser towns, the effective political and social units are based on traditional groupings and are usually very small in area and population, extending barely beyond the village or complex of villages. The gulf between the village on the one hand and Djakarta on the other is a wide one, and the problem of administering these lower units would not be touched either by the creation of a federation or by the surrender of wide powers of autonomy to provinces. In either case it would still be necessary to meet more immediate local needs below the state or the province. It may be argued, indeed, that a major task facing any government in Indonesia today is that of extending its authority to the base of society—of securing "government in general" in a situation where immediate local consciousness is stronger than any feeling of national identity. And local government planning at these lower levels must take account of this fact. It must aim to meet not merely the demands for greater powers made by the politically self-conscious, but also the need for administration, central or local, to reach the larger number of politically unsophisticated.

Briefly (and if for the moment the presence of complicating factors which are not strictly regional in character is disregarded) it would seem that there are at least two distinct problems wrapped up in the idea of regionalism in Indonesia. There is the need to satisfy feelings of broad local consciousness related sometimes to ethnic identity, sometimes to economic identity, sometimes to distance from the centre or to population distribution, or to a combination of these. And there is the need to provide general government. It may appear odd that, for two such different tasks, the one general solution should have been considered applicable. But this has been the case. In the long-drawn-out efforts to frame a fundamental law for local government, the two problems were dealt with as though they were one. The local government law which eventually emerged and the earlier measures which it replaced had a number of features in common, including the fact that they all provided for a hierarchy of local authorities. Provision was made for the establishment, as self-governing regions, of large areas, at first termed "provinces" and later "first-level regions"; of smaller divisions (second-level regions) within these; and within these, in turn, of smaller subdivisions still. First-level regions, with their representative and executive councils, were intended to satisfy those feelings whose existence gave substance to the Dutch arguments for a federation—the feelings of cultural self-consciousness or of economic disabilities or the resentment of Javanese domination. At the lower levels the council system was designed with an eye to securing orderly administration as well as developing local initiative. Or, rather, it was hoped optimistically that these would be the two sides of the coin—that the development of local initiative might prove able to assume the burdens of administration hitherto borne by the centre.

Here lay the most controversial aspect of planning, for

the central government, even though its original blueprint envisaged the ultimate shedding of some of its responsibilities, argued that this must be a gradual process. In the meantime, it was necessary to preserve a delicate balance between the surrender of powers to the lower regional governments and the retention of central control over them. Successive governments sought to do this by integrating the whole local government system into the existing centralized administrative system, at least until such time as the local governments themselves could be trusted as instruments to assist in the maintenance of central authority. In consequence the Republic's arrangements for local autonomy from 1950 to 1956 had something of a colonial flavor about them. This was true not merely in form—the system of units and organization used at the local level stemmed from, and bore many detailed resemblances to, the old Dutch programs of administrative and political decentralization—but also in essence. To put it in other terms, though Indonesia had become an independent sovereign state, its task at the local level was not altogether different from that of an alien government attempting to establish and preserve its authority in the "subject" society, at least in regard to those matters which touched its own interests. This naturally affected the form in which local self-government could immediately be granted, whatever the long-term plan.

The administrative corps on which the centre relied to maintain its general administrative control was itself an inheritance from the colonial past. Organized on a territorial basis, the present central administrative structure has taken over the prewar forms as they had existed in Java. It comprises a highly developed pyramid of command with its apex in the Ministry of Home Affairs in Djakarta and with authority passed down through a descending scale of levels to the base of society. Below the Ministry comes the main division, the province. Provinces in turn are divided into Residencies, Residencies into *kabupatens* (the prewar regencies), *kabupatens* into *kewedanaan* (districts), and *kewedanaan* into *ketjamatan* (subdistricts). Below the *ketjamatan* lies the *desa* or village complex (the official administrative term is *kelurahan,* which derives from the chief official of the *desa,* the *lurah*).[8] The officers administering this pyramid of territorial divisions—governors in charge of provinces, Residents in charge of Residencies, *bupatis* of *kabupatens,* and *wedanas* and *tjamats* of *kewedanaan* and *ketjamatan* respectively—form a distinct and highly efficient service of the central government, the *pamong pradja.* It is an

[8] Although the term "village" is used frequently in these pages and is sufficient for our purposes in indicating broadly the traditional unit of rural society, it is important to realize that the term is not precise and to notice that it ignores the great variety of village organization in Indonesia. The *negeri* of Minangkabau, for example, is very different from the *marga* of South Sumatra, as both are from the *desa* of Java. Ter Haar broadly distinguishes over twelve main forms of community organization (B. ter Haar, *Adat Law in Indonesia* [New York, 1948], pp. 60 ff.). Even within the one ethnic division there may be important differences. The Javanese *desa,* to take one case, does not present a completely uniform pattern everywhere. In some instances the group of hamlets has great coherence, in others the individual *pedukuhan* (hamlet) has preserved a sense of identity such that it rather than the *kelurahan* remains the effective unit. (See, e.g., G. William Skinner, ed., *Local, Ethnic, and National Loyalties in Village Indonesia* [Yale University Cultural Report Series, Southeast Asia Studies; New Haven, 1959]. Note the definition [p. 3] of "local" loyalties as those "focussed at or below the highest unit whose administrative officer is selected or elected by the villagers from among themselves.")

elite service. Its officers are responsible for the co-ordination at each level of the activities of the several technical ministries, health, agriculture, education, and so on, as well as for the maintenance of law and order—in a word, for all the many aspects of government. It is Indonesia's mandarinate. At the base of the pyramid the *tjamat* or subdistrict officer has maintained the vital link between the government and the rural population in general. He conveys information concerning national policies as far as they affect the village and, indeed, may be said to provide the village with its picture of the outside world. He mobilizes support for novel projects. He is an arbiter between conflicting pressures. He is, in effect, the government.

This organization was taken over in its essentials from the old Inland Administration (*Binnenlands Bestuur*) of the Dutch. In colonial times the service had been divided on racial lines and was composed of a European and an Indonesian element. The higher ranks in the hierarchy—governors and Residents [9]—were Dutch. Below the Resi-

[9] The Residency was at first the major territorial division in the administration. The office of Resident had its origins in the days of the Dutch East India Company. Its functions, magisterial and administrative, were extended during the British interregnum. Thereafter the office changed little in form, though the duties became more extensive as government itself expanded. By the mid-century Residents were regarded as "the hub round which everything turns" (quoted in De Kat Angelino, *op. cit.*, II, 138). They were responsible for general administration, for co-ordinating the several fields of government in their areas, and for supervising the work of the Indonesian officials below them. Their primary function as described by one observer was "not to enforce the law but to give effect to the policy of Government" (Furnivall, *op. cit.*, p. 261). When, in the 1920's, provinces were formed for the purpose of developing regional autonomy, the provincial division was used as

dent the regent, formerly a hereditary office, was the highest level of the service in Java to be staffed by Indonesians. But it would be a mistake to regard the service as merely a colonial hang-over. These lower ranks derived from a more ancient tradition for they preserved the administrative forms of earlier Javanese kingdoms, and, until toward the end of the Dutch period, they continued to be filled by persons of aristocratic origin (*prijaji*). It was this *prijaji* character which gave the service its standing in the eyes of the community. In fact, much of this element still remains. Outside Java the pattern was a little different. In Sumatra, for instance, the European service penetrated one stage lower. Sumatra immediately before the Second World War was a "government" divided into Residencies. Beneath the Residents, assistant Residents administered divisions approximating roughly a Javanese regency. Beneath that division in turn a European controller administered a lower subdivision, below which came districts and subdistricts under native officials. In still other areas where local rulers were recognized by the Indies government, European officers advised rather than administered and guided indirectly the internal administration of the principality. The system as reconstituted after the revolution made a bid for greater uniformity by extending the Javanese pattern of units to other areas where possible, but in its main outlines there was little change. Under the Republic, as before it, the *pamong pradja* has represented the eyes, ears, and hands of the central government. Its role in the early years of inde-

---

an administrative division as well as a major region of self-government, and the extra rank of Governor was superimposed above that of Resident.

pendence can hardly be overestimated, and the main problem attending the development of local self-government has been how far a local government system should be kept separate from, integrated with, or used to replace the centre's own territorial administration. Were there to be two governments in each region or a single government with a dual aspect?

As plans for the extension of local self-government developed, the part to be played by the *pamong pradja* became of crucial importance. The question was not a new one; it had already emerged clearly after the administrative reforms of the twenties. As has been seen, officers of the central administration had been cast for a pivotal role—that of chairmen of local councils—in the early experiments in political decentralization. But since the councils were intended not merely as a forum for local opinion but also as an aid to the centre in its task of government, there was present the implication that a full flowering of local government would, in due course, remove the need for a territorial administration. Writing at the end of the twenties, De Kat Angelino argued that "the developing autonomous life will slowly overgrow the administrative corps and make it superfluous."[10] In the postwar plans for autonomy it was again assumed that the administrative service would eventually wither away. But during the early transitional period the service continued to occupy its old position, combining the central administrative duties with the leadership of local councils.

The question of whether this arrangement was to continue was important for each of the two aspects which have been noted as belonging to the broad problem of

[10] *Op. cit.*, II, 358. See also p. 382.

regionalism and local government in Indonesia. At the level of what might be called regionalism proper—the existence of strong local consciousness over a comparatively wide area—the conflict between centre and regions was, in part, a conflict over the division of powers whether within a federal or a unitary system. And the operations of the *pamong pradja* represented one aspect of central power which the regions felt to be an encroachment on their autonomy. To successive central governments, on the other hand, the whole idea of Indonesian unity seemed bound up with the maintenance of the service.

For the second aspect, that of preserving order and carrying on the many functions of government at the lower levels, the question was equally vital. Were local authorities mature enough to shoulder the burdens of administration on behalf of the centre? The centre tended to feel that they were not and that therefore the *pamong pradja* should continue to perform at least an auxiliary role. In consequence, three main issues of planning emerged: the issue of supervision of local governments, the issue of the extent of the powers to be enjoyed by local governments, and the issue of the character of the lower levels of local government. This controversy came to centre primarily on the first of these, the issue of supervision, though, of course, this was intimately connected with the other two. The wider the powers which were to be conceded to local authorities, the more likely was the centre to demand a solid supervisory machinery. And in particular, since control of a rural population was an important task of government, the centre would be reluctant to transfer its functions in that regard to newly established councils. The ideal instrument of supervision in the eyes of the centre was the *pamong pradja,* and this corps was, at the same time, the centre's channel of communication to the mass of the population. It was hardly surprising, therefore, that contending views on the many aspects of planning a local government system should focus primarily on this one issue—what was to be the future role of the *pamong pradja,* and how soon could it be discarded?

These questions run like a communicating thread through the various aspects of the local government problem to be discussed in the following pages: the extent and character of local powers, the problem of creating new authorities to reflect the wishes of the immediate locality, the problem of staffing local services and of providing an adequate financial basis for local governments. There were increasing concessions by the central government to meet regional demands, until, by the end of 1958, when the new pressure for guided democracy was making itself felt, the centre had granted in principle the full substance of autonomy. The first nine years of the Republic saw, in effect, an attempt to meet the problem of regionalism by creating appropriate machinery for local self-determination. It was not, in the end, a successful attempt, and it was followed by a withdrawal of some of those concessions which had been granted. But it is worth examination as a coherent plan. Its main features emerged in the course of a prolonged struggle, but in their final form they constituted a framework for a thoroughgoing system of local government.

2

The Planning of a Local Government System

ANY study of Indonesian local government must face at the outset a rather confusing body of legislation. Several attempts were made to draft a measure which could give statutory authority for the creation of local authorities and provide a suitable legal framework within which they could operate. Although a broad family resemblance runs through all the enactments which have appeared, the individual differences between them are important, and it is necessary to examine them in some detail. In legislative terms the high-water mark in developing local responsibility was reached in Law 1 of 1957, which was approved by Parliament, after long controversy and substantial redrafting, in December 1956, proclaimed in the following January, and gradually implemented during the two subsequent years until, in September 1959, its central clauses were suspended by a presidential edict. Law 1 [1] replaced

[1] Law 1 is a "basic law" (*undang-undang pokok*). After its passage by Parliament further legislation was required actually to establish the system of local government for which it provided.

It is necessary to distinguish between various instruments: a the earlier basic laws under which many local authorities had already been established: RI Law 22 of 1948, a law of the original Republic of Indonesia (Jogjakarta), and NIT Law 44 of 1950, a law of the State of East Indonesia (*Negara Indonesia Timur*) passed during the period when it formed a constituent member of the short-lived United States of Indonesia (December 1949–August 1950).

In considering the character of this earlier legislation it is, perhaps, helpful to make a preliminary distinction between two broad types of situation to be found in the archipelago. On the one hand there are the areas such as Java, Madura, and, to a lesser extent, Sumatra and Borneo, where the central government, both in colonial times and at present, has maintained its own centralized administrative system reaching right down to the basic territorial unit—the village. The organization of this administration has already been described. Secondly, there are the areas such as the greater part of Celebes, the Moluccas, and the Lesser Sundas, where a type of indirect rule obtained. In these areas agreements (the long contract or the short declaration) between the Indies government and the local rulers had granted a degree of recognition to principali-

---

basic law (*undang-undang pokok*); a law (*undang-undang*); an emergency law (*undang-undang darurat*) which could be issued in certain circumstances by the government in advance of parliamentary approval; a government regulation (*peraturan pemerintah*) issued under the authority of a law; a ministerial regulation (*peraturan menteri*) issued by a Minister. The establishment of autonomous governments required legislation or emergency legislation. The surrender of particular powers, the provision of a procedure for selecting representative councils, and so on were the subjects of government regulation. The provision in detail of a procedure for selecting executive councils was the subject of ministerial regulation.

ties (*swapradjas*) as self-governing states within the colonial framework, and the lower administrative structure was thus more independent of the centre. It was an extremely limited independence, of course. The earlier form of agreement, the "long contract," was developed at a period when Holland was dealing with rulers of some substance, controlling fairly extensive territories, and it enumerated in some detail the respective powers to be enjoyed by the Indies government and the "self-governing state." At the end of the nineteenth century, when Dutch power was being extended more widely and more effectively through the islands, a briefer and more blanket form of submission was adopted. In signing this "short declaration" rulers recognized Dutch sovereignty, renounced their right to the conduct of their own external relations, and agreed to accept regulations prescribed by Holland for their internal government. They were thus brought effectively under Dutch control, and their independence amounted to little more than the right to administer policies imposed by a higher government. The adoption of the short declaration to replace the earlier type of agreement did not necessarily affect those principalities which had already accepted the latter, and some states such as Jogjakarta and Surakarta in Java, Pontianak in Borneo, and Deli in Sumatra continued under the long contract until the end of Dutch rule. But the short declaration became the normal basis for government in the indirectly ruled parts of the colony, to be found particularly in the eastern islands. Out of over 250 states only 17[2] remained under the old style of agreement. (The location of some of the major principalities is shown in

[2] Schiller, *op. cit.*, p. 81.

Map 2. Space does not permit the inclusion of the great bulk of the tiny states which were recognized in Celebes, the Moluccas, and the Lesser Sundas.)

Since the ruler of a self-governing state was required to enforce decisions of the Indies government, it may be argued that there was little practical difference between such a territory and an area under direct rule.[3] The formal difference, however, was important for it affected the character of the administration. In the case of the directly ruled areas, immediately above the *desa, negeri,* or other basic unit of village organization, stood the central government or at least its lower administrative reaches. In the case of the indirectly ruled areas the meeting place between the government and the governed was not the village, but the self-governing state. Above the *swapradja* stood the government. Below it lay its own administrative organization maintaining contact with the village. Both geographically and politically this distinction can only be maintained in very broad terms. Although most of the self-governing states were in the eastern part of the archipelago (i.e., to the east of Java), in the western part of the archipelago there were also several important self-governing states. To mention merely some of the more important examples, there were the four princely states, Jogjakarta, Surakarta, Mangkunegaran, and Pakualaman of Central Java; there were Deli, Serdang, Langkat, and Asahan in East Sumatra; and in Borneo there were Kutaï, Pontianak, and Sintang. And in the eastern part of the Indies there were areas under direct rule such as Lombok and Minahasa. Further, there were wide differences in size and competence and organization between one self-

[3] Furnivall, *Netherlands India,* p. 258.

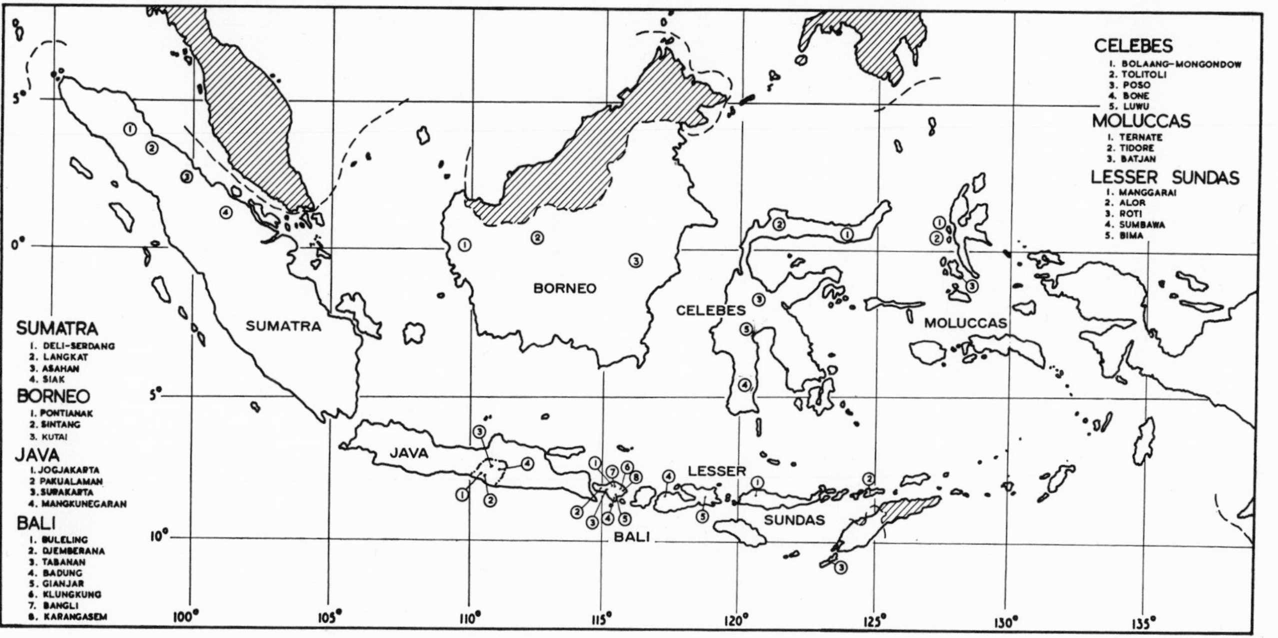

Map 2. General location of some of the major self-governing states recognized under long contract or short declaration by the Indies government.

governing state and another, just as there were innumerable forms of social organization for the directly ruled communities. The contrast between Deli-Serdang (population 371,763) or Bima (population 199,661) and such tiny units as Waidjelu (population 2,984) or Laura (population 5,661) was considerable, and administration of the latter came very close to direct rule.[4] But nevertheless an awareness of the broad distinction between the two types of situation, and of the fact that the two were, on the whole, geographically separate also, is important for an understanding of postwar experiments in local government.

In view of these different situations, it proved difficult for the independent Republic of Indonesia to prepare a uniform system which could be applied to the whole country. RI Law 22 of 1948 had originally been intended to fulfill that role, since the Republic, which had proclaimed its own existence in August 1945, claimed authority over all Indonesia. The actual operation of the law was more limited: from 1950 to 1957 it was the basis for the establishment of local governments in Java, Sumatra, and Borneo. Law 44, as the corresponding basic law for the State of East Indonesia, continued during these years to form the basis for local government in the eastern islands, which were now constituted as the three eastern administrative provinces of the unitary Republic—Sulawesi, Maluku, and Nusa Tenggara. The new Law 1 of 1957 attempted to provide arrangements of sufficiently flexible character to meet the circumstances of both areas.

Although Law 1 of 1957 introduced important modifi-

[4] These population figures are taken from the 1930 Census.

cations in the local government system envisaged by the earlier legislation, some features remained common to all three laws—e.g., the idea of local legislative and executive councils and the hierarchical arrangement of local governments. The important differences between the new law and its predecessors concerned three points: the method of supervising local government activities (the element of supervision was greatly narrowed); the extent of the powers to be surrendered (the new conception envisaged greatly enlarged powers for local government); and the actual establishment of the lowest level in the hierarchy for which the law provided (this was left as an unsolved question, and no such lowest level governments have yet been established). The changes which were made represented reluctant concessions to parliamentary pressure, and it is impossible to understand the character of Law 1 except in the light of the very acute controversy which attended its birth. Perhaps the best method of indicating the character of the issues will be to deal in some detail with the provisions of RI Law 22 of 1948 [5] (and, briefly, by way of comparison and contrast, with those of NIT Law 44 of 1950) which lay down the broad outlines of the system and then to indicate very briefly the nature of the changes made by Law 1 of 1957. The more important of these will be dealt with more thoroughly in the chapters which follow.

[5] For a close legal analysis of the terms of this law see Gerald S. Maryanov, *Decentralization in Indonesia: Legislative Aspects* (Cornell Modern Indonesia Project, Interim Reports Series; Ithaca, 1957).

RI LAW 22 OF 1948

Units of Local Government

In laying down the basic forms which were intended to provide the pattern for the eventual development of autonomous local governments in Indonesia, Law 22 of 1948 took, as its point of departure, the central administrative system which the Republic had carried over in its essentials from the prewar Dutch administrative system as it had existed in Java. Law 22 sought to modify the extreme centralization of the administrative system by transforming three of the levels of the hierarchy into levels of local government. The levels in question were the province, the *kabupaten,* and the *desa* or its equivalent. Provinces, *kabupatens,* and *desas* were to become "self-governing regions" (*daerah swatantra*) possessing wide powers of autonomy over their own affairs.[6] Provision was made also for municipal governments at two levels. Large towns were to be equivalent in status to a *kabupaten,* and small towns were to be equivalent to a *desa.* Finally, in addition to these "ordinary" self-governing regions, rural and urban, there was provision for the formation of "special regions" (*daerah istimewa*) composed of units or groups of units which, because of their character or historical traditions, did not lend themselves to the ordinary classification. The so-called "self-governing states" (*swapradja*) which had been brought under Dutch au-

[6] The remaining administrative divisions—Residency, *kewedanaan,* and *ketjamatan*—were not mentioned in the law, though its explanatory appendix appeared to look forward to the gradual disappearance of these units. In practice they were retained for the time being.

thority by means of the short declaration or the long contract and which had been subject to a species of indirect rule in colonial days were expected to fit into this category. These states possessed a traditional organization for which the Republic was prepared to make special arrangements. A special region according to its size and level of development might be equivalent in status to a province, a *kabupaten,* or a *desa.*[7]

A distinction was made between two types of power to be exercised by a *swatantra,* whether "ordinary" or "special." There was the right to deal with matters described as the "household affairs" (*rumah tangga*) of the region.[8] In these matters the regions were to exercise powers of autonomy. Secondly, there were other fields in which local governments might perform an auxiliary role, assisting in the execution of central government tasks delegated to them by law or of tasks belonging to and delegated by a higher local government level.[9] Such "co-operating administration" was termed *medebewind.* The powers of autonomy were not enumerated in detail in Law 22, but it was provided that they were to be elaborated subsequently in the further establishing legislation which was required actually to establish each region as a region of local government under the basic law.[10] Establishing legislation eventually listed such fields as irrigation, maintenance of roads and public buildings, supervision and development of agricultural programs, control of fisheries, maintenance of health services, maintenance of veterinary services, matters of social welfare, supervision of marketing and distribution.

[7] Article 1 (2).
[8] RI Law 22, Articles 1 and 23 (1).
[9] Article 24.
[10] Article 23 (2).

Institutions of Local Government

The institutions through which regional self-government would be conducted were to be similar for all three levels. For each local government region were to be established two councils—a representative council (*Dewan Perwakilan Rakjat Daerah,* usually abbreviated DPRD), to be elected in a manner to be determined by law,[11] and an executive council (*Dewan Pemerintah Daerah,* usually abbreviated DPD), to be elected by and from the members of the representative council according to the method of proportional representation.[12] The representative council, the DPRD, was entrusted with legislative powers in the fields falling within the competence of the region. Legislation was not to concern itself with matters which were already dealt with in legislation of the central parliament or of a higher level of local government, nor was any level of local government to deal with matters falling within the defined sphere of action of a lower level. More generally legislation of a local government was not to conflict with legislation of the central parliament or of a higher level of local government.[13] The executive council, the DPD, whose members were collectively and individually responsible to the DPRD, was entrusted with the day-to-day conduct of government,[14] executing decisions of the DPRD, administering the various fields of activity belonging to the region, and performing such other functions as were specifically conferred in the law.[15]

[11] Article 3 (4). [12] Article 13 (1).

[13] Article 28. [14] Article 34.

[15] E.g., certain powers of supervision of the conduct of local governments at a lower level and of the budgets of lower local governments were given to DPD's also. Powers in *medebewind*

In each region there was to be a head of the region (*kepala daerah*) who was to serve as the chairman of the DPD as well as general supervisor of the local government in question. This office was not to be entirely elective. It was to be filled by appointment made by a specified authority representing the central government, but such appointments would be made in each case from a list of at least two and not more than four candidates submitted by the DPRD of the region concerned. Thus the *kepala daerah* of a province was to be appointed by the President from the list of candidates nominated by the DPRD of the province. The *kepala daerah* of a *kabupaten* or a large town was to be appointed by the Minister of Home Affairs from a similar list proposed by the DPRD concerned. And the *kepala daerah* of a *desa* or a small town was to be appointed in a similar fashion by the *kepala daerah* of the province in which it was situated.[16] It was provided that a *kepala daerah* could be removed by the appropriate authority at the request of the DPRD concerned, though it was not obligatory for the authority to accede to such a request.[17]

In the case of a "special region" different arrangements prevailed. Here the *kepala daerah* was to be appointed by the President from the traditional ruling family of the area (if it still retained power), with the proviso that the

might be surrendered to either a DPD or a DPRD (Article 24). If such powers were surrendered to the DPD, it would not be responsible to the DPRD for its handling of that function.

[16] Article 18 (1, 2, 3).

[17] Explanatory appendix, par. 24. The power of the central government to remove such an officer on its own initiative without any request from the DPRD was not specifically provided, but it appeared to be assumed by officers of the Ministry of Home Affairs.

appointee must be suitable in terms of his ability, justice, and loyalty. Normally the *kepala daerah* would be the traditional ruler. This was, in fact, the essential difference between an "ordinary" and a "special" local government. In the latter existing rulers, because of their prestige and their continued command of the loyalty of their subjects, would be recognized, and they were to serve as the appointed heads of their regions, though the two councils were now to be associated with them. In making the appointments attention was to be paid to the customary law of the region.[18]

Supervision

Although some measure of autonomy was conceded in principle to local governments under this law, the central government was anxious to retain a measure of supervision over the activities of these governments, even in those fields specifically surrendered to them. Various methods of supervision were provided. In the first place the *kepala daerah,* in addition to his chairmanship of the executive council, was to exercise certain specific powers of control on behalf of the central government. His signature was necessary for ordinances of the legislative council.[19] He was also empowered to delay the operation of decisions of either council if they appeared to him to conflict with

[18] Although the method of appointing the regional head was the only formal difference between a special and an ordinary region, in practice the only such region which has been established (Jogjakarta) possesses rather more power than its ordinary counterpart —a province—since it retained, in large measure, the powers it had formerly exercised as a *swapradja* in addition to those specifically defined in its establishing law.

[19] Article 28 (6).

higher legislation or to run counter to the general interest. In the event of such a delaying veto the matter was to be reported within seven days to the President in the case of provinces and to the DPD of the next highest level in the case of lower local governments. If no contrary decision was made by those authorities within three months, the original decision was to come into effect.[20] This power of the *kepala daerah* was called "preventive supervision."

As implied in this arrangement, a second feature of the control system was to be found in the fact that the three levels of autonomy, like the six levels of administration, were hierarchically arranged. Provinces, while concerned with the field of activity specifically assigned to them, possessed a supervisory power over *kabupatens* and large municipalities within their boundaries, and so on down the scale. Indeed, it was through this hierarchy of authorities that the preventive supervision of the *kepala daerah* was made effective, since the imposition of his delaying veto automatically brought the whole question before a higher level. But besides considering cases in which a *kepala daerah* of a lower level had exercised his preventive veto, DPD's were given a power of preventive supervision of their own over lower levels with regard to certain matters, primarily financial, which were specified in the law. The matters in question were the remuneration and traveling expenses to be granted to members of the DPRD (Article 7), the preparation by a DPRD of a guide for the conduct of affairs by the DPD (Article 15), the remuneration of DPD members (Article 16), the terms and conditions for appointment to and employment in the civil service of a region (Article 21), regula-

[20] Article 36 (1, 2, 3).

tions enacted jointly by more than one region to cover matters of common interest (Article 27), and regulations concerning criminal offenses (Article 29), the raising of loans (Article 33), and the annual budget (Article 39). Regulations governing these subjects were not to go into effect until they had been approved by the appropriate higher authority—by the President in the case of provinces and by the DPD of the next highest level in the case of other councils. If the higher authority made no decision to the contrary within three months, the regulations so referred could go into effect, except that the authority concerned had the power to impose a further three months' delay if it wished.[21] In the case of rejection of a regulation, provision was made for an appeal to the DPD of the next highest level again (or to the President in the case of regulations of second-level governments which failed to secure the approval of the provincial DPD).

The hierarchical organization of local governments enabled provision to be made for a third type of control device. In addition to their power of preventive supervision and their power to decide questions referred after the exercise of the preventive veto of a lower *kepala daerah*, DPD's had the power to repeal decisions already made by the DPD or DPRD of the level below them, if they conflicted with the general interest or with higher legislation. This type of action was termed "repressive" supervision.[22] For provinces this power rested with the President.

Finally, provision was made for the direct intervention of the central government itself where, in the opinion of the centre, a regional government was neglecting its tasks.

[21] Article 30. [22] Article 42

In these circumstances a central instruction could be issued in the form of a government regulation requiring the local government to act in a certain manner.[23]

The Position of Kepala Daerah

As has been suggested, the intentions of this local government system were twofold. The institution of a measure of self-government at the provincial level was intended to satisfy the feelings of regional and cultural identity existing among various ethnic groups within the archipelago and to provide for the facts of broad regional suspicion of the centre and of fears of Javanese predominance within the unitary state. Autonomous provinces constituted an alternative to the creation of constituent states in a federal system. Secondly, there was the need to provide "government in general"—to fashion new instruments of government at all levels for a society in transition. The proposed creation of the second- and third-level local governments in *kabupatens* and in villages was directed toward that end, and it was at these levels that the supervisory machinery provided under the Act was regarded as particularly important. From the government's point of view the vital link in the supervisory system was the position of *kepala daerah* or regional head, and here it is relevant to compare the postwar plan with the prewar local government system.

In some respects this system of regional units and authorities outlined in Law 22 followed the pattern set, somewhat halfheartedly, by the prewar Dutch experiments in political decentralization. As has been noticed, provinces, regencies, and municipalities had been estab-

[23] Article 25.

lished during the twenties and thirties, with councils able to exercise a measure of responsibility over local matters. There were, of course, vital differences between these and the new councils provided for in Law 22. Election of members on the basis of universal suffrage and the disappearance of the European members of councils were natural changes in the postrevolution situation. But, in view of its semielective character, this position of *kepala daerah* represented, possibly, the greatest single innovation made by the new law, for it involved a major change in the relationship between the central government's administrative service and the local government system. In the prewar experiments the head of the local government system at each level was the central government's chief executive officer in the region. The Governor of a province was also chairman of the provincial executive council. In a *kabupaten* the regent, also essentially a central official, possessed a similar dual function. Thus a close connection was preserved between the central administrative hierarchy and the system of local autonomy, similar to that existing in Holland itself and in certain other European countries. Law 22 proposed, in theory though not, as it turned out, in practice, to dispense with that tie. The office of *kepala daerah* and chairman of the DPD was still to be combined with that of chief administrative officer of the region. But an elective element was introduced in that appointment was to be made, as has been noticed, from a list of nominees chosen by the representative council. Thus the chief executives of regions would no longer be members of an official service though they would still combine two types of activity. In theory the full flourishing of the new local government system was expected to eliminate the need for a separate territorial administrative service of the central government.[24] The local governments themselves were expected in time to take over, on behalf of the centre, the responsibility for the administration of lower units within their territory (e.g., *kewedanaan* and *ketjamatan* within a *kabupaten*) if such administration continued to be required. Although Law 22 is not clear in defining his position and duties, it would seem that the *kepala daerah* was intended to co-ordinate local and central activities. The explanatory appendix to the law, in fact, described him as a representative of the central government, with reference to such administrative duties,[25] but the same document described him elsewhere as an organ of the regional government.[26] His power to delay decisions of the DPD and DPRD were to be exercised, of course, on behalf of the centre.

Briefly, according to Law 22 the *kepala daerah* was intended to exercise a dual function. As chairman of the DPD he was to be head of the local government with some responsibility to the DPRD. Secondly, he was entrusted with the supervisory powers over his councils under Article 36. But, in addition to these two specific functions, there was a third type of duty to be performed

[24] Article 46 (2) provided that administrative divisions would continue to exist until they were abolished. The appended explanation to the law makes it clear that such abolition involved also the abolition of the *pamong pradja*. In particular the office of Resident was expected to become obsolete in the very near future. (See note on Article 46 and also explanatory appendix, par. 35. Government Regulation 38/50 transferred the powers of the Resident to the provincial DPD, but it was not implemented.)

[25] Law 22, explanatory appendix, par. 35.

[26] *Ibid.*, par. 22.

on behalf of the centre, though it was not defined in the law. As head of the region the *kepala daerah* was to be the representative of the central government in the area, supervising the execution of governmental tasks which did not fall within the competence of the local government and exercising the same type of co-ordinating function as had formerly fallen to the lot of the appropriate officer of the *pamong pradja,* or central administrative service, i.e., the Governor in the case of a province, the *bupati* in the case of a *kabupaten,* and the mayor (*wali kota*) in the case of a town. It might be said that the new proposal reversed the prewar arrangement. Formerly a central administrative official was appointed as head of the region. Now the incumbent of the office of regional head was also to perform some of the duties formerly belonging to a central administrative official.

Obviously the concept of the dual role of the *kepala daerah* had its theoretical difficulties. The fact that he was an organ of the local government, bearing a responsibility together with his colleagues on the DPD to the representative body on the one hand and having responsibility to the higher levels of administration on the other, left open the possibility of a conflict of interest between the two capacities—a conflict which was particularly likely to occur in view of his specific power to delay measures of the local councils which appeared to him to be contrary to the general interest or to run counter to the measures of higher governments. The exercise of this temporary veto was not intended always to be left as a matter of discretion. Since the *kepala daerah* owed a duty to the central government, it could be assumed (and was in fact assumed) that he could be instructed by the Ministry of

Home Affairs to delay any matter which was known to be pending and in which the Ministry felt itself to have an interest contrary to that of the elected authorities of the region. If used in this way the veto power could become the central element in the system of supervision which the centre considered it necessary to maintain over local bodies. Obviously the position of *kepala daerah,* as provided in the law, called for great qualities of skill and tact if a clash of interest was to be avoided.

As it happened, the innovation proposed by the law was not to be implemented for a considerable time. The law itself provided an escape clause [27] which enabled the central government to appoint individuals to the position of *kepala daerah* for the time being, without any reference to the wishes of the representative councils in the regions concerned. The centre availed itself of this loophole. Of major importance was the fact that in so doing it simply appointed the appropriate members of its own administrative service, the *pamong pradja,* thus reverting to the prewar practice of placing an official at the centre of the local government. For the provisional period these officials combined several tasks. They were chairmen of executive councils and heads of autonomous governments at their respective levels. At the same time, they supervised the operations of the autonomous governments on behalf of the centre. And with these duties they combined their normal responsibilities as central government servants—the co-ordination of central matters and the performance in general of territorial administration. Thus a *bupati* was not merely *kepala daerah* of an autonomous *kabupaten.* Since the *kabupaten* still remained an administrative di-

[27] Article 46 (4).

vision for those central government purposes falling outside the scope of autonomy, the *bupati* continued also to be the officer to whom the lower administrative ranks of *wedana* and *tjamat* were responsible and who, in turn, was responsible to the Resident, the Governor, and, through them, to the central government. The same collection of tasks devolved upon the Governor at the provincial level. In other words, whereas the law envisaged regional administration eventually being taken over by the autonomous governments, at whose head would stand a man who combined the functions of local leader with some of those formerly possessed by a central administrative official, for the time being, through the retention of the central administrative service, an even greater integration of autonomous government and central administration was achieved.

The preservation of the connection between the official hierarchy and the local government system remained until 1957, and it became the major item of controversy during this period.

NIT LAW 44 OF 1950

While RI Law 22 of 1948 was used as the basic local government law for the whole western part of the archipelago, for the eastern islands which had together formed the State of East Indonesia (*Negara Indonesia Timur*) a law of that state (NIT Law 44 of 1950) had already been promulgated before August 1950. This law had continued to serve as the basic law for local government within the administrative provinces of Sulawesi (Celebes), Maluku (Moluccas), and Nusa Tenggara (Lesser Sundas) into which East Indonesia was now divided, except that the administration of the law was transferred from the State of East Indonesia to the central Ministry of Home Affairs. In general the main principles of NIT Law 44 resembled those of RI Law 22. The same type of hierarchy of autonomous levels was planned, with the executive council at each level exercising a general supervision over the local authorities of the next lowest level. Naturally, because of the very different administrative history of these islands, the actual territorial divisions which were selected to become autonomous units were not identical with those of Java. East Indonesia had no counterpart to the *kabupaten,* for instance. Before the war the area had been a patchwork of self-governing states of varying size and development, together with several directly ruled areas. Many of the principalities were far too small to be effective as units of self-government immediately below the provincial level, and, as a means of securing a greater degree of uniformity, the Dutch, in setting up the State of East Indonesia, had attempted to fashion a new territorial form, the "*daerah*" (the term literally means simply "region"), based on unions or federations between contiguous communities which might be ethnically or culturally different, but which were politically and economically interdependent. In Law 44 the *daerah* unit was used as the second level of autonomy, below the province, and it was rated as roughly equivalent to the *kabupaten* elsewhere. (In practice, as will be seen, the thirteen *daerahs* established by 1950 were further subdivided in subsequent years, to meet local demands and, in some cases, to make the unit more internally coherent.) The third level of autonomy was to be composed of the constituent parts of the *daerah* unit.

Provision for the appointment of a regional head was precisely the same as that laid down as normal procedure in Law 22. An important difference between the two laws, however, was that Law 44 had no escape clause which enabled the central government to make direct appointments to that office during a transitional period. The rank of *kepala daerah* in East Indonesia was thus filled by the centre in each case from a list of nominees submitted by the DPRD, except, of course, in the case of "special regions," where, as in western Indonesia, a member of the former ruling house was to be appointed.

A further difference between the two major areas, though this was not written into the basic legislation, related to the method by which powers were to be conferred on the local bodies. It has been brought out that, in the areas where Law 22 operated, powers were to be surrendered to the local government by the central government. In the case of East Indonesia the reverse procedure was followed. The powers assumed by the central government were defined, and the undefined remainder were left to the local government until such time as this distribution was revised by the centre. This method followed that used by the Indies government in making its contracts with *swapradjas* in the past. The net result was to leave local governments with a greater range of powers, at least on paper, than was the case in the rest of the Republic. It will be seen that the method by which powers were to be distributed was one of the issues at stake in the preparation of a new local government law to embrace the whole of Indonesia. On this question, as on others, the central government was forced to compromise between its own desire for a uniform system and its need to recognize local demands.

Law 22 and Law 44, between them, provided a broad legal basis for the actual institution of local governments after 1950. How far they were adequate to meet the twin problems of regional feeling and efficient administration naturally depended upon the manner in which they were applied.

APPLICATION

It was perhaps not surprising that the early application of these two measures should be severely limited. Law 22 was drafted during the actual conflict with Holland, and, at that stage, it could be little more than an earnest of good intentions for the future. And Law 44 was, in any case, more limited in its intended scope, since it was to apply only within the State of East Indonesia. After the formation of the unitary state, it was clear that a new all-embracing law was required to replace both of these interim measures, but this was not an easy task during the early years of independence. Apart from the inevitable major differences in basic point of view which were carried over from the federal period, there were many problems of practical detail which could be clearly formulated only in the light of experience. The variety of social situations to be dealt with and the consequent difficulty of imposing a uniform solution, the smallness of the village unit which was envisaged as the basic level, the lack of experience on the part of those who would have to run local governments at the lower levels, the complicated preparations necessary before electoral procedures could be introduced either at the national or the local level, and many other problems—all combined not only to prevent the full implementation of the provisional measures but also to delay agreement about the shape of a permanent basic law.

In fact, there were three main points at which the provisional system in western Indonesia failed to correspond with the plan set out in the provisional basic legislation. One of these has already been noticed. For the time being the use of the escape clause of Law 22 enabled the central government to appoint the *kepala daerah* directly, rather than to select from lists of nominees submitted by representative assemblies. The appointment of the appropriate members of the central administrative service either made available to local authorities the training and experience of these officers or, alternatively, subjected local wishes to closer central supervision, depending on the point of view.

A second departure from the plan concerned the areas established as self-governing regions. In 1950 three provinces were established in Java, together with Greater Djakarta (Djakarta Raya) and the Special Region of Jogjakarta (Daerah Istimewa Jogjakarta), and three were established in Sumatra. In 1953 Borneo was constituted as a province. (These initial subdivisions were later subjected to some modification as new provinces were carved out of existing ones in order to meet particular separatist demands.[28]) At the second level of autonomy *kabupatens* and large municipalities were established (or reestablished) in Java and Borneo. In Java the regency as an autonomous as well as an administrative division had existed in colonial times, but in Sumatra and Borneo the

[28] See below, Chapter III.

unit was a transplantation—a fact which presented some minor difficulties.[29] But this was the limit. Although the basic law provided for three levels of autonomy, in fact the only third-level local governments to be established, even in Java where the system was most complete, were small municipalities (*kota ketjil*). Nowhere was the *desa* or its equivalent made into an autonomous area under the provisions of the new law. From provision made during the colonial period customary units such as the *desa* of Java, the *negeri* of western Sumatra, or the *marga* of southern Sumatra had secured a measure of formal recognition, and customary procedures had been subjected to some degree of adaptation to the needs of centralized government. The Javanese *desa,* for instance, though the details of its organization vary from place to place, already elected its headman, the *lurah,* it possessed its own officials (*pamong desa*), and its village assembly was already a functioning body with at least some basis in custom. It is difficult to say how far the institution of village meetings still conformed to traditional patterns and how far, under Dutch rule in its various phases, the processes of discussion and election in the *desa* had assumed an entirely new character. The point is that a working system of supervised autonomy over immediately local matters already existed in the *desa,* and it would have been a little odd to have imposed on that system the novel and more formal arrangements prescribed for *kabupatens* and prov-

[29] Autonomous *kabupatens* were at first established in Sumatra by Governor's decrees, not law, and they lacked the powers of regulation and execution enjoyed by their Javanese counterparts. They performed primarily an advisory role. In 1956 further legislation under Law 22 gave these councils a proper statutory basis and brought them into line with *kabupaten* DPRD's in Java.

inces by Law 22. For that reason, and for the reason also that the *desa* was subsequently judged to be too small in terms of area and population to serve effectively as the basic unit of local government, the Ministry of Home Affairs began to have second thoughts about the wisdom of Law 22 insofar as it concerned the *desa*. The product of the second thoughts will be described below. Here it is sufficient to point out that, although representative assemblies and executive councils were established at the *kabupaten* and provincial levels, the village continued to operate on what had come to be its customary lines—autonomous up to a point, but autonomous in a manner not prescribed by the new law.

Thirdly, the local government system during the provisional period was not able to operate on a basis of the intended electoral procedures. Law 22 foreshadowed a universal franchise for local councils, but provided that the details of the electoral system were to be elaborated in separate legislation.[30] In 1950 an electoral act was passed[31] providing for the indirect election of DPRD's of the higher levels. Electoral colleges for provincial and *kabupaten* and large municipality elections were to be composed of electors chosen by *desas* or their equivalent.[32] In fact, however, this law was not used except in one instance. In 1951 an election was held for the DPRD of the Special Region of Jogjakarta on the basis of Law 7.[33] But elsewhere the central government argued that

[30] Article 3 (4). [31] Law 7/50.

[32] Articles 8, 57, and 69.

[33] In the eastern part of the archipelago a number of local elections were held, notably in Minahasa, Makassar, and Sangihe-Talaud, but on the basis of local electoral regulations.

problems of inadequate administration in the regions and the difficulty of securing uniformity in the surrender of powers to areas of widely differing experience and capacity made it impossible to establish fully autonomous bodies immediately. For these reasons the government relied on another escape clause in Law 22 which allowed for the appointment, not election, of "temporary councils" (DPRD *sementara*) in a manner to be determined by government regulation. In 1950 the controversial Government Regulation no. 39 was issued under Law 22 and provided for the appointment of representatives on the basis of established party and other organizations. Political parties and groups such as labor unions or women's organizations were entitled to representation on *kabupaten* or municipal councils if they possessed a central executive and were established in at least three *kabupatens* in a province and with *ketjamatan* branches in those *kabupatens*. Members of the provincial DPRD's were to be chosen by the DPRD's of *kabupatens* and large towns, which were thus to act as a kind of electoral college for the representative councils of the first level of autonomy.

Government Regulation 39 may have appeared to offer a reasonable solution to the problems of the transitional period, but it contained a technical defect which brought it under fire in Parliament. A procedure was laid down in the regulation for selecting candidates put forward by major parties and other organizations up to the full number of seats provided, in the establishment law, for the DPRD of the province, *kabupaten*, or municipality concerned. But it was further provided that, when the full number of candidates had been selected, parties and organizations still unrepresented were entitled to one member, and the size of the councils was to be increased accordingly beyond the stated figure to enable this extra representation to be achieved. This provision was open to easy abuse. It was possible for recognized parties who had already secured their representation on councils by the normal procedure to attempt to increase their representation by forming suborganizations specifically for the purpose of claiming extra seats. The suborganizations, theoretically independent, could then claim one representative under the provision allowing for the extra members. The Masjumi Party was criticized as the main offender,[34] and other parties, in particular the PNI (Indonesian Nationalist Party), felt that they had been outwitted. Finally Parliament agreed to a motion introduced by Hadikusumo of the PNI calling for the disallowance of the regulation and the freezing of councils already established according to the procedures it prescribed. As a result of this motion no further councils were established for the time being, though those already formed were allowed to continue in operation till other arrangements were made. In areas where the regulation had not been

[34] In the *kabupaten* of Blitar (East Java), to give one example, the establishing law provided for a council of 10. Under the normal procedure laid down in Government Regulation 39, the Masjumi Party obtained 2 representatives and 8 other parties and groups obtained 1 each. The council seats were thus filled. Then, under the extra membership clause, membership was given to 7 other groups—farmers' organizations, women's organizations, youth organizations, labor organizations. All of these associations had been founded by the Masjumi or were Islamic in basis and connected, at least indirectly, with the Masjumi. On a council now swelled to 17, members of Moslem organizations had thus secured an effective representation of 9 members—an absolute majority.

applied, the powers of councils were to be exercised for the time being by the *kepala daerah.*[35]

This unsatisfactory state of affairs dragged on, in fact, until after the long-delayed general election for the national parliament in 1955. The successful holding of the election, in spite of the fear which had preceded it,[36] made local elections much more of a practical proposition and gave more reality to the long-drawn-out preparations for the creation of a permanent local government system. As a first step it was decided to prepare a new electoral law. The indirect method of election prescribed by Law 7/50 and used in Jogjakarta was now considered unwieldy, expensive, and insufficiently representative, and in 1956 a new law (19/56) provided for direct elections. At the same time it was decided to dissolve the "temporary" councils (DPRD *sementara*) where they existed under Regulation 39 and to create new "transitional" councils (DPRD *peralihan*) in all areas, to fill the gap until elections under Law 19 were actually held. The transitional councils were still to be composed of appointees, but they at least possessed a genuine representative character in that they were based on the returns of each local government area in the 1955 general election. Parties were entitled to nominate candidates for appointment to councils in proportion to their general election performance. The first regional elections under Law 19 were eventually held in 1957 in the provinces, *kabupatens,* and municipalities of Java.

In addition to these three shortcomings in the pro-

[35] Emergency Law 7/54.

[36] See H. Feith, *The Indonesian Elections of 1955* (Cornell Modern Indonesia Project, Interim Reports Series; Ithaca, 1957).

visional system of local government the central government was slow in transferring powers to the two levels of autonomy which had been established. By 1956, certainly, a fairly wide range of tasks had been surrendered to provinces, but *kabupatens* and other second-level local authorities had received effective initiative only in the fields of health and public works by that date. Finally, no satisfactory financial provision was made for local government. Local sources of revenue were inadequate, and local bodies were thus dependent (almost completely dependent in the case of provinces) upon grants-in-aid from the centre.

These departures from the pattern of decentralization outlined in Law 22 provide a key to the outstanding issues on which agreement was difficult to reach and which therefore stood in the way of the drafting and the passage through Parliament of a new basic law after the formation of unitary Indonesia in 1950. The character of the office of *kepala daerah* was in particular a matter on which Parliament and the Ministry of Home Affairs were sharply divided. The official view favored the continuance of what had originally been regarded as a strictly temporary, emergency device—the direct appointment of officials to the office. Parliamentary opinion, on the contrary, demanded that the office be a political one and that supervision in general be restricted to a minimum. The question of local government powers, too, was a matter on which it was felt that the centre was too cautious. And naturally the financial independence of local governments was of great importance to the regions themselves, particularly to those outside Java who considered that they were unfairly treated by Djakarta, especially in view of their contribution to Indonesia's general economic stability. The creation of third-level autonomous governments was again a major stumbling block. In this case the problems arose not from clashing viewpoints, but from the sheer technical difficulty of implementing the provisions of the law.

Attempts to solve these difficulties were drawn out over several years, during which the whole question of regional autonomy remained a major national issue. In January 1951 passage of the Hadikusumo motion calling for the disallowance of Regulation 39, the freezing of councils established under it, and the preparation for the introduction of fuller local autonomy was one of the factors leading to the fall of the Natsir Cabinet.[37] The Masjumi-PNI–dominated Sukiman government which succeeded it, though committed to an implementation of the January motion, made no further progress than its predecessor. The Wilopo Cabinet (1952–1953) did widen the powers

[37] The Natsir government was dominated by Masjumi and supported by PSI (*Partai Sosialis Indonesia*), PIR (*Persatuan Indonesia Raja*), and Parindra (*Partai Indonesia Raja*). The PNI was in opposition. On the question of local government the PNI considered that the Masjumi had succeeded, through the misuse of Regulation 39, in securing extra representation out of all proportion to their strength. The motion brought forward by Hadikusumo (PNI) reflected the party's dissatisfaction, and it was supported also by two of the government parties, PIR and Parindra, whose continued backing was necessary for the government's majority. The motion was accepted by Parliament on January 22, 1951, and, in consequence, Assaat, the Minister for Home Affairs, offered to resign, since he held the view that the motion could not be implemented at that time. When the Cabinet supported the position of the Minister and refused to accept the decision of the House, PIR withdrew its two Ministers from the Cabinet and the government, recognizing that it no longer commanded the confidence of Parliament, took the only course open to it, and resigned.

enjoyed by provisional local councils, but was unable to move toward a general settlement. In 1954 the first Ali Sastroamidjojo government prepared a draft bill designed to replace both Law 22 and Law 44 and to create a basis for a uniform local government system for the country as a whole. It was withdrawn, however, after an unfavorable reception in Parliament, and the question remained in cold storage until after the general elections. In 1956 a radically amended draft was presented by the second Ali government, but again met with strong parliamentary opposition. Only after prolonged negotiations between the Minister and party leaders was a compromise agreement reached. The bill in its final form was accepted in December and promulgated in the following January as Law No. 1 of 1957.

LAW 1 OF 1957

The new local government law followed the broad pattern of Law 22 in proposing a hierarchy of local governments each composed of representative and executive councils; but it differed from them in important respects. It modified the proposals of the earlier legislation in respect to the number of levels to be established in the local government hierarchy. And it revised the whole supervisory system proposed in Law 22, including the role to be played by the regional head. The effect of the latter change was to take out much of the "built in" character of the supervisory machinery of Law 22, to weaken the character of the office of regional head, and to strengthen the independence of DPD and DPRD in their handling of matters falling within the field of autonomy. The dualism still present within local government under Law 22 was to be removed, and for local matters the two councils were to be in control of their own household, subject only to an external supervision from the centre. The measure represented a triumph for the political parties which had fought for a fuller measure of independence at the local level.

The nature and implications of the changes will be discussed more fully in succeeding chapters. It will be sufficient here to indicate briefly the main points of difference.

Units of Local Government

Law 1 like Law 22 provided for three types of self-governing region—"ordinary regions" (*daerah swatantra*), "special regions" (*daerah istimewa*), and municipalities (*kotapradja*). And as with Law 22 provision was made for up to three levels of local government. But whereas Law 22 has referred specifically to provinces, *kabupatens*, and *desas* (with municipalities and special regions equivalent to any of these), the new law spoke more vaguely of Level I, Level II, and Level III. This change avoided any suggestion of exporting Javanese terminology. Although *kabupatens* had been established between 1950 and 1956 in Sumatra and Borneo, both as administrative divisions and as autonomous regions under Law 22, the unit was developed essentially in the former administration of Java. And, given the wide variety of forms of village organization throughout Indonesia, the use of the term *desa* was particularly misleading. The terminological changes were not intended to alter the general intention of the old law. First-level regions were intended to provide for major territorial divisions of the country. Although existing boundaries might subsequently be changed, it was specifically provided that, in the first instance, autonomous provinces already created under Law 22 were automatically to become *daerah swatantra* Level I under the new law, and *daerah istimewa* of provincial status (Jogjakarta was the only example) were to be *daerah istimewa* Level I.[38] Similarly second-level governments were to be roughly equivalent to autonomous *kabupatens* established under Law 22, and *kabupatens* already established under that law were automatically to be second-level governments under the new law.[39] (Governments established under NIT Law 44 of 1950 were to continue to operate under that law until special provision was made for them under the new law.) A further difference was that, whereas Law 22 had provided for large municipalities (equal to a *kabupaten*) and small municipalities (equal to a *desa*), the new law removed this difference and made all municipalities second-level regions. (Greater Djakarta, formerly a municipality with the status of a province, continued to be an exception and remained as a first-level region.)

Finally there is the fact that, unlike Law 22 which spoke of establishing three levels of local government, Law 1 provided for the establishment of "at the most" three levels of local government. It has been noted that, under Law 22, no third-level governments were in fact established, with the exception of small municipalities. Long before the drafting of the new law it came to be held that, even in Java, the *desa* was not a suitable unit for establishment as a *daerah swatantra*. Consideration was given to the amalgamation of *desas* into larger units which could then be given autonomy, but such a proposal obviously bristles with difficulties. In consequence the

[38] Article 73. [39] *Ibid.*

new law left the question open. There are very considerable issues of principle involved in this, and it will be more convenient to postpone consideration of them until after other aspects of the new law have been described.

Powers

Law 1 of 1957, like its predecessor, provided that local authorities could exercise powers of two types—autonomy and *medebewind,* the latter to be given as formerly by the centre or a higher level of autonomy either to the DPD or to the DPRD. However, powers of autonomy were more simply—and more widely—defined in the new law. Article 31 provided that the DPRD of a self-governing region could deal with all its "household affairs" except those surrendered by this law to another authority. The explanatory appendix to the law expanded further on the meaning of this clause and interpreted it to mean that the local government could handle all matters of local concern which were not dealt with by the central government or a higher regional government. Without lessening the general application of this clause, Article 31 further provided that it was still possible for the central government, as before, to specify in the establishing regulation the matters which could be dealt with by the regional government.

This broad invitation to local government to take over the regulation of matters not pre-empted by the centre was the natural conclusion to a gradually changing emphasis already evident in the later application of Law 22.

Kepala Daerah

On the particularly difficult question of the character of the office of regional head, Law 1/57 went further than the provisional legislation. It has been seen that both RI Law 22/48 and NIT Law 44/50 provided not for straight-out election, but merely for the partial election of the *kepala daerah,* i.e., the selection, by a specified authority acting on behalf of the central government, of a *kepala daerah* from a list of at least two and not more than four candidates advanced by the DPRD. This provision (withheld in practice in Java, Sumatra, and Borneo, but applied in the eastern islands) was intended as a compromise between the prewar system where the *kepala daerah* was a central government official and the complete surrender of choice to the local government itself. Law 1/57 boldly removed the element of compromise and made the office entirely elective. The *kepala daerah* was now simply to be elected by the DPRD either from its own membership or from outside it, having regard only to capacity and knowledge.[40] (This was seen as an interim arrangement. It was intended that eventually the election would be made, not by the representative council, but by direct popular vote. This was not regarded as immediately practicable, and hence, for the initial phase, the DPRD was to make the selection.[41]) The only safeguard from the point of view of the central government was that the result of the election of a *kepala daerah* was to be

[40] Article 24.

[41] Actually Law 1 provided that the *kepala daerah* was to be chosen by a procedure to be fixed by law (Article 23 [1]), but that pending the passage of such a law the *kepala daerah* was to be chosen by the DPRD, having regard to the qualities of ability and knowledge required by the office. The explanatory appendix to the law made it clear that the law to fix the method of selection would again be based on the idea of the office as a popular one to be filled according to the wishes of the region. The idea of direct popular election was specifically foreshadowed.

ratified by the President for first-level regions and by the Minister of Home Affairs or an authority nominated by him in the case of second- and third-level regions.

The conversion of the office in this way from a semi-official semipolitical position to a purely political position was accompanied by certain changes in the functions attached to the office. The result was that the *kepala daerah* as envisaged in the new law was a much less significant figure in himself than had originally been intended. This was partly because he was now stripped of the supervisory functions which Law 22 had vested in him (even the power to sign regional regulations was now transferred to the chairman of the DPRD) and partly because he was no longer to possess the general co-ordinating functions envisaged in Law 22. (As has been noticed, this aspect of the *kepala daerah*'s proposed functions was indicated in the explanatory appendix to Law 22 rather than in the actual provisions of the law, but it seems clear, nevertheless, that the *kepala daerah* under that law was intended to inherit some of the powers formerly held by the *pamong pradja.*) In other words, he was no longer to be a chief executive—a sort of elected *bupati* or Governor-cum-local government head. He was to be merely an elected chairman of the executive council. The effect was to enhance the power and independence of the two councils within their own sphere.

The law was silent on the question of whether or not, in view of this limitation of the *kepala daerah*'s powers, the *pamong pradja* was to remain in existence for central government administration. Certain of the provisions relating to the supervision of local government suggested that this might be intended.

Supervision

With the change in the character of the *kepala daerah* the centre had to make other arrangements for the general supervision which it was anxious to exercise over local governments. Certain elements were retained of the supervisory machinery of Law 22. Local governments were still to form a pyramid with the higher levels exercising some control over the lower, both repressive and preventive. Decisions of either legislative or executive councils which conflicted with higher law or ran counter to the national interest could still be delayed or repealed by the next highest executive council (by the Minister in the case of first-level regions).[42] Councils (or the Minister in the case of Level I) also possessed a power of preventive supervision over lower councils in the case of specified matters. As before, regulations on these matters were not to be effective until approved by the next highest level.[43] But the immediate supervision of the *kepala*

[42] Article 64.

[43] The list was similar to that of Law 22: remuneration and traveling expenses to be granted to DPRD members (Art. 12), to DPD members (Art. 22), and to the *kepala daerah* (Art. 28); the preparation of a general guide for conduct of affairs by the DPD (Art. 21); the rules of procedure for councils (Art. 16); the surrender of powers by one region to a lower region (Art. 31); the definition of offenses punishable by a sentence of six months or more or by a fine of Rp.5,000 or more (Art. 39); joint action taken by more than one region (Art. 42); regulations covering terms and conditions for appointment to and dismissal from the civil service of a region (Art. 53); regulations concerning regional taxes (Art. 56); and the annual budget (Art. 61). In most of these matters local councils were further limited in that a general guide was to be laid down for them by a government regulation or, in the case of regional powers of taxation, by a law. In this way the centre was

daerah for which Law 22 provided—his presence as chairman and his ability to refuse to sign regulations—was no longer available. Alternative control devices could hardly make up for this loss, for it is difficult to overestimate the effect of the personal influence of an official who was actually present at a meeting and whose authority and prestige might well swing a discussion in the desired direction. And it is obviously much more difficult to delay or cancel a regulation once it has actually been formulated, passed, and signed than it would be to secure its quiet withdrawal in the course of discussion, or even at the point of signature. As a general substitute for this the new law gave special supervisory powers to the central government. Article 69 provided for a general government supervision over the local administration. The manner of supervision was, however, left open, to be defined later by government regulation. And, more specifically, there was provision for the Minister of Home Affairs "or an authority designated by him" to delay or veto local ordinances for second- and third-level governments if they conflicted with higher legislation or with the general interest and if the appropriate higher DPD (first and second level respectively) neglected its duty to take action.[44] (For first-level regions the power to delay or veto already rested with the Minister or an authority designated by him—Article 64.)

These two clauses could, conceivably, keep the door open for the retention of the central administrative corps,

---

able to secure a degree of uniformity in such matters as civil service regulations, remuneration and expense allowances for council members, the method of selecting the DPD from the DPRD, and so on.

[44] Article 65.

though perhaps in a modified or disguised form. The authority designated by the Minister could easily be the Governor for first-level local governments and the *bupati* or the *wali kota* for second- and third-level governments. However, as will be seen more fully below, the government, as a matter of policy, yielded to party pressure that even this loophole should not be used. In December 1957 a ministerial instruction took the first practical step toward the disbanding of the *pamong pradja* by transferring *bupatis* to Residents' offices. With this step the already generous provisions of Law 1 would seem to have been given as liberal as possible an interpretation. The law as implemented gave scope to the elected councils to become the genuine governments of their areas, free not only from the close supervision, but even from the competition, of the territorial administration representing the central government. The centre would operate its own agencies in the regions—its railways and its post offices, its hospitals and its agricultural extension programs—but for these it would no longer need to possess its own separate "government as such" in each region and at each level.

THE END OF THE EXPERIMENT

Although Law 1/57 reflected a fairly thoroughgoing approach to local government, it did not solve Indonesia's regional problems. Indeed, its enactment coincided with a period of heightened tension between Djakarta and the outer islands which was to culminate in open rebellion a year later. Against this background of national crisis the whole experiment in fuller autonomy was soon to be drastically curtailed. In July 1959 Indonesia, by presidential decree, returned to the Constitution of 1945, a constitution which, in the eyes of the President, offered a suitable framework for the development of his plans for guided democracy. In the following September a presidential edict suspended those provisions of Law 1 relating to the election and the powers of the DPD and to the election of the *kepala daerah.* Briefly the edict provided, instead, for a return to the idea of an appointed regional head, and it created a new type of executive council, responsible not to the DPRD but to the *kepala daerah* himself. At the time of writing the implications of the edict have yet to be worked out in practice, but their general tendency is clear enough. They represent not merely a modification of detail, but a reversal of the central intention of Law 1. Regional autonomy was to be confined within narrow bounds, and the element of central control, so greatly weakened in Law 1, was reimposed in a firmer manner than ever before.

It is proposed in the following six chapters to examine the main theoretical and practical problems involved in the preparation and implementation of Law 1. Attention will then be given to the effect for regional government of the return to the 1945 Constitution. Finally, an attempt will be made to outline the broader aspects of regional policy and to consider how far the local government plan could offer a genuine solution.

3

Areas and Units

THE year 1950 saw the initial series of establishing laws by which local government areas were set up and councils created in the western part of the archipelago under Law 22. In subsequent years further measures gradually extended the area in which the law applied. In eastern Indonesia, through the implementation of Law 44, a similar process was under way, though it was more gradual in character. The local governments established in these areas may have been limited in character in the ways already outlined, but, by 1957, when the new comprehensive law was proclaimed, there had at least been considerable progress in defining regions on a uniform pattern throughout the country as a whole, thus securing a greater degree of standardization in what had been a very varied situation.

Uniformity was indeed desirable. As a result of many factors—the methods by which Dutch authority had been extended over the outer islands in the first place, the character of Dutch experiments in political decentralization in the twenties and thirties, the *ad hoc* practices of the Republic during the revolutionary struggle, the creation of new states to counterbalance the Republic during the same period—there existed in 1950 a wide range of units possessing autonomy on a great variety of legal bases. There were municipalities possessed of powers which derived from prewar Dutch enactment. There were self-governing states drawing their authority from the old long contracts and short declarations made by the Dutch with existing rulers. There were new units created by Holland for tactical reasons during her conflict with the Republic (e.g., the *daerahs* of East Indonesia) and based to a greater or lesser degree on prewar forms.[1] There were the "National Committees" (*Komite Nasional Indonesia* or KNI) set up within the Republic in the course of the struggle. Some of these survived into the period of independence and served as the basis for councils until such time as more uniform provision could be made. The application of Law 22 in Java, Sumatra, and Borneo and of Law 44 in the remainder of the country gradually reduced the differences as autonomous governments were established in varying degrees of completeness under the new laws or as local governments already established under other enactments were brought under the new laws and were thus given a new statutory authority.

[1] Schiller, *op. cit.*, pp. 89 ff., distinguishes eleven types of local government form used by Holland during her efforts to lay the foundations for a federal state of Indonesia. Of these six are described as being based upon, or as resembling, prewar forms—self-governing lands (*swapradjas*), neo-lands or *neo-swapradjas,* federations of *swapradjas,* neo-group communities, local autonomous units of Java and Sumatra (e.g., regencies), and municipalities. The remainder are described as governments novel in origin and structure and include the *negaras* or states, the *daerahs* of East Indonesia (which really break down into *swapradjas, neo-swapradjas* or federations of *swapradjas*), supervisory districts of East Indonesia, autonomous constitutional units (special regions), and the federal district.

Of the islands subject to Law 22, a distinction must be made between Java on the one hand and Sumatra and Borneo on the other. In Java, where the decentralization experiments of the Dutch had been carried out with most completeness at both the provincial and regency levels, it was possible to use prewar foundations in applying the provisions of the new law. Three provinces had been established in Java under the decentralization legislation of 1922: West Java (1925), Central Java (1930), and East Java (1928). These had the advantage of being on the whole ethnically homogeneous, West Java being Sundanese and Central Java and East Java predominantly Javanese. Beneath the provinces regencies as well as municipalities had also been given a degree of autonomy. The task of the Republic in establishing provincial divisions in Java under the new law was therefore comparatively simple. In 1950 the three provinces of West, Central, and East Java were established.[2] The four self-governing states which the Dutch had recognized in Java could not, of course, fit into the new scheme without adaptation. Two of these states, Jogjakarta and Pakualaman, whose rulers had aligned themselves with the Republic's struggle for independence, were together constituted as a special region (*daerah istimewa*) with the status of a

[2] The original provinces set up in 1925, 1930, and 1928 respectively were, of course, very different in constitution from those established by the Republic. In colonial times the provincial council was composed of nominated as well as elected members, though the latter were in a slight majority. Representation was given to three national groups—Dutch, Indonesian, and foreign Asiatic. For the Indonesian members a system of indirect elections was established whereby the members of regency and municipal councils were electors for the provincial council. Communal distinctions were now removed, and provision made for election of all members.

province. The Sultan of Jogjakarta was appointed as the *kepala daerah* of the region, and the ruler of Pakualaman became deputy *kepala daerah*. In this way the prestige of the two rulers was preserved and something of the special position of their status was retained, but within the framework of the new legislation. In fact, Jogjakarta was in many respects the reverse of conservative. Even during the struggle for independence it had become the centre of pilot experiments in the introduction of democratic procedures at the village level. The remaining two states, Surakarta and Mangkunegaran, were deprived of their separate political identity and absorbed into the Province of Central Java. One further region of provincial status was established in Java—the municipality of Greater Djakarta, which was thus treated as a special case, distinct from the normal big municipality which was equal in status to a *kabupaten*. Below the provinces the creation of *kabupatens* and municipalities again presented no difficulty. As in the three provinces, it merely meant a formal reconstitution, under the new law, of entities already in existence.

In Sumatra and Borneo, on the other hand, the prewar creation of autonomous communities had not proceeded as far as in Java, and the creation there of provinces and *kabupatens* thus meant innovation, not the following of a firmly set pattern. Apart from the more limited degree of Dutch administrative penetration in these islands, they lacked the relative homogeneity of Java, with its division between two major ethnic groups only—Javanese and Sundanese—and with its broad similarity of social patterns and of village institutions from one end of the island to the other; they were thus less fertile soil for political exploitation.[3] As a halfway house to autonomous provinces a "government" had been established in Sumatra and another in Borneo in 1938. It was proposed within these areas to develop lower autonomous communities of a variety of kinds, not modeled on the Javanese regency but adapted to the existing customary pattern. In the meantime, however, at the "government" level, power was to be vested in the Governor, who was not merely to carry out the central government's tasks, but to exercise powers which might later be transferred to autonomous provinces of Sumatra and Borneo. The Governor's task was, indeed, to prepare for that next step,[4] but no further development had taken place before war intervened. Thus the implementation of Law 22 by the Republic meant the formation of essentially new units in these two islands.

In 1950 three provinces were created in Sumatra (North, Central, and South), and in 1953 Indonesian Borneo was constituted as the single Province of Kalimantan. For reasons which will be discussed more fully below, but which were closely connected with the absence of previous political experiment in these two islands, these divisions proved not entirely satisfactory. In 1956 it was decided to subdivide some of these regions, and several new provinces were thus carved out of existing ones: a Province of Atjeh was separated from the remainder of North Sumatra, and Kalimantan was divided into three provinces instead of one—West, South, and East Kalimantan. Again, further subdivision took place shortly after the Husein coup in Central Sumatra and the establishment of the authority in that province of the

[3] De Kat Angelino, *op. cit.*, II, 403, n. 3.

[4] Schiller, *op. cit.*, p. 88.

Banteng Council in December 1956. In 1957 the central government attempted to retain at least some authority in the area by meeting demands from Djambi and Riau for separate provincial status. These provinces were established by emergency law in 1957, and the remainder of the old Central Sumatra became, at least formally speaking, the Province of West Sumatra. In the same year a fourth province was established in Kalimantan by the division of South Kalimantan into two units, Central and South Kalimantan. Thus the original establishment under Law 22 of nine units of provincial status between 1950 and 1953 had been altered by subdivision until at the end of 1957 there were fifteen such units in western Indonesia.

While the establishment of provinces in Sumatra and Borneo was more a matter of trial and error than had been the case in Java, the establishment of lower-level *swatantras* proved less difficult, though here also there was no previous foundation on which to build. Whereas in Java the *kabupaten* had existed previously both as an administrative and as an autonomous unit, those set up in Sumatra and Borneo were new from both points of view. In Kalimantan preparations were already in progress, before the establishment of the province, for the creation of regions of equivalent status to a Javanese *kabupaten*, and the establishment of the province was accompanied by a further emergency law to bring these regions into being officially. In parts of Sumatra such regions had been established by Governor's decree in 1949, i.e., before provinces themselves had been created.[5] These

[5] This stemmed from the *ad hoc* arrangements for the revolutionary period, when there was a National Committee (KNI) for Sumatra as a whole, for the Residencies of Sumatra, and for dis-

councils had no real power, or at least no powers had been formally surrendered to them by the centre. In fact, their activities were limited to discussion and advice to *bupatis* and assistance to the provincial government in the execution of provincial tasks. In 1956 further legislation under Law 22 at last regularized the situation by formally creating *kabupatens* (as well as re-establishing municipalities) in the Sumatran provinces.[6] Councils were thus given a statutory basis and brought into line with *kabupatens* and municipal DPRD's in Java.

In the eastern islands of Indonesia, subject to NIT Law 44, slower progress was made. As with Sumatra and Borneo, the prewar plans for political decentralization had not proceeded beyond the "government" stage. A "Government" of the Great East was established at the same time as the Governments of Sumatra and Borneo. During the struggle for independence East Indonesia, established as one of the constituent states in the planned federal Indonesia, had not proceeded beyond the enactment of a basic law when the unitary state was created in 1950. Between 1950 and 1957 no autonomous provinces were created. During that period the provinces of Sulawesi (Celebes), Maluku (Moluccas), and Nusa Teng-

tricts. But the fluidity of the military position and the establishment by the Dutch of the "State" of East Sumatra (*Negara Sumatra Timur*) after the first police action make it difficult to give any general statement about formal constitutional arrangements in the island during this period.

[6] Laws 8, 9, and 12/56 established small municipalities, large municipalities, and *kabupatens* in Central Sumatra; Emergency Laws 4, 5, and 6/56 established *kabupatens* and large and small municipalities in South Sumatra; Emergency Laws 7, 8, and 9/56 established *kabupatens* and large and small municipalities in North Sumatra.

gara (Lesser Sundas) were administrative divisions only, and consideration was given to the desirability of further dividing these regions before conceding self-governing institutions at the provincial level. In 1957 the first autonomous first-level *swatantra* was at last created under the new basic law—that of Maluku.[7] In 1958 Nusa Tenggara was divided into three first-level *swatantras*—Nusa Tenggara East (consisting of Flores, Sumba, and Timor), Nusa Tenggara West (consisting of Lombok and Sumbawa), and Bali.[8] In 1960 by Presidential Regulation no. 5 of that year, Sulawesi was divided into two administrative provinces. At the end of the year a government regulation in place of a law constituted these two provinces as autonomous regions, thus completing the construction of first-level regions throughout Indonesia.

At the lower levels the situation was more complex than was the case in the western islands. The State of East Indonesia had enjoyed a more substantial existence than the other *negaras* established by the Dutch before 1949, and though it had not formed provinces within itself, it had attempted, as has been noted, to evolve the new types of autonomous units at the second level to which were given the somewhat misleading name of *daerah*. The *daerah* of NIT was built on a variety of foundations, but in general it aimed at welding—by union or federation—smaller units, whether principalities or directly ruled areas, into more viable units. In Bali, for example, the existing *swapradjas* were at first united

[7] Emergency Law 22 of 1957, followed by the establishment—or re-establishment—of second-level governments within the province (Emergency Law 23/57).

[8] Law 64 of 1958.

to form one *daerah,* with effective power in the hands of a Council of *Radjahs* (*Dewan Radjah-Radjah*), though an elective body was also created. Legislation was, theoretically, the task of both councils jointly, but, in practice, the Council of *Radjahs* had power to enact ordinances alone in cases of disagreement. Broadly similar arrangements were established in Sumbawa (federation of 3 *swapradjas*), Sangihe-Talaud (federation of 6 *swapradjas*), Central Sulawesi (federation of 15 *swapradjas*), Sumba (federation of 16 *swapradjas*), and Flores (federation of 9 *swapradjas*). As a variation on this pattern the *daerahs* of South Sulawesi, North Sulawesi, and North Maluku were composed of a mixture of federations of *swapradjas* and *neo-swapradjas.*[9] (South Sulawesi was composed of a federation of 30 *swapradjas* and 8 *neo-swapradjas;* North Maluku was composed of a federation of 3 *swapradjas* and 1 *neo-swapradja;* and North Sulawesi —a more complicated example still—was composed of a federation of 1 *swapradja,* 1 *neo-swapradja,* and four federations of *swapradjas.*) In addition there were other areas, such as the formerly directly ruled areas of Minahasa and Lombok, which were now each constituted as a single *neo-swapradja,* with its own council, and there were reconstituted municipalities such as Makassar and Ambon.

Although these territories had been formally established during the existence of the State of East Indonesia, the degree to which they possessed institutions of self-government in active operation varied widely. Where

[9] A *neo-swapradja* was an area which was to be granted all or part of the powers vested in *swapradjas* under the self-governing regulations of 1938.

daerahs were composed of federations of *swapradjas*, though many councils were formed even before the enactment of Law 44/50, these were for the most part merely advisory in character. The substance of power continued to rest with the individual rulers. The *daerahs* had the right to make their own electoral regulations, but only Minahasa (including, until 1953, the city of Manado) did so. (Provision was made there for the direct election of a DPRD, a method which has since been adopted in the latest local electoral law for the whole of Indonesia, in contrast to the system of indirect election laid down in an earlier local electoral law for the areas operating under Law 22.) Other councils were elected under Governor's emergency regulation (e.g., Makassar) or were appointed on a basis of representation of political parties. In any case the giving of a final shape to the local government system of Sulawesi, Maluku, and Nusa Tenggara under NIT Law 44 was delayed pending reconsideration of the precise areas which were to be established as autonomous units immediately beneath the provincial level. The *daerah* units as defined during the existence of the State of East Indonesia were regarded as being roughly equivalent to a *kabupaten* and were intended to take over the powers exercised formerly by Residents. The object was therefore to form territorial units of sufficient size and development to make that possible—hence the federation of small *swapradjas* into larger units. But after the formation of the unitary state there was pressure from particular areas for the division of *daerahs,* if not into their constituent *swapradja* parts, at least into smaller groupings. For example, the large *daerah* of South Sulawesi which consisted of 30 *swapradjas* and 8 *neo-swapradjas* was divided by government regulation of the unitary Republic, 1953, into 7 *daerahs* still of the same (i.e., *kabupaten*) status. In 1957 3 of the 7 were subdivided further into 8 *daerahs*, thus giving a total of 12 *daerahs* where there had originally been 1. In all, the original 13 *daerahs* of East Indonesia had become 29 *daerahs* by the beginning of 1957 with further subdivision in prospect.

The introduction of Law 1/57, under which final arrangements were of course to be made, altered the picture somewhat, for it involved a change in the conception of what was a suitable unit to receive the status of second-level government. The change, as it happened, accentuated the existing trend toward the breakup of the old *daerah* unit. Legislation creating new second-level governments, or bringing existing ones into line with those in western Indonesia, had to wait upon the creation of autonomous first-level governments under Law 1 to replace the existing administrative provinces. With the establishment of Maluku, Nusa Tenggara Timur, Nusa Tenggara Barat, and Bali it was possible to make a start on the settlement of lower regions. In Maluku the existing *daerah* divisions—North Maluku, Central Maluku, Southeast Maluku, and the city of Ambon—were preserved when these regions were converted into 3 second-level regions and 1 municipality under Law 1.[10] But in Nusa Tenggara 6 original *daerahs* became 26 second-level regions. In Nusa Tenggara Timur the 3 *daerahs* which had existed under NIT Law 44 were divided into 12 second-level regions.[11] In Nusa Tenggara Barat 2 *daerahs* became

[10] Emergency Law 23/57.

[11] Law 69/58. The 3 *daerahs* which had existed before had been composed altogether of 44 very small *swapradjas* and 3 other *adat*

6 second-level governments.[12] And the island of Bali, formerly the 1 *daerah,* was divided once more into its 8 parts.[13] The 8 *swapradjas* of Bali had continued to retain their identity, of course, even within the *daerah.* The significant change that was made in 1958 was that they became ordinary regions of the second grade, not special regions. Finally in Sulawesi second-level regions were established by Law 29 of 1959 in advance of the establishment of the two first-level regions into which Sulawesi was divided in 1960. Ten second-level *swatantras* were established in the area later to become North Sulawesi and twenty-seven in South Sulawesi.

FIRST-LEVEL REGIONS

The establishment of provinces, or first-level *swatantras* as they were termed after the passage of Law 1/57, was intended to provide a solution for the first of the two aspects which have been mentioned as belonging to the problem of local government—the need to allow for broader regional awareness. According to the general plan, many areas which had been, or might have become, states in the federal system were to be constituted as provinces, and the exercise of reasonable powers of autonomy at this level would, so it was hoped, allay the suspicions of Java to be found in the outer islands, and

units. In the new dispensation some of these *swapradjas* are constituted on their own as second-level regions (e.g., Manggarai, Sikka). Others continue to form part of federations though on a smaller scale than formerly. For example, Daerah Sumba had formerly been one federation of 16 *swapradjas.* It now became 2 second-level *swatantras* composed of 9 and 7 *swapradjas* respectively.

[12] Law 69/58. [13] *Ibid.*

the suspicions of the centre to be found even within Java, and would provide an adequate outlet for local patriotism, local ambitions, and local initiative. And there was no great difficulty arising from variety of social patterns; the province was an artificial unit anyway.

The apparent regional separatism of the period 1956–1958 and especially the climax of revolt in West Sumatra and North Sulawesi in February 1958 may appear to point to the conspicuous failure of the whole plan. A more cautious judgment should be recorded at this point. The centrifugal tendencies of these months might well derive from causes other than the decentralization plan itself—the slowness of implementation of the basic legislation, for example, or the presence of other sources of discontent having little to do with regional feeling properly so called. These possibilities will be considered below. However, in addition to any other factors which may have been present, there were certain difficulties attendant upon the actual demarcation of boundaries and upon the decision to constitute particular areas as provinces which cannot be ignored. The experience of Sumatra may serve as an example.

It has been seen that whereas the Republic, in setting up first-level governments in Java, had been able to use the prewar divisions determined during the decentralization experiments of the twenties there was no such basis outside Java. Nor could the hasty attempts made by the Dutch before the transfer of sovereignty to establish states and special regions really offer a very stable foundation for the later application of the decentralization plan. Apart from the environment of conflict within which these experiments were made and the severe limitations which were placed on genuine local initiative, the establishment of these regions was dictated more by the accidents of military fortune than by any consideration of the suitability of particular areas to be so constituted. The Dutch were able to set up these governments only in areas which they could control. The independent Republic inherited these arrangements and was slow in moving toward a more rational and coherent solution to the problem. The result has been that many of the provincial divisions established after 1950 were arbitrary in character, bearing little relation to ethnic divisions or to earlier administrative boundaries. The earlier administrative divisions of the colonial period were not necessarily "natural," but they at least set habits. In Sumatra this was clearly illustrated. Provincial boundaries as first defined departed radically from the prewar administrative divisions in the island, and the provinces in consequence lacked adequate coherence as autonomous regions. In Central Sumatra, for instance, the lumping together of Minangkabau, Djambi, and Riau as one province was followed by the growth of a separatist movement in Djambi and Riau. Since communications from the west coast to the eastern parts of the province left much to be desired, there was some ground for the feeling that the two latter areas were not essentially part of the same natural geographical division as Minangkabau. Nor were there cultural affinities to offset the geographical differences. Indeed, it would not be entirely untrue to say that, until 1956, the Government of Central Sumatra was really the old West Coast Residency in a new guise. In this case the old administrative division had a greater reality than the new province. Similarly the new Province of North Sumatra extended far beyond the confines of the former East Coast Residency and was also an unwieldy and unsatisfactory entity. The government of the province was most effective where it coincided with the administrative machine already established, comparatively ineffective in the remoter parts of the province, as in Tapanuli (formerly a separate Residency), and at its minimum in Atjeh where Darul Islam [14] remained in control of most of the area.

But it was not easy to define rational boundaries. In 1956 the central government acted to rationalize the situation in North Sumatra by subdividing it and establishing Atjeh as a separate province.[15] The Husein coup in Central Sumatra in the following December prompted similar action there to bring provincial boundaries more into relation with administrative history, with social facts, and with local wishes. In 1957 Djambi and Riau were formally established as provinces (first-level governments), leaving the west coast as West Sumatra. West Sumatra, which kept itself outside the control of Djakarta, refused to recognize the new dispensation. It continued to term itself "Central Sumatra" and to claim authority still over the two new provinces. In fact, Djambi acknowledged Djakarta, and so did the Riau archipelago. The mainland portion of Riau province, however, remained loyal to Bukittinggi. A partial explanation of these loyalties may be found in the military dispensation in Sumatra, for the political situation in 1957 coincided with the lines of military authority in the island. Sumatra was divided into

[14] A movement of revolt in West Java, Atjeh, and South Sulawesi, dedicated to the formation of an Islamic state. The movement, begun in West Java during the revolutionary period, has continued since independence and has spread to the other areas.

[15] Law 24/56.

two military regions: Military Region I with its headquarters at Medan and Military Region II with its headquarters at Palembang. The boundary between these two regions did not coincide with the political divisions of the island, but cut across the Province of Central Sumatra. Minangkabau and Riau lay within Military Region I, though they formed a distinct area command with its headquarters at Padang. Djambi fell within Military Region II. The Husein revolt was, in effect, a revolt of the Padang Area Command, and it was, perhaps, natural that the mainland part of Riau should go along with the Husein regime. Conversely Djambi, since it had been militarily tied to South Sumatra even when it had been included within Central Sumatra politically, continued to look to Palembang rather than to Padang and remained loyal to the central government after it had become a separate province.[16]

The principle of creating smaller first-level divisions has obvious advantages, advantages of coherence, manageability, and perhaps, of ethnic homogeneity. The suggestion has been made that the last factor is so important that it should be the principal factor in determining which areas should be granted first-level autonomy—that existing divisions should be reconsidered and a greater number of smaller regions defined so as to coincide with ethnic groups (*suku bangsa*). There are obvious attractions in the proposal, but as a general principle it has

[16] A further difficulty attended the formation of the new provinces. Because of the opposition of West Sumatra it was not possible to make a proper transfer of archives and personnel from Bukittinggi to the capitals of the new provinces. The latter were thus founded in a vacuum without the continuity which should have come from a division of the large provincial administration.

certain difficulties. In some cases it would create divisions too small to exercise effective powers of self-government at the first level. And, although ethnic loyalties are clearly of great importance, it may be wondered whether their character is such as to form a natural basis for regional autonomy. A sense of ethnic identity is most fully developed where there are continuous or regular contacts outside the group. Where a population has been comparatively sheltered from such stimulus, its members may take their *suku bangsa* so much for granted that it may not offer a clear focus for loyalty.[17] Ethnic consciousness is perhaps most effective as an ingredient in regional consciousness when it has been reinforced by the coincidence of an administrative division, as in West Sumatra or Atjeh.

A disadvantage of the tendency toward smaller first-level divisions is that of the potential poverty of the small region. Although a large and sprawling province might prove an unsatisfactory unit by reason of its internal diversity, the financial resources of a *swatantra* should, as far as possible, be adequate for its responsibilities. This test is not, however, conclusive. The facts of geography as well as the strength of local loyalties may sometimes justify the subdivision of a large area. Difficulties of communication between the main centres of population, as in Kalimantan, would seem to suggest the rationality of the subsequent subdivision of the old single Province of Kalimantan.

There can probably be no entirely satisfactory set of criteria to apply to this problem of defining regions, however, since any rational plan is likely to be upset by particular regional demands for recognition. Since it proclaims its

[17] For a discussion of this point see Skinner, *op. cit.*, p. 7.

willingness to meet legitimate local demands, the central government, in determining the actual delimitation of particular provinces, must consider not merely what divisions are convenient. It must also consider what divisions, if they are desired, are reasonable and, perhaps, what divisions are expedient. Where a demand exists for the creation of a new province, the question must be examined in terms of the size, population, background, and competence of the area concerned. But it may sometimes be necessary, on grounds of expediency, to concede provincial status to an area which does not measure up to a list of tests of that kind. As may be seen in Table 1, provincial status has not presupposed any equality of population. It is possible, however, to exaggerate the difficulty. Indeed, to ask in general terms what are the criteria which should be used in defining a province is to beg the question, for it assumes a necessary equality as between such regions, without indicating in what respects they are to be equal. It should be possible theoretically to concede first-level status without indicating that the region so established should enjoy governmental services of the same quality and complexity as other regions of the same grade. It would possess the right to handle all matters belonging to first-level governments. But the size of its civil service, the dignity of its public buildings, and the manner in which it was able to execute its proper duties would have to depend on the resources available to it.

Something of this view lay behind the terminological changes made in the hierarchy of autonomous regions by Law 1/57. It has been seen that Law 1 replaced the terms province, *kabupaten,* and *desa* by the vaguer terms Level I, Level II, and Level III. Although the verbal change

Table 1. Populations of individual provinces *

Atjeh	1,550,000	Central Java	17,200,000	South Kalimantan	1,440,000
North Sumatra	4,340,000	East Java	20,150,000	East Kalimantan	440,000
West Sumatra	2,600,000	Greater Djakarta	2,081,000	Bali	1,790,000
Riau	970,000	Special Region of		West Nusa Tenggara	1,780,000
Djambi	670,000	Jogjakarta	2,100,000	East Nusa Tenggara	2,200,000
South Sumatra	4,170,000	West Kalimantan	1,490,000	Sulawesi	6,600,000
West Java	16,069,000	Central Kalimantan	430,000	Maluku	770,000

* Estimated figures for 1958 supplied by the Biro Pusat Statistik.

was primarily designed to avoid the offensiveness of using Javanese terminology, it was also thought that the vaguer language might allow for greater flexibility in applying the basic local government pattern to individual circumstances. It should make it easier to establish, as equivalent regions within the meaning of the act, regions which varied widely in area, population, wealth, and ethnic composition, but which it is convenient to handle in the same way for local government purposes. This point may be pushed too far. Even the old laws did not prevent variety in application. For example, though no *kabupatens* were established in the eastern islands of Indonesia, it was proposed to regard the *daerah* unit as roughly equivalent to a *kabupaten* for practical purposes. The new law, in breaking away from the connotation of the old terms, should make this easier. The term "province" was perhaps less open to variation in application. Although there was no exact definition of the criteria, whether in terms of area, population, or resources, which would indicate the desirability of conferring provincial status on a particular region, the term tended to suggest an area which, in a federal Republic, might have possessed the economic basis and the social coherence such as to justify its establishment as a constituent state. The less definite term "Level I" by contrast left open the possibility of creating autonomous governments with first-level powers in areas which possessed strong local feeling, but which would not ordinarily have qualified for provincial status. The case of Bali may be taken as an example. It was originally held that Bali, though it was too big to be a second-level *swatantra,* was too small and too poor to justify its separation from Nusa Tenggara and its elevation to first-level status by itself. Even when it was decided, in 1957, that Nusa Tenggara was too unwieldy an area to receive autonomy as a unit, the intention was still to divide it merely into two units—a western part in which Bali was to be lumped together with Lombok and Sumbawa and an eastern part consisting of the remaining islands of the group. In the proposed smaller Province of West Nusa Tenggara it was intended to establish the individual principalities of Bali as second-level governments and to discard altogether the new unity which had been achieved by the formation of a single *daerah* in the island under the State of East Indonesia. Finally, however, it was resolved to recognize the essential coherence of the island and its difference from its neighbors and to confer first-level status on it. Acceptance of this solution did not suggest that Bali was on all fours with, say, the first-level region of East Java and entitled to roads, hospitals, and the like, on the same scale.

If this point appears labored, it is because there has in fact been—and Bali notwithstanding there continues to be—a tendency for regions to demand better services, such as roads, schools, or hospitals, merely on the ground that other regions of the same formal status are better provided for in this respect. This type of false comparison has helped to add bitterness to the complaints of less populous regions that they have been neglected by Djakarta; and it would require more than a terminological adjustment to remove such grievances. It is not easy to see why the problem should exist at the provincial level when it does not arise at lower levels. In the case of municipal governments, for example, there appears to be no difficulty whatsoever in accepting the principle that equality of status does not necessarily mean equality of power or function, and the changes made by Law 1 in removing the distinction between large and small towns is accepted as a sensible improvement. Under Law 22 Surabaja was a *kota besar,* a large municipality equal in status to a *kabupaten,* whereas Pasuruan was a *kota ketjil,* a small municipality equal in status to a *desa.* Under the new law they are both *kotapradja, tingkat II*—second-level municipalities. That obviously does not mean that Pasuruan can demand the services or the quality of administration necessary for a city the size of Surabaja, and nobody suggests that it should. But in the case of first-level governments the principle does not appear to be easily accepted.

SECOND-LEVEL REGIONS

The definition of second-level regions in the western islands has not been a subject of controversy. In Java the lines of *kabupaten* division were well established, and elsewhere too it has been possible to find administrative divisions suitable for treatment as autonomous regions. The demands for second-level autonomy are, in any case, not as vociferous as those for first-level autonomy—except, perhaps, in the case of towns. It is difficult to draw a satisfactory dividing line between those smaller towns which should receive municipal status and those which should not. But apart from urban areas the encouragement of self-government at this level does not appear as a response to any very strongly felt local need. Indeed, it may be argued that the whole idea of an intermediate stage of autonomy represents an attempt to find an alternative to the old administrative system and that it therefore derives rather from the needs of the central government than from the need to satisfy genuine pressure for the exercise of local initiative.

In view of the history and character of the Javanese *kabupaten* it is not surprising that this should be so. From an administrative point of view this has been, perhaps, the most important link in the chain of command. At this level all of the affairs of the region have been effectively centred in the hands of the *bupati,* who has been the terminal point for the lines of authority passing down through *wedanas* and *tjamats.* The *bupati,* of course, was responsible in turn to the Resident and the Governor, but theirs was a much more general supervision than that which he exercised over the officers below him. It is doubtful, however, whether the *kabupaten* could be as effective a unit from the point of view of autonomy as it has been from the point of view of administration. It is too small in territorial extent to offer a point of focus to broad regional feeling, yet not small enough to fall within the horizon of the village. It will be seen in a later chapter that, with some exceptions, members of second-level councils are not drawn from the rural population, and the questions which are discussed by them are not usually those of most concern to the rural population. There are, it is true, identifiable regional matters which can be handled well enough at this level—water supply in towns which do not have municipal status, roads, and other public works—but these matters touch the interests of a small elite rather than those of the general village inhabitant. It might even be argued that the establishment of a lower and more basic level of autonomy would render the second level superfluous. The needs of the population could then be served adequately by the local council for immediately local matters and by the provincial government for matters of more general concern. Even pending this arrangement the responsibility for *kabupaten* tasks might be better redistributed between provinces and municipalities. They do not require a special intermediate level of local self-government.

This view has in fact been argued in certain quarters. In particular it has found advocates in the Special Region of Jogjakarta, where local government experiments were originally directed to the establishment of a strong third level of autonomy based on the amalgamation or federation of individual *desas*. The success of this approach, it was argued, would remove all necessity for a second level of autonomy between the *daerah* government (= provincial) and the village unions.[18] Jogjakarta was a special case, of course. This region is composed of two former *swapradjas,* and before the war the two rulers possessed the usual powers allowed to *swapradjas* under the long contract. In this situation *kabupatens* during the colonial period remained as administrative units only and did not enjoy the preliminary experience in local government as did *kabupatens* in the directly ruled parts of Java. *Desa* organization was weaker also, or at least *desa* loyalty was modified by loyalty to the ruler. For this reason the reorganization of *desas* into larger units has been easier than might prove to be the case elsewhere, while the newly created autonomous *kabupatens* have less of a vested interest in their own continued existence than is the case

[18] See Soenarjo Dipodiningrat, *Proces Demokratiseering dan Otonomiseering Pemerintahan di Daerah Istimewa Jocjakarta* (Jogjakarta, 1954) and *Pembentukan Daerah Otonom Tingkat ke III* (Jogjakarta, 1956).

elsewhere. In East Indonesia, by contrast, the *daerah* unit established under NIT Law 44/50, theoretically of the same status as a *kabupaten,* appears to be a more effective unit for the expression of local aspirations and might offer grounds for the view that there the third rather than the second level should be dispensed with.

The Jogjakarta approach has not been unchallenged. In 1957 Dr. Hatta, former Vice-President, argued the contrary case in a press article.[19] Hatta argued that a multilevel system of self-government was inevitably hierarchical in character and was likely to be undemocratic; power would tend to accumulate in the higher and more remote levels. In these circumstances the province would represent such an important centre of power that its component parts would wish to become provinces, and there would be pressure, of the kind already described above, to draw provincial boundaries more narrowly. This in turn would threaten the role of the autonomous *kabupaten.* Hatta's own suggested solution was to lay the emphasis of self-government on the *kabupaten,* giving it a directly elected assembly and making the province primarily a coordinating level. The province, certainly, would possess an assembly, but composed of *kabupaten* delegates rather than of directly elected representatives. The *kabupaten* would be the main level between village and centre for the exercise of local initiative and the expression of local feeling.

Whether or not *kabupaten* self-government could be given a more effective life than it has possessed hitherto, it is clearly the case in practice that the level has remained important from the view of the centre, and it was natural

[19] *Pedoman,* April 27, 1957.

that autonomous institutions at this level should be expected to carry something of the old administrative load. Law 22 of 1948 foreshadowed the gradual disappearance of the old administrative corps as autonomous government got under way, and in spite of a rear-guard action by those who feared the effect of such a development the initial steps were taken, for good or ill, toward that end. In the resulting situation the autonomous *kabupaten* could become responsible not merely for the co-operating administration (*medebewind*)—i.e., the execution of tasks delegated by the centre or the province—for which the law provided, but for the assumption of the task of lower regional administration. Until a third level of autonomy was established, it would presumably be necessary to maintain the lower ranks of the *pamong pradja* to carry the authority of government to the base of the pyramid. But it was possible that the control of these tasks might be transferred to the autonomous side. The *wedanas* and *tjamats,* at present officials of the centre, might thus become servants of the *kabupaten* council. That, at least, was the theory. If, on the other hand, the third level of autonomy did eventually develop an effective life, the need for the *kabupaten* either as a convenient administrative division or as a level of autonomy would be correspondingly reduced.

THIRD-LEVEL UNITS

The whole idea of a third level of autonomy has undergone considerable change since the enactment of Law 22/48, partly as a result of the obvious defects of the provision made for the third level by that law. Present in the original planning was the idea that the lowest level of autonomy, designed to satisfy the needs of the immediate locality, should be grounded as far as possible in customary organization. Both provinces and *kabupatens* were artificial creations, overarching all traditional forms. The object was to use, below these, units which enjoyed (if the term may be allowed) a "natural" existence or which could command a traditional loyalty from their members. But to use a customary unit poses its own difficulties. The more firmly a unit is grounded in custom, the less easy it is to introduce new procedures.

Societies are never static, of course. It is commonly asserted that Indonesian society has been more successful than most in resisting the pressure of external influences,[20] and during Dutch rule it was a matter of deliberate policy to respect customary law, to safeguard land, and, in general, to preserve the village as a social unit.[21] Nevertheless, the combined impact of alien rule and of an alien economy could not but leave its mark, in varying degrees. Indeed, at the level of administration the very policy of recognizing and making use of the traditional leadership in the village itself, paradoxically, tended to change the character of that leadership. The government was anxious to find one chief with whom to deal, and from the period of the Culture System onward it therefore tended, through a misunderstanding of village organization, to confer upon individuals powers which they did not possess in custom and to alter their whole position in the village scheme.[22]

[20] E.g., J. C. van Leur, "On Early Asian Trade," in *Indonesian Trade and Society* (The Hague, 1955), p. 95.

[21] J. S. Furnivall, *Colonial Policy and Practice* (Cambridge, Eng., 1948), pp. 241, 263.

[22] In the same way the use of regents both by the Dutch East India Company and by the later Indies government had the effect

Even to regulate and formalize customary procedures in village government was to introduce change. Yet, whatever changes may have occurred, village organization in its various forms continues to possess vigorous life. It was unfortunate that the term *desa* was used in Law 22, since the *desa* of Java has no exact counterpart elsewhere. It is a territorial unit very different in character from, say, the *negeri* of Minangkabau, partly based on kinship, or the *marga* of South Sumatra, or even the *desa* of Bali. Use of the term obscured the actual multiplicity of local forms which might well affect the organization of a local government system. However, the terminological changes of Law 1 removed the suggestion of using Javanese terminology. The term "Level III" involved no presuppositions about the ideal character of the lowest level of autonomy.

Even if allowance is made for the wide variety of village forms to be found in Indonesia, the creation of a third level of autonomy would pose the problem of grafting new procedures on to those already established. To form democratic councils on patterns suggested in Law 22/48 or Law 1/57 would presuppose a fairly "open" society. Social change is proceeding rapidly in Indonesia, but each of the various forms of village organization, because of the strength of customary obligations and procedures, is

---

of altering the character of existing authorities. For example, see J. Bastin, *The Native Policies of Raffles in Java and Sumatra* (Oxford, 1957). Village authorities, like regents, were used for the purposes of government. "Under the Culture System the village was used to promote cultivation for the State; under the Liberal system it was adapted to the requirements of planters; under the Ethical system it was used to promote welfare along western lines" (Furnivall, *Colonial Policy*, p. 241).

still to a great extent a closed society of its own. (This is, of course, a matter of degree. Some villages have already been brought within the orbit of a wider economy and society and have been the subjects of a greater breakdown in traditional patterns than is the case with others.) Further, even if it were easy to transform customary procedures in the desired fashion, the village unit which represents the core of social organization in Indonesia is considered by the government to be, for the most part, too small to serve as an effective unit of autonomy. It was really this which gave the Ministry ground for reconsideration of its early plan. During the drafting of the bill which was eventually to take shape as Law 1/57 attention was given to the possibility of creating third-level governments of a more reasonable size in areas formed by the amalgamation or the federation of individual *adat* units, but this would have been an ambitious plan since it would involve nothing less than a substantial modification of customary organization.

Reference has already been made to the Jogjakarta experiment on these lines. Arguing that the *kabupaten* was an artificial unit which had its uses only so long as a lower level was not in existence, the government of the special region has sought experimentally to combine neighboring *desas* either by union or by federation.[23] In

[23] The choice between union or federation was not regarded as one of principle, but merely one of convenience (Soenarjo Dipodiningrat, *Pembentukan Daerah Otonom Tingkat ke III,* p. 48). The practical difference was not unimportant, however. If *desas* were amalgamated, the individual *desas* would become merely administrative units under the authority of the DPD of the third-level autonomous region. If federation was the method adopted, the individual *desas* would continue to possess forms of autonomy that they had possessed in the past (*ibid.,* appendices I and II, pp. 54–55).

the *ketjamatan* (subdistrict) of Pakem, for instance, 16 *desas* comprising 60 *pedukuhan* (hamlets) and representing a population of over 23,000 were reduced to 5 *desas* each with a DPRD and DPD instead of the traditional forms of village assembly. However, in view of the special circumstances of Jogjakarta, it might well be expected that such an approach elsewhere might be defeated by the strength of custom. The primary units might well prove to have more staying power than the new.

The plan of the Ministry of Home Affairs was that, since the *desa* was too small, the third level of autonomy might be based upon the *ketjamatan* or something like it in terms of area and population. It was argued that although the *ketjamatan* has been purely an administrative division up to the present time and has had no existence in custom it was still a small enough unit to fall within the horizon of the *desa* population. The *ketjamatan,* both in the colonial period and at present, has been a crucial level of administration in Java since it is the point at which the *adat* unit, the *desa,* comes into contact with the central government machinery. Regular meetings, usually weekly or fortnightly, between the *tjamat* and the *lurahs* (village heads) of his area provide the means whereby central government requirements, explanations, and requests are passed down to the *desa.* These meetings are not for the purpose of discussion and decision, but for the purpose of paternal instruction by the *tjamat* to the *lurahs.* Whether or not this administrative unit could be transformed into an autonomous unit—and, if it were, what would happen to the "natural" level of autonomy, the *desa*—is extremely problematical. It might be possible to establish a representative council for a whole *ketjamatan,* either by the process of amalgamating *desas* or on the basis of a federal association of *desas,* as in Jogjakarta. In either case it is likely that such a council, in its decision making, would still have to recognize the existence of a separate, vigorous, and prior process of decision making in the individual *desas* themselves. The actual execution of *ketjamatan* council decisions, for instance, might well be forced to depend upon the consent and co-operation of traditional *desa* leaders, whether the status of those leaders was still formally recognized or not. Particularly would this be likely to be the case where the individuals elected to the central council were different from the traditional authorities as constituted before the amalgamation or federation. For reasons such as these the government, though it did desire to use, as its basic level of autonomy, the *ketjamatan* or something like it in area and population, also recognized that, at least in Java, the strength of the customary unit was such as to make such a transition a remote possibility for the time being. Hence it adopted the more flexible wording of Law 1, which, instead of providing for three levels of autonomy, allowed, more vaguely, for the formation of *up to* three levels. The lowest level was to be set up where circumstances made it convenient: where, that is to say, there already existed traditionally organized units of suitable size and coherence to be adapted to the tasks of modern local government or where it appeared possible to create new units.

In broad terms there are four types of situation to be handled. First of all there is the situation to which reference has just been made, where geographically small units exist with a strong base in custom, as in Java. Here, for the reasons mentioned, the establishment of a third level based on, say, the *ketjamatan* would be difficult.

Hence in Java the Ministry's plan has so far been limited to the creation of first- and second-level governments only, and this limitation is seen by responsible officials as necessary for an indefinite period of time. Whether the innovations in Jogjakarta may stimulate experiments elsewhere depends on how far the circumstances of Jogjakarta are regarded as essentially different from those outside the special region. Secondly, there were areas where, in colonial times, the Dutch had attempted to evolve more manageable units through the amalgamation of *adat* units. In the Karo plateau of East Sumatra, for instance, 250 villages were reorganized first into 15 large unions for administrative purposes and then into 5 self-governing territories subject to the short declaration. Although an attempt was made in this centralization to preserve indigenous forms, it was obvious that these would undergo very radical change in the process.[24] Thirdly, there are areas where custom has collapsed or been submerged under the pressure of new forces. The environs of Medan provide an example. Here the original population has been swamped by newcomers drawn in by estate enterprise. Where this has happened, at least there would be no problem arising from the strength of custom that would prevent the definition of a satisfactory unit for the role of Level III. Finally, there are situations where, without amalgamation, there already exists in custom a suitable foundation for third-level government under the Act. The *negeri* of Minangkabau, though it is approximately

[24] W. Middendorp, "The Administration of the Outer Provinces of the Netherlands Indies," in B. Schrieke, ed., *The Effect of Western Influence on Native Civilisations in the Malay Archipelago* (Batavia, 1929).

equal in size of population to a Javanese *desa,* covers a more extensive area, and it has already had some experience in the operation of a council system modified by Dutch regulation. Moreover, it controls more adequate sources of revenue—e.g., unlike the Javanese *desa* it secures income from market administration which is a *kabupaten* or municipal preserve in Java. It may well prove a suitable subject for experiment as an autonomous unit of the third level. The same applies to the *marga* of South Sumatra where a complex administration under council control and on a basis, often, of financial independence already exists.[25] Again, some of the smaller *swapradja* in East Indonesia might be similarly adapted, perhaps after an interim period in the form of third-level special regions. In larger *swapradja,* where the administrative system of local rulers has already weakened the identity of the village as a self-contained unit, it may be possible to repeat the experiments of Jogjakarta. But in all cases the creation of the lowest level of autonomy must be a matter for trial and error and for the adaptation of modern procedures to the character of the society in question.

In general the core of the problem lies in the difficulty of determining which units in Indonesia have genuine substance. In Java the *desa* has substance in a way that higher units do not have it. As has been noticed earlier, the autonomous *kabupaten* is really a product of social change. It serves the interests of the elite, which has never belonged to, or has escaped from, the *desa.* So long as

[25] Notice, for example, the budget of the *marga* of Kajuagung, Kabupaten Ogan and Komering Ilir. In 1957 it had an income of Rp.247,987 and an expenditure of Rp.130,538.

effective social organization continues to be based on the small unit, the higher levels of local government must be, to some extent, divorced from the mass of the population. And it is the existence of the gap between government and the great mass of the governed which gives local administration in Indonesia something of a colonial character still. General government is the function of the Ministry of Home Affairs. It is not without significance that the building which today houses the Ministry in Djakarta is the same as that which once housed the central administration of the Indies (*Binnenlands Bestuur*) before the war. There has necessarily been more carry-over than might have been expected in the types of functions performed within its walls.

There is also a further point to be noticed. The caution of the Ministry of Home Affairs in experimentation has, perhaps, not been solely due to the difficulties which have been mentioned, though these have provided a prime ground for delay. There was also, no doubt, a political element present. There has been a natural reluctance to open the village to the full play of rivalry between political parties. In particular there has been a fear that an unsophisticated rural population may be suitable material for exploitation by what is considered to be irresponsible political leadership. More bluntly, the PNI leanings of the *pamong pradja* and the PSI (Socialist Party) affiliations of some of the senior civil servants have helped in the past to explain a fear that the creation of the third level may deliver the village to the PKI (Communist Party) whose skill in grass-roots organization has already been demonstrated in local as well as national elections. Hence there was the desire that the existing system of village government and administration should continue to function, but outside the provisions of the local government law and subject, as at present, to the control exercised by the central government through the chain of authority extending down through *bupatis, wedanas,* and *tjamats.*

The problem of the role of the centre has been brought into sharper focus in the long-drawn-out debate on the future role of the *pamong pradja* which will be examined in the next chapter.

SPECIAL REGIONS

Although Jogjakarta has been the only example on a significant scale of the formal transformation of a *swapradja* into a *daerah istimewa* (three small *swapradjas* were established as special regions, Level II, in Kalimantan), there has been a certain amount of experimentation with *swapradjas* in East Indonesia as a preparation for the creation of more special regions in the future.

Jogjakarta was exceptionally suited to special-region treatment from the beginning. One of the conditions of the special-regions idea was that less developed principalities might get gradual practice in manipulating a council system and acquire experience in the technical aspects of daily administration. But Jogjakarta was already, in most respects, like a fully fledged province. Its councils and its administrative system were already well developed. It has owed a good deal of its model character to the skill and ability of its ruler, Sultan Hamengku Buwono IX, who, in addition to holding high office at the national level (he was Minister of Defense in the Hatta Cabinet, Republic of the United States of Indonesia, Deputy Prime Minister under Natsir, and Defense Minister in the Wilopo Cabinet), has proved an adventurous administrator in his own state. While the Ministry of the Interior hesitated to create third-level local governments in the areas under its direct control, the Sultan of Jogjakarta, as has been seen, pushed ahead with the amalgamation of *desas* and the experimental creation within them of councils on the Law 22 pattern. In applying this policy he was not merely seeking a fuller implementation of the local government law, but was trying to demonstrate his own distinctive view—that if a properly functioning basic level could be created there was no need for an intermediate level as well.

The Sultan plays a double role, that of a political leader and administrator and that of the head of a royal house. As the latter, in the palace, he maintains all the apparatus of state: the forms and ceremonies, the attention to precedence laid down by tradition. But outside the palace, in his role as *kepala daerah,* he becomes in outer appearances the normal provincial Governor. The dual personality, however, is not entirely complete, and, as regional head, the Sultan still carries the mystical aura of his hereditary position. He thus has a considerable advantage in his handling of unruly councilors who cannot entirely shed their feelings of awe before authority. But this characteristic no doubt belongs to a transitional phase.

Jogjakarta's maturity was demonstrated in 1951 when it was the second region of any level to hold elections (indeed, the only region to hold elections under the earlier electoral law, Law 7 of 1950).

In East Indonesia, with the long-delayed establishment of autonomous provinces, it became necessary to decide what was to be done with the many tiny *swapradjas* which had been grouped together to form the much larger *daerah* units. Attention has already been drawn to the tendency to redivide the *daerahs* into smaller groupings, and this was now pushed further. Of significance was the fact that the new groupings of units which were accepted were established as ordinary second-level local governments, not as special regions. The second-level region of West Sumba, for instance, comprised nine *swapradjas,* but was itself an ordinary region. And the *swapradja* Manggarai, which was big enough to be recognized as a second-level region by itself, became an ordinary region. Within the second-level regions the individual *swapradjas* could preserve their own identity, just as did the *desas* within a Javanese *kabupaten.* They still owed their legal existence to the short declaration binding them to the central government as the inheritor of the old colonial government, and they were to that extent independent of the authority of the executive council of the second-level government above them. Since no third-level units were yet to be established, the ultimate fate of these small principalities was left open. They could conceivably lend themselves to special-region treatment at that level.

Between the exceptional example of Jogjakarta and the small principalities which might lend themselves to establishment as special regions of the third level there are many gradations, not all of which are appropriate units for creation as special regions at either the third or second level. Here again the problem of size has been a major one. In East Indonesia the combination of smaller units, some of them *swapradjas,* was intended to rationalize the situation and to create a manageable number of second-level units. The form of combination varied according to circumstances. In spite of the apparent rationality of the arrangements, however, many of the new units failed to acquire a genuine existence (this was partly due, perhaps, to delays in implementation of the law, such that many of the divisions were not even given a chance to come into being), and the constituent parts remained the effective groupings. In this connection it is worth looking once more and in greater detail at the case of Bali. The history of the arrangements adopted there may serve as an example which can focus at one point a number of the problems to be faced in Eastern Indonesia.

Bali was composed of eight principalities [26] which had been recognized before the Second World War as self-governing states within the limitations of the short declaration binding them to the Indies government. After the war they were combined, as has been seen, to form the one *daerah* within the State of East Indonesia. This was not a completely unheralded development, for there had been some political experimentation immediately before the war. In 1938 the eight rulers had established advisory councils (*Paruman Negara*) within their respective states. The members were nominated and their powers were purely advisory, but the innovation was a preparatory step in the modification of the powers of the rulers. In the same year, in an attempt to enable at least some concerted action in matters of common concern, the eight rulers established a council (*Paruman Agung*) consisting at first merely of themselves. In the following year the council was enlarged to include two advisers from each *swapradja*. The council was chaired by the Dutch Resi-

[26] Buleling, Djemberana, Tabanan, Badung, Gianjar, Klungkung, Bangli, Karangasem.

dent of Bali and Lombok. After the war, when Holland again resumed control of the island, the *Paruman Agung* was re-established, but upon the establishment of the State of East Indonesia the idea of a union of the eight *swapradjas* was placed on a somewhat different basis with the formation of Daerah Bali as one of the thirteen *daerahs* of East Indonesia in 1947. The island became one unit for the administrative purposes of the government of NIT and also, though to a lesser degree, for the purposes of local autonomy.

Daerah Bali could have been described as a federation of *swapradjas.* With the formation of the new unit the single council, *Paruman Agung,* was replaced by two distinct bodies: a Council of *Radjahs* (*Dewan Radjah-Radjah*) and a "popular" assembly (which retained the earlier name, *Paruman Agung*) composed of 40 members, of whom 34 were elected by indirect election—5 from each of the five major *swapradjas* and 3 from the three lesser ones.[27] Provision was also made for the nomination by *Radjahs* of representatives of minorities. The powers entrusted to the "lower" house were extremely limited, and in the few years for which the machinery lasted the government of Daerah Bali was little more than government by the rulers, who acted, however, in a concerted fashion through their own council. For example, though legislation nominally depended on agreement between the two houses, there was provision, "when circumstances demanded rapid action," for the *Dewan Radjah-Radjah* to

[27] The *desas* elected representatives to an electoral college which chose the three representatives of the *swapradja* on the *Paruman Agung.*

enact measures on its own authority.[28] In 1950, however, with the passage of NIT Law 44, the government of the *daerah* was brought into line with the terms of the new basic law. The *Dewan Radjah-Radjah* and the *Paruman Agung* were abolished and were replaced by a representative assembly and an executive council (DPRD and DPD) on the standard pattern. The former was chosen at first in a manner similar to that prescribed for Western Indonesia by Government Regulation 39/50. The *kepala daerah* was chosen by the central government from the nominees of the DPRD. In 1956 Daerah Bali came under the provisions of the transitional regulations which were applied elsewhere, and a new transitional DPRD was appointed on the basis of the general election results of the preceding year.

Although, at the *daerah* level, postwar Bali continued the earlier experiment in amalgamation, it was reasonable nonetheless to question the reality of the new unit. During the postwar period the application of Law 44 to the island as a whole was matched by similar provision within each of the constituent principalities which became, in effect, special autonomous regions of the third level. Executive councils were established to replace the old advisory *Paruman Negara*, and the traditional ruler was, of course, appointed as *kepala daerah* in each case. After the passage of Law 1/57 the whole position in Bali, as in East Indonesia generally, came under review. Just as it had proved expedient in 1952 and 1953 to subdivide many of the *daerahs* established under Law 44, so in Bali there were doubts as to the suitability of the island as a whole being

[28] Est. Law 15, Aug. 1947, Article 29 (3).

retained as a single second-level *swatantra*. Indeed, if the model of a Javanese *kabupaten* is kept in mind, it would seem that a single *swapradja,* though slightly smaller in population than a typical *kabupaten,* was much closer to the *kabupaten* in terms of area, scale of responsibility, and general function in both the administrative and the autonomous scheme of things than was the *daerah*. Consideration was therefore given to the possibility of constituting each *swapradja* not as a third-level but as a second-level *swatantra,* either "special" or "ordinary." This would have meant abolishing the *daerah* and admitting the failure of a bold experiment. As has been seen, this was at first proposed. The proposal to divide Nusa Tenggara into two first-level *swatantras* and to include Bali with Lombok and Sumbawa as one of these involved the constitution of the eight individual *swapradjas,* not the *daerah* as a whole, as second-level *swatantras*. The question was solved, however, by the decision to retain the unity of Bali by making it by itself a single first-level region.

This decision still left open the question of whether the second-level regions were to be special regions or not. The question had been under consideration for some time. In two of the states the *Radjahs* themselves had wished to step down from the position of *kepala daerah*. And it was also reported that, in 1957, in conversations with the Governor of the province, another four had indicated that they too were agreeable to the conversion of their principalities into ordinary regions. The change would make little practical difference, perhaps. There did not appear to be a great deal of public feeling on the question, and DPRD's refrained from discussing it. In these circumstances the actual establishment of Bali as a first-level region in 1958 was accompanied by the establishment of eight second-level regions—"ordinary"—to coincide with the eight principalities.

This decision was in line with general informed feeling, which, by this time, had come to regard the concept of the special region as something to be applied only in very exceptional circumstances. The decision in other parts of Nusa Tenggara to create ordinary second-level regions was also consistent with the trend. It would seem that Jogjakarta was likely to remain an interesting survival—a solitary exception to the rule of adopting a uniform pattern of local government wherever possible, at least for the second level and above. The special region, if the idea survives at all, may be applied in future only to very small units.

The problems associated with the definition of suitable areas for constitution as areas of local government must depend for their solution in great part upon experiment. The early years of planning, despite the attempt to secure uniformity, have provided a wealth of experience in different regional forms at different levels. This experience will continue to offer a basis for whatever adaptions are made in the future.

4

The Regional Head and the Problem of Supervision

THE central issue in the controversy which surrounded the preparation of Law 1/57, and which continued to surround its implementation, concerned the degree of control to be retained by the centre and the method by which that control was to be exercised. Briefly, the choice lay between the continental system whereby the central figure in the local government system is an official of the centre (the burgomaster in Holland or Germany, the prefect in France) and a system more akin to that of Britain in which control is exercised through the operation of the courts in ensuring that local authorities do not overstep the powers conferred on them and through the limitations of finance rather than through an official entrusted with supervisory functions. The Indies before the Second World War adhered to the former system. As De Kat Angelino argued:

It brings experience and discipline into relation with spontaneous initiative and enthusiasm for the public good. It makes people used to the idea that autonomous life can only exist within the sphere of organic unity permeating every local section of the greater community.[1]

By contrast, it has been noticed that Law 1 resolved the controversy by choosing to make the office of *kepala daerah* elective. In view of the importance of this provision it will be as well at this point to embark on a full discussion of the issues involved in the change.

The compromise arrangement of Law 22 whereby the centre was to appoint a *kepala daerah* from a list selected by the DPRD was intended to satisfy local demands for a fuller measure of autonomy, while giving the centre at least some opportunity of securing a man agreeable to itself on whom it could rely to carry out the supervisory functions still allotted to the *kepala daerah* (i.e., the delaying of local ordinances which appeared to conflict with higher legislation or were contrary to the general interest and the general co-ordination of local and central government tasks). It is fairly obvious that this sort of compromise was bound to be unsatisfactory since it could not hope to meet the requirements of either side. Indeed, an arrangement whereby nominations would be made by representative bodies and appointments by the central government was likely to attain the worst of both worlds. In spite of the retention of an element of appointment the central government could not count, with any degree of certainty, on being able to find even one man in a list of four candidates chosen by the DPRD who was suitable for appointment from its point of view. Given the operation of normal political party competition for control of the local legislature, it was only to be expected that the legislature's nominees for the office of *kepala daerah*

[1] De Kat Angelino, *op. cit.*, II, 402.

would be political leaders of the community whose interests and sympathies would be bound up with their party and their region. The centre, on the other hand, sought a regional head who could see with the eyes of the centre as well as with those of the region and with the eyes of an official as well as with those of a politician. Such a combination of virtues in the one man was not impossible, but it was unlikely. From the point of view of the region itself the compromise was again bound to be unsatisfactory since the limitation placed upon the free choice of *kepala daerah* implied a general limitation on the powers of local government.

It was therefore not surprising that the central government should have availed itself of the escape clause provided in Law 22 which allowed the direct appointment of the *kepala daerah* for the time being, and of major importance was the fact that the central government, in exercising its power under this clause, should simply have appointed the appropriate members of its own administrative service, the *pamong pradja*. Governors became *kepala daerah* of provinces, *bupatis* became *kepala daerah* of *kabupatens*, and mayors became *kepala daerah* of municipalities.[2] This practice reversed the intention of Law 22 and, in effect, constituted a straight return to the prewar method whereby an official was installed at the centre of the local government. The implications of the change may be appreciated more clearly if intentions of Law 22 are examined briefly once more.

In providing for a semiresponsible *kepala daerah* Law

[2] This was the general rule, but there were exceptions in the case of higher appointments. Not all governors were selected from within the service.

22 referred to the office as possessing a "dual function." In reality, as has been suggested already, it would have been more accurate to distinguish three functions rather than two:

1. The chairmanship of the executive council
2. Supervision of executive council and legislative council
3. Territorial administration and general co-ordination to be performed for the central government by an official of that government

Law 22 placed the first two of these in the hands of the *kepala daerah* (his dual function) and assumed that the third function would gradually become superfluous or, alternatively, become the duty of the local government. In practice, with the appointment of officials as *kepala daerah,* all three functions were retained and were concentrated in the hands of a single person in each area. Strictly speaking, however, the distinction remained between the duties of governors, *bupatis,* and mayors as *pamong pradja* on the one hand and the dual functions of the *kepala daerah* on the other. For example, the general co-ordinating and administrative duties of the *pamong pradja* did not pass to the local government, whose field of activity was to that extent restricted. Provinces, *kabupatens,* and municipalities remained administrative divisions for those central government purposes falling outside the scope of autonomy, and governors, *bupatis,* and mayors continued to be the officers to whom the lower administrative ranks were responsible. But in another respect the distinction was blurred. Whereas, according to Law 22, the supervisory function was to be exercised as part of the responsibility of the *kepala daerah,* not as part of that of the *pamong pradja,* the appointment of members of the *pamong pradja* to that office tended to confuse the separate roles and undoubtedly strengthened the element of supervision.

These consequences were deliberate. The decision to appoint directly to the office, rather than from a list of nominees submitted by the legislative council, as well as the accompanying practice of appointing existing officials, was due partly, no doubt, to the fact that if the position had been given the semiresponsible character envisaged in the law the government would have been faced with the necessity of making immediate readjustments in its administrative system in order to cope with the considerable body of unemployed officials which would have been created. The plan was to allow the *pamong pradja* to become superfluous gradually, not at one stroke. But there was also present the conviction that close official control and supervision of autonomous governments were a necessity for the time being. Although in theory a *kepala daerah* appointed from a list of nominees according to the normal procedure laid down in Law 22 was intended to owe loyalty to the centre as well as to the elected council and was intended to exercise supervision over the local government on behalf of the centre, the officials who were actually appointed owed loyalty to the centre by virtue of the structure and traditions of the administrative service itself, and they were thus far more independent of the pressures of local politics. Indeed, with the training and traditions of official service behind him a member of the *pamong pradja* would naturally be expected to be a different type of person from a *kepala daerah* appointed by the prescribed procedure and to interpret in a different way the obligation to balance the desires of his regional council against more general considerations of national interest. Any *kepala daerah* appointed from a list submitted by a legislative council would surely be extremely reluctant to impose any check upon the resolutions of either his executive or his legislative councils, which would be composed of his political colleagues, presumably of like mind with himself. In such circumstances it would be natural for the national interest to be interpreted in such a way as to make it consistent with local demands.

As it was, the reverse was the case. The Ministry was able to rely with certainty upon the obedience of its servants in imposing a delay on local ordinances and in subordinating local wishes to its own interpretation of the national interest. The supervisory machinery established under Law 22 was much more effective when the Ministry was in a position simply to instruct its officials to impose a veto with regard to any controversial matter which was known to be pending. It could then ensure that the matter was raised by stages through the hierarchy of local governments until it was eventually brought officially to its own notice. For example, a *kabupaten* decision vetoed by the *kepala daerah* would be referred to the executive council of the province, as required in Law 22. If the executive council of the province approved the original decision of the *kabupaten* legislative council or executive council, that approval would constitute a decision of the provincial executive council which might then be the subject of a similar delaying veto by the *kepala daerah* of the province, and the matter would then pass for decision to the Minister acting in the name of the President. The watchdog function of the *pamong pradja* was, of course, intended to produce the same effect where the central government had no prior warning and had issued no prior instruction.[3]

In general, then, the exercise of the duties of *kepala daerah* by the person who was at the same time the central government's chief executive in the region concerned meant that the role of these officers as central government servants was more apparent than their role as leaders of the local government and that the prestige of the local government was overshadowed by that of the centre even where local matters were concerned. The character of the system as it operated in practice was reflected most clearly, perhaps, in the accepted titles of regional heads. It is

[3] In the cases studied by the author there were a number of examples of both uses of the preventive veto—by central instruction to the regional heads of provinces and *kabupatens* and by the original initiative of regional heads themselves. Where matters on which the central government had a contrary interest did manage to slip past the supervision of the *kepala daerah,* it was sometimes possible for the centre to impose a repressive veto under Article 42, even on levels lower than the province. In one case studied, an ordinance of the DPRD of Bogor (*kota besar*) had been approved by the *wali kota/kepala daerah.* Since it concerned the remuneration of DPRD members, it was subject, under Article 7 (2), to the preventive supervision of the DPD of the next highest level—the Province of West Java. The provincial DPD in fact approved the ordinance, and this decision was, in turn, approved by the Governor of the province. The Ministry, however, was opposed to the original measure. Since it was, by this time, too late to secure the veto of the *kepala daerah,* the Ministry was forced to resort to a presidential "repressive" veto, under Article 92 (1), of the provincial DPD decision approving the *kota besar* ordinance. In this way an ordinance of a second-level local government was revoked at two removes, as it were. Such a procedure, however, would not have been possible had the original ordinance been that of a third-level government, not a second-level government.

worth noting that, though in strict terminology the term *kepala daerah* was supposed to denote a different function or area of activity from that of a Governor, or *bupati,* or mayor, and though the official designation of these officers was *Gubernur/Kepala Daerah, Bupati/Kepala Daerah, Wali Kota/Kepala Daerah,* in practice the *pamong pradja* rank was invariably used by itself—Governor, *bupati, wali kota.* And this practice was more consistent with the facts as they had been up to that time.

Objections were raised in principle against the combination of the two positions in the same hands, on the grounds that it was no more than a device for disguising the continuance of central control. At the same time it must be admitted that, in practice, the system had worked surprisingly well. It is true that there were cases where governors and *bupatis* found themselves at odds with their councils. But these were exceptional. For the most part regional heads had managed to establish a good working understanding with their councils. Although party representatives in Parliament had directed their fire at the retention of a veto power in the hands of central officers, these attacks did not seem to have awakened strong echoes in the regions themselves, where the issue of central supervision appears to have been of much less moment in practice than one would expect in theory. In fact, the power of veto was rarely used. The credit for that fact must lie partly with the political skill of governors and *bupatis* who were able, by personal contact with council members, to resolve potential differences between councils and centre before they became issues in the councils. In exercising this skill a Governor or *bupati* was, of course, aided by the mere fact that he was in a position to impose a veto if it did come to the point. But, in addition to this legal power, there was a more intangible factor present also—the fact that he was a person of authority. The *mystique* of authority still counts for much in political relations in Indonesia. A Governor or a *bupati* or a mayor was the more easily able to reach a good understanding with the members of his council, considered as individuals rather than as party representatives, because of the mere fact that he embodied in his person the authority of the central government in the region. His authority was a genuine and traditional authority which may be contrasted with that of the DPD or, for that matter, with the power of the Army which gradually came to play an expanding role in the local field. The new organs of local government had not yet built up a basis of authority in tradition, whereas the Army was obeyed through fear, not authority. But a member of the *pamong pradja* was able to secure a large measure of unforced obedience deriving in part, at least so far as Java is concerned, from the aristocratic origin of the service. *Prijaji* authority is closely connected with the whole system of Javanese mysticism which sees society as the reflection of a cosmic order.[4] Even the modern civil servant of more humble origins, engaged in the tasks of daily routine, still walks to some extent in the borderland between this world and another and receives respect because of his higher place in the cosmos. Although a commoner, he has the vestiges of *prijaji* power about him. It is a paternal authority which he represents. He is the father of his

[4] See, e.g., C. Geertz, "Religious Belief and Economic Behaviour in a Central Javanese Town: Some Preliminary Considerations," *Economic Development and Cultural Change,* Jan. 1956.

people, and it would be unwise for the student of political relations in Indonesia to ignore the special flavor expressed, for instance, on the occasions when a *bupati*—or for that matter one of his subordinates, a *wedana* or *tjamat*—speaks paternally to the *lurahs* of his region. Even at the more sophisticated level of *kabupaten* or provincial political activity something of the same relationship survives.

Naturally this attitude to authority may be expected to change. There were signs even during the provisional period that the chairman of the representative council, a person chosen by the council itself, was coming to be an important focal point in local affairs. He was empowered to call meetings of *fraksi* leaders (a *fraksi* is a party or a group of parties or of individuals who have agreed to act together in the council), and in this way he managed the negotiation of agreed decisions and the facilitation of the handling of business in the council. His role could help to weaken the traditional position of the *bupati* or the Governor. Again, the tendency of members of the *pamong pradja* to acquire a party affiliation blurred the distinction between official neutrality and the conflict of political pressures, especially when some members of the administrative service were seeking political office. Although the connection was by no means universal, there was a tendency for members of the *pamong pradja* to join the Nationalist Party (PNI), and that party undoubtedly looked to regional officials for a great deal of its local influence.[5] It was argued by some that the *pamong*

[5] H. Feith, *The Indonesian Elections of 1955,* p. 33, and *The Wilopo Cabinet, 1952–1953* (Cornell Modern Indonesia Project, Monograph Series; Ithaca, 1958), p. 51.

pradja as a service should stand aside from politics. But this was a difficult ideal to achieve, since, in recent years, many higher appointments in the service had been made partly, at least, for political reasons. An ambitious regional officer could hardly be blamed for attempting to safeguard his future advancement by acquiring political connections.

But these were long-term elements of change. In the situation as it existed until the close of 1956, though the political affiliations of the administrative official had laid him open to the charge of using his influence in matters of national politics, as in the elections of 1955, his neutrality in local government politics seemed not to have been seriously impaired, and so far his prestige was such as to overshadow that of popular representatives. In these circumstances his special position within the system of autonomy had not, except in a few difficult cases, constituted the source of friction which one might have expected from a study of the formal machinery of local government or from a consideration of parliamentary criticisms of the system.

It was against this background of practice during the provisional period that the drafting of the new basic local government law took place. In fact, the preparation of the law tended to develop into a tug of war between the Department of Home Affairs, which was well satisfied by the working of the provisional supervisory machinery, and political leaders in Parliament and the regions who were anxious to remove any suggestion of paternal control. The role of officials and the degree to which they should continue to exercise powers of control over local authorities emerged as the major point at issue between successive governments and Parliament. It was the intention of each government which concerned itself with the problem to retain a greater measure of supervision than had been envisaged in the old Law 22 (this intention reflected closely the departmental view), and it was the aim of party leaders in Parliament to resist such a plan.

Briefly, the government's case for withholding full autonomy had rested on several considerations. There was a paternal fear that inexperienced local councils would prove inadequate to the tasks confronting them. Although the government regarded full autonomy as a desirable goal, it found it difficult to believe that the regions were ready to receive full responsibility immediately. It is never difficult to find evidence to support an assumption of that kind. Nor was it simply inexperience which was feared. There was also the fear of positive irresponsibility, and indeed there have been cases enough to lend substance to such a fear.[6] But perhaps more important than either of these arguments was the fact that, though provinces and *kabupatens* might be given certain powers of self-government, there still remained the problem of administering the basic unit—the *desa,* or *negeri,* or *marga,* or whatever other form its organization might take. The theory behind Law 22 may have envisaged the transfer of this responsibility to the autonomous *kabupaten* pend-

[6] As one instance there may be quoted the situation in West Java where local councils increased the remuneration of members beyond the prescribed scale for attendance at meetings. In such cases as this the Ministry was unable to rely on obedience to instructions which it could legitimately issue to councils. Of similar character was the action of many councils with a strong Moslem majority in refusing to seat a Communist member on the executive council when that party was entitled to a seat.

ing the establishment of a third level of autonomy. In practice the centre was reluctant to allow such a transfer. When a third level of local government, based on villages or collections of villages, was established, the need for a central administrative service should disappear as envisaged in Law 22, or at least be greatly reduced and changed in character. At that point the lower regional administration, if it was still considered to be necessary, could be allowed to become the responsibility of the autonomous *kabupaten*, with *wedanas* and *tjamats* acting as the servants of the *kabupaten* executive council. In the meantime there remained the fact that *kabupaten* councils were not really representative of the agriculturalist, and their activities did not directly reflect village needs. Members of councils at this level were, for the most part, drawn either from the ranks of the civil service or from small traders, religious leaders, and teachers.[7] Only isolated exceptions were drawn from the agricultural population. Even if fuller autonomy were to be conceded to the *kabupaten* level (in the sense of restricting the veto of the *kepala daerah*), the central government could not willingly surrender full responsibility for the care and control of the village to councils which did not adequately represent the village population. In the "special regions"—*swapradjas* or federations of *swapradjas*—the situation was rather different. There local governments, as a matter of history, had already been responsible for the administration of lower territorial subdivisions. But for the remainder of the archipelago, where the local administration of the central government had always been more detailed and more thorough, the government considered it necessary, for the

[7] See below, Chapter V.

time being, either to retain this channel of communication in its own hands (which also meant preserving as a central responsibility the duties of general administration) or to institute a very close supervision by appointed officials over the administration of lower districts by legislative and executive councils.

At first the latter alternative was preferred. When the new legislation for local government was under consideration between 1954 and 1956, two alternative solutions to the problem, opposite in character, but each designed to establish a firm supervisory system, were put forward in succession. The draft bill of 1954 suggested a simple and direct solution, namely, that the existing provisional method of direct appointment of an official as the *kepala daerah* be made permanent. The *kepala daerah* of provinces would be appointed by the President, of *kabupatens* and large municipalities by the Minister, and of lower units by the *kepala daerah* of the province concerned. Naturally it was intended that, in making these appointments, the government would continue its practice of appointing members of the *pamong pradja.* Emphasis was laid in the bill not on the dual character of the *kepala daerah,* but rather on his character simply as an official of the central government. "The *Kepala Daerah* has the role of supervising all the measures of the regional government in the interests of the State as a whole. Because of this it is provided that the *Kepala Daerah* shall be an official who is appointed and dismissed by the central Government." In this way it was hoped to continue the practice of balancing the power of autonomous local governments by placing at their centre the same individual who was also responsible for the administration and co-ordination of central government activities in the region concerned. With his power of veto over the decisions of both local councils he could exercise an effective supervision over their actions and policies.

It was, perhaps, not surprising that this feature of the bill should arouse strong and successful opposition, and a new draft, prepared in 1956, tried to secure something of the same object but by different means. Instead of integrating the autonomous hierarchy with the administrative hierarchy it was now decided to make a clearer separation between the two. In the new draft the *kepala daerah,* far from being an official, was to be simply a political figure, appointed by the legislative council itself in the case of provinces and *kabupatens* and directly elected by the people in the case of lower levels. (The selection had still to await confirmation from above, but this was seen as an emergency safeguard only.) At the same time the character of the office was also to be changed. There was no longer any question of the regional head having a dual role. The accompanying explanation to the draft law described him as being simply "an organ of the regional government." The supervisory powers which had been entrusted to the *kepala daerah* in 1948 and again in the 1954 draft were now to be vested in the hands of a new officer at the provincial level—a commissioner (*komisaris*)—who was to stand outside the local government system and who was empowered, on behalf of the President, to delay decisions of provincial, *kabupaten,* and municipal councils where they conflicted with the national interest and to delay or revoke those of third-level councils. The draft bill was silent on the details, but it was intended that the *pamong pradja* would be retained, though as a distinct and separate service, and that the position of *komisaris* would, in fact, be occupied by the governors of provinces. Below them former *bupatis* and mayors, no longer themselves empowered to interfere directly in the workings of local councils in their area, were intended to keep a quiet eye upon council deliberations and to serve as a spy system on behalf of the centre.

The new proposals clearly offered a much watered-down system of central control as compared with the proposals of two years earlier. The combination of the office of *kepala daerah* with that of central official made the imposition of a check upon council decisions at all levels a simple matter. It would obviously be much more difficult for the Governor in his role of *komisaris* to delay enactments of *kabupaten* councils than it had been, formerly, for the *bupati,* who was himself chairman of the DPD, to withhold his consent to ordinances. Nevertheless, the new draft did not go far enough to meet parliamentary opinion. Debates on the new bill in November 1956 were marked by sharp criticism of the institution of the new office of *komisaris,* and the Minister of Home Affairs, at that time Sunario (*Nahdatul Ulama*—NU), was unable, in a conference with party leaders, to convert them to his view. The outcome was the passage of a severely amended version which became the new basic law for local government—Law 1 of 1957. The terms of this law have already been given in some detail,[8] but, at the cost of a little repetition, it will be necessary to notice again here the changes made in the position of regional head.

In the amended version, as has been seen, the *kepala daerah* remained a political figure as in the earlier draft.

[8] See above, Chapter II.

He was to be chosen according to a procedure still to be determined by law, but, pending such further provision, he was to be chosen by the legislative council. As an integral part of this change the office itself was cut down to size. It was no longer to denote the wide range of executive functions suggested by the term itself, "head of the region." Instead, the *kepala daerah* was to be merely the chairman of the executive council, responsible along with his colleagues to the representative council and losing office if the executive should be overthrown by the representative council.[9] As *kepala daerah* he would possess a certain prestige, no doubt. But his real power had decreased while that of the DPD had grown.[10]

From the point of view of supervision the main feature of the new law was the dropping of the proposed supervisory official, the *komisaris,* and, therefore, by implication the complete separation of the administrative service from the local government system. The only remaining provisions for higher control over local government were that decisions of legislative and executive councils which

[9] This at least was to apply so long as the *kepala daerah* was chosen by the DPRD. A change in the method of selection as foreshadowed in Law 1 would have to be accompanied by corresponding changes in the office. If the *kepala daerah* were to be chosen by direct popular election, he would have an authority quite distinct from that of the DPD.

[10] Only two special duties are conferred on the *kepala daerah* by Law 1: the proclamation of regional regulations (Article 37) and, in the case of a neglect of duty by the regional government such as to require intervention by the central government, the assumption of interim responsibility for the running of regional affairs pending central action (Article 50). Later when legislation was prepared to effect the transfer of *pamong pradja* powers to regional governments, it was decided that these powers would be transferred to the DPD, not to the *kepala daerah.*

ran counter to the national interest might still be repealed by the next highest executive council in the hierarchy (by the Minister in the case of provinces), that decisions in certain specified fields must still await the approval of the next highest executive, and that the Ministry itself was to have a power of direct intervention in a manner to be determined by government regulation. (The Minister also had the power to delay or revoke decisions of second- and third-level councils if the appropriate authority—the next highest executive—neglected its duty. The Minister apparently had the right to decide when a neglect of duty had taken place.[11]) But in spite of these provisions it was clear that the new law had left the central government in a much weaker position with regard to the daily running of local governments than would have been the case if the local government system had been closely integrated with the administrative system, as proposed in 1954, or if the former had at least been indirectly supervised by the latter, as proposed in 1956.

Nevertheless, as far as the terms of the law were concerned, it would seem that there was still room for the *pamong pradja* to exist as a corps, and though its members would be restricted, formally speaking, to matters falling outside the sphere of autonomy, they could still, no doubt, be used to observe unobtrusively the work of councils and to report to the Ministry on the performance of autonomous governments at various levels. In fact, however, there was a possibility of a more extensive role for the service, for the law left a wider loophole still. The powers of supervision conferred upon the Minister—power to delay or revoke decisions of first-level councils (Article

[11] Article 65.

64) and second- or third-level councils (Article 65)—could be delegated to "an authority nominated by him." This could be the *pamong pradja.* Again, the blanket clause enabling a general central government supervision of local government work (Article 69) provided that the method of supervision was to be defined by government regulation. By this means, also, it was possible to confer formal authority upon the *pamong pradja* in the field of local government. The actual term *komisaris* was dropped, but it would seem that the same sort of solution was still legally possible, though introduced by the back door as it were.

The use of the administrative corps in this way was, of course, a matter of policy which remained undecided at the time of the proclamation of the law. Whether or not such a solution was adopted, it appeared more than ever necessary, in the official view, that the service should not be allowed to wither away or be transferred to the control of local authorities. There would still, in effect, be two distinct governments in each region, that of the centre and that of the region, and no doubt there would be a competition for prestige between Governor (or *bupati*) on the one hand and *kepala daerah* on the other. This would be likely to show even in apparently trivial matters—whose would be the official residence which had formerly been occupied by the Governor/*kepala daerah*? Would it pass to the region, or would it remain the property of the centre? A much sharper distinction would be necessary between central tasks and local government tasks than had existed in practice during the provisional period, so that a clear division of responsibility would exist between the DPD and the officers of the *pamong pradja* who would be placed in each region as chief executive officers of the centre. The responsibility for what is called "general government," and, in particular, the administration of the village in areas where this had previously been the task of the central government and where a third level of autonomy had not been established, was intended to remain within the field of central responsibility, though one of the original purposes in developing an elaborate multilevel local government system had been to relieve the burden of central administration. The *pamong pradja* was to continue to serve as the government's channel of communication to the base of society. To put it in another way, general administration might be regarded as a specialized function of central government similar in character to its functions in technical fields such as health, education, or agriculture. Just as there existed ministries of health and of agriculture, with their branch offices at the provincial level and below, so there was still to be a Ministry of Home Affairs with its technical duties to perform, except that, in this case, the "branch offices" would be the offices of the Governor, the Resident, the *bupati*, and so on.

But the Ministry of Home Affairs was not to be allowed to salvage even this much of its paternal system of supervision after its parliamentary defeat on the terms of the bill at the end of 1956. Although the application of this approach depended on the omissions of Law 1 rather than on its positive provisions, and was, therefore, a matter of government policy, government policy could not be fashioned independently of party and other pressures. During 1957 the battle shifted from the nature of the office of *kepala daerah* to the future role of the administrative corps; and just as the government was forced to retreat on the former issue, so it retreated also on this. Some months after the gazettal of the law and against the background of separatist tendencies in Sumatra and Sulawesi, it was decided by the then Minister, Sanusi Hardjadinata, that steps would be taken after all to abolish the *pamong pradja* by gradual stages. The political developments of 1957 had delayed the implementation of Law 1. Although regional elections were held in Java in the course of the year, the declaration by the President of a state of siege and war and the actual interruption of ordinary civil administration in large areas of the country made it impossible to proceed immediately with the election of the *kepala daerah.* Under the emergency legislation military authority was issued for the temporary continuance of the practice of appointing officials to this office. As the year proceeded, however, the Djuanda government gradually became convinced of the necessity not merely of hastening the implementation of Law 1 and of other measures already decided on (e.g., the transfer of certain taxing powers to the regions and the establishment of a more clearly defined financial relationship between local and central government), but of making more drastic concessions than had hitherto been intended. These included the decision to make specific transfers to local governments of large areas of what had been central responsibility. Consistent with this process was the eventual decision to dispense with the central administrative service, not merely in its supervisory capacity, but even for the control and co-ordination of central tasks.

This decision was given formal expression in a ministerial regulation of December 5, 1957, which laid down three phases through which the decision would be implemented. During the first phase the tasks of the *pamong pradja* were to be transferred gradually to the local authorities, but these authorities would receive help in the execution of such tasks from members of the *pamong pradja* who would, however, remain servants of the centre and who would, meanwhile, retain responsibility for duties not yet transferred to the regions. The second phase would see the actual control of these activities by local government departments staffed by local officials. The third phase was one of stabilization, in which central and local responsibilities would be clearly defined. Only three aspects of "general government" would remain in central hands by this stage—control of police, co-ordination of the tasks of the several central government ministries operating in the area, and the task of supervision of first-level governments. And the responsibility for these tasks would no longer be that of the *pamong pradja,* but would be divided among other central departments. In the intervening period the ministerial powers of supervision laid down in Articles 64 and 65 of Law 1 were to be exercised on behalf of the Minister by governors, and the office of Governor was to remain until after the completion of phase three.

In the course of 1958, legislation was prepared to effect a transfer of *pamong pradja* powers to local governments in accordance with this three-phase plan, and it was passed early in 1959 as Law 6 of that year. It will be convenient to reserve for separate consideration the issues of local government authority which were involved in that transfer.[12] At this point our concern is merely with the fate of

[12] See below, Chapter VI.

the *pamong pradja* as a service. The initial steps in the direction of implementing the first phase of the plan and beginning the disbandment of the *pamong pradja* were taken quickly. They involved the transfer of *bupatis* from their *kabupatens* to the office of the Resident, where they would act as assistants in the more general co-ordination of services and the supervision of lower administration which was conducted at that level. As vacancies occurred in the rank of *bupati,* they would not be filled. In *kabupatens* the tasks which were still to be handled by a central official were to be taken over by the *patih*—the chief secretarial assistant of the *bupati.* (It should be noted that although the *patih,* formally speaking, would possess the authority of the *bupati* for the time being he would lack the prestige of the higher rank, and he would, in effect, be merely a stand-in.)

The government's decision did not pass unchallenged. The professional association of the *pamong pradja*—the SSKDN (*Serikat Sekerdja Kementerian Dalam Negeri*)—naturally opposed the measure. And its legality was doubted. The position and power of the *bupati* had been created over a long period of time by a whole series of Dutch enactments. It was held by some that a position created by law could not be abolished by a simple ministerial instruction. This line was taken by the Governor of East Java, R. Samadikoen, who, with the co-operation of the military authorities in the region, decided simply to ignore the December 5 instruction. He failed to transfer *bupatis* from their *kabupatens,* and he filled vacancies in the position as they occurred. (His action in these respects was legalized by *Peperda*—the Regional Military Authority—under the terms of the emergency law of December 1957.) In the Special Region of Jogjakarta the DPD on its own initiative went much further than the instruction. On the ground that Law 1 did not mention the *pamong pradja,* the DPD resolved to remove *bupatis* from their position and to place the lower ranks of the service directly under the control of second-level executive councils. The decision led to a direct clash between the Special Region government and the SSKDN, culminating after some months in a threatened strike by the *pamong pradja* of the region. Jogjakarta was a special case because of the position of the Sultan and the loyalty of the *pamong pradja* to him personally. The strike was avoided through the action of the Sultan in inviting the direct intervention of the Minister of Home Affairs, but the incident symbolized the directness of the conflict between the idea of local council government and the tradition of *pamong pradja* government.[13] However, the situations in Jogjakarta and in East Java were exceptional. Elsewhere steps were taken to obey the policy laid down by the Minister and in the gradual manner prescribed.

In the meantime elections had been held in Java for the actual position of *kepala daerah* under the terms of Law 1, and it is interesting to notice the general character and background of those who were first elected to the position in its new form. A surprising feature of the elections was the high proportion of successful candidates who were

[13] An account of the conflict in Jogjakarta and of the special difficulties in which the Sultan was placed by virtue of his combined position as traditional ruler and as chairman of a democratic council is given by S. Soemardjan, "Social Changes in Jogjakarta" (unpublished thesis, Cornell University, Ithaca, 1959), pp. 189 ff.

drawn from the *pamong pradja* itself, a total of 34 out of 98 positions.[14] Eleven were elected to the position of *kepala daerah* in regions where they had held office as *bupati* or *wali kota*, 5 other *bupatis* were elected as *kepala daerah* of second-level regions other than their own, and one former Governor (of Kalimantan) was elected as *kepala daerah* of a first-level region (East Java). Seventeen were elected to levels other than those at which they had served as officials (e.g., *wedanas* elected as *kepala daerah* of second-level regions). The latter general category included the *kepala daerah* of the Central Java first-level government, who had formerly been the *wali kota* of Semarang. It is worth noting that a substantial majority of those members of the *pamong pradja* who were elected —22 out of the 34—were members of the PNI, a reflection of the appeal of the PNI to official ranks in general. But these officials, though elected by representative councils and loyal, presumably, to those councils and to their parties, might be expected, by and large, to possess at least the cast of mind and general attitude of which the centre would approve. They now represented local interests, but they would still possess an appreciation of the needs of central government, as well as experience in administrative difficulties, which could be important in political leadership. Of the remaining regional heads, a further 33 were civil servants from other central departments, a fact which is not surprising when one remembers

[14] This figure excludes the Special Region of Jogjakarta and the second-level regions within it. The 98 regions comprise 4 first-level regions (West Java, Central Java, East Java, and Greater Djakarta), 18 *kotapradjas*, and 76 other second-level regions (ex-*kabupatens*).

that officials formed the most important single element in Indonesia's political elite.[15]

The December 5 instruction, in laying down procedures for the disbandment of the *pamong pradja*, appeared to mark the end of a long-drawn-out struggle between centre and regions on the question of supervision and to represent a decisive victory for one point of view over the other. The issues had been quite clearly defined during the provisional period under Law 22. In fighting a rear-guard action for the maintenance of an effective supervisory system, successive governments—or rather their official advisers in the Ministry of Home Affairs—were undoubtedly moved by the desire for good government. The close connection proposed between the autonomous system and the administrative hierarchy appeared a neat and simple way of securing this. It was hoped that the combined functions of the official/*kepala daerah*, far from being a potential source of friction, might enable guidance and intervention to take an unobtrusive form. That, of course, would have required a high degree of understanding on both sides. Whether or not that was an impossible hope, the prewar method as it was re-established during the provisional period did reflect a consistent point of view, albeit an authoritarian one. On the other side it was argued that the Ministry was being too paternal and too cautious and that, in the interests of good government, it had been too distrustful of local bodies and too reluctant to allow them a reasonable scope for experiment and error.

[15] It is interesting to notice the high proportion of officials from the Ministry of Information—also a PNI stronghold—who secured election as *kepala daerah*.

The various proposals of the postwar years had not really bridged these two approaches. Law 22, as has been argued, could not hope to satisfy either the centre's demand for official supervision or local demands for greater independence. Subsequent drafts were equally unsatisfactory. And even Law 1/57, so long as the centre was determined to retain its centralized administration, represented an uneasy compromise between the political pressures demanding fuller autonomy and the official approach based on the view that autonomy must, for the time being, serve the purposes of general government. The ministerial instruction of December 1957, by proposing the gradual elimination of the administrative corps, offered one clear-cut solution.

Whether or not official fears about the consequences of such a thoroughgoing solution would be borne out only time could tell—and time was not to be allowed. The ministerial instruction of December 1957 may have appeared decisive, but the battle was not yet quite over. It will be seen below that the reversal of the intentions of Law 1 by Presidential Edict 6 of September 1959 was equally clear cut and uncompromising.

5

Councils and Party Politics

"THE regional government is composed of the regional representative council and the regional executive council." So it was laid down in straightforward terms in Law 1/57, which in this respect made no change from the plan embodied in Law 22/48.[1] Within the terms of that general statement the representative council with its legislative functions and its ability to appoint, dismiss, and exercise a general control over the executive council was clearly to be the basic institution in the whole local government system—the embodiment of local aspirations and the local expression of popular sovereignty. The theory did not always accurately reflect the facts, and the process of making the DPRD's effective centres of power was a slow one. Attention has already been drawn to the preliminary stages through which representative bodies had passed since the formation of the unitary Republic: the "temporary" councils (DPRD *Sementara*) appointed under the compromise Government Regulation 39 of 1950 and the "transitional" councils (DPRD *Peralihan*) formed in 1956 on the basis of the returns of each region in the 1955 general election. The latter were designed to bridge the

[1] Law 1/57, Article 5 (1). The wording is taken over from Law 22/48, Article 2 (1).

gap between the earlier *ad hoc* arrangements and the formation of properly elected bodies under the new electoral law of 1956.[2] The first regional elections were held in Java in 1957. But these preliminary stages served to lay the formal foundations of the council system which was to be accepted in essentially the same form in the basic law of 1957.

They were foundations only. At the time of the proclamation of the law the operation of the system was still far from complete. Apart from the fact that elections had not yet been held, the councils were still under the chairmanship of an appointed Governor, *bupati,* or mayor and still subject in their decision to his power of veto, as well as to his general moral authority. So long as an appointed official remained at the centre of the local government system, the scope left for the exercise of genuine initiative by representative and executive bodies was limited: the independent powers which were theirs in theory were balanced in practice by the weight of central prestige symbolized in his person. Secondly, only a limited range of powers had actually been transferred. The proclamation of the new law offered a prospect of early escape from

[2] There had been an earlier stage still during the revolutionary period when local committees (Komite Nasional Indonesia or KNI) were established as a means of mobilizing nationalist feeling. These, like the central assembly (Komite Nasional Indonesia Pusat or KNIP), usually reflected a broad interparty agreement. They were at first constituted on the initiative of local leaders, but later were regularized by the republican government and in some cases were filled by election (Kahin, *Nationalism and Revolution in Indonesia,* p. 140). The "temporary" councils established under Regulation 39 thus really replaced one temporary device by another more formal one.

these limitations. The change in the character of the office of *kepala daerah* was in itself enough to throw new responsibilities on the council system as a whole. The subsequent government decision to go even further and to dispense gradually with the *pamong pradja* confirmed the change. And the foreshadowing of early elections and of the transfer of wider powers, as well as of greater financial responsibility, opened wider possibilities for councils.

These were changes of genuine substance; wise or not, they gave real content for the first time to the formal local government structure and provided an adequate institutional framework for the play of local politics,whether activated by purely local issues or by the activities of national political parties.

The size of representative councils at each level varied slightly from area to area. Law 22 had provided that the number of members of both the DPRD and the DPD should be fixed in the establishing law required to create each area as a *swatantra,* and the establishing legislation of the years 1950–1953 set a general pattern for the future. In Java all provincial representative councils were composed of 60 members. *Kabupaten* councils varied between 20 and 30, and municipal councils between 10 and 25.[3] Law 1 of 1957 altered the basis according to which council membership was determined: it was now made dependent upon the size of the population of the region concerned. In first-level regions the representative council was to consist of 1 representative for every 200,000 inhabitants, with a minimum size of 30 representatives

[3] Small town councils ranged at first between 10 and 15 members, and large towns between 15 and 25.

and a maximum of 75. And similar bases were prescribed for the second and third levels.[4] For existing *swatantras* the practical consequences of the change were slight. The first-level councils in Java were all swelled to the maximum figure of 75 members, and most second-level councils to 35 members. The practice of regular meetings was firmly established by 1957. The law prescribed at least one DPRD meeting every three months (Article 14), but in practice they were being held more frequently, usually once a month.

Membership of representative councils has reflected the narrowness of Indonesia's political elite.[5] Even at the *kabupaten* level council members could hardly be regarded as representative of the rural community which formed the great mass of constituents, and at the provincial level the connection was still more tenuous. By far the greatest single occupational group to be found on councils has been formed by civil servants, a fact which is reminiscent of the local bodies established during the colonial period.[6] Other groups were small traders, reli-

[4] In second-level regions there was to be 1 representative for every 10,000 inhabitants, with a minimum of 15 and a maximum of 35 council members; for third-level regions there was to be 1 representative for every 2,000 inhabitants, with a minimum of 10 and a maximum of 20 council members.

[5] The formal requirements for membership were very broad: members were to be Indonesian citizens over 21, domiciled in the region concerned for at least six months previously, literate, of sound mind, not an undischarged bankrupt and not deprived of voting rights by judicial decision.

[6] Civil servants formed from one-third to one-half of the membership of eight second-level councils studied by the writer in East Java and of four in West Sumatra. In the transitional representative council of the Province of East Java, appointed in October 1956, 23 of the 69 members were civil servants.

gious leaders, teachers, labor leaders, and industrial workers. Only an isolated few have been drawn from the ranks of the peasantry. This fact constitutes an important, if inevitable, limitation upon the reality of political decentralization in contemporary Indonesia, and, as has been brought out, it was one factor which helped to justify the reluctance of the central government to relinquish the control it had maintained in the past through its administrative corps.

While regional legislatures were finding their feet during the provisional years, their executives also were acquiring initial experience and were beginning to assume responsibility for the administration of local services. The size of executive councils under both the provisional and the permanent laws was laid down in the establishing law for each *swatantra,* having regard to the size of the DPRD in each case. In fact, they varied between four and six members, among whom was divided, on something like a portfolio basis, the executive responsibility belonging to the region—health to one, public works to another, and so on. There were, of course, wide differences in the degree of development from area to area and from level to level. The executive council of a fully fledged province already controlled, by 1957, a considerable administrative organization. In East Java, for instance, behind the impressive Governor's Office and Secretariat in Surabaja stands a separate administrative complex housing the offices of the autonomous government of the province—health, agriculture, public works, veterinary services, and so on—which exist here on a scale hardly to be matched in the humbler and more homely circumstances of, say, Bukittinggi or Palembang. At the *kabupaten* level in Java there was also in existence a smoothly running organization whether in a large *kabupaten* such as Malang or a small one such as Pasuruan, though the executive opportunities open to the *kabupaten* were at that stage severely limited by the slender character of the functions transferred to that level. Outside Java, with some notable exceptions such as Minahasa, the second-level executives were in a much less developed state. But at least the first steps had been taken in the direction of uniformity, as in the establishment of the new *kabupatens* of Sumatra.

In addition to their administrative duties, an important function of executive councils was that of supervising lower levels of local government. There was the specific responsibility of approving regulations of lower councils dealing with matters for which the basic law had prescribed such a procedure.[7] And there was the more general responsibility of checking all lower legislation to ensure that it was consistent with higher legislation and not in conflict with the national interest. The latter responsibility, involving as it did an interpretation of the national interest, conferred very wide powers of intervention on regional executives. In fact, these powers were considered as being in the nature of a formal safeguard, to be used in emergency situations rather than as enabling or encouraging a regular and continuous intervention in the domestic affairs of lower regional governments. In practice their use was extremely restricted. In those cases noted by the writer, rejection of regulations of a lower council on grounds of the general interest was extremely rare. Intervention was confined almost entirely to the

[7] See above, Chapter II, "RI Law 22 of 1948" and "Law 1 of 1957."

securing of adherence to the law and consistency with the measures of higher local governments. And even on these points supervision was usually of an informal character. Regulations of a second-level council were considered first by the legal section of the first-level administration, which tried to pass on to the first-level DPD only those regulations which were legally in order. Where there were legal objections to a measure, it was referred back to the lower council for alteration. Thus, when a regulation was eventually brought forward for the consideration of the higher DPD, approval was likely to be automatic. The supervisory powers were operating, in effect, within a framework of practice already well established and deriving from the experience formerly provided by the apparatus of central administration at each level.

An important peculiarity of the council system in Indonesia was to be found in the relationship which the executive was intended to bear to the legislature. The basic law provided that the executive council should have a "collegial" character and that it should be collectively responsible to the representative council.[8] The two concepts were closely connected. "Collegial" responsibility was the responsibility of the individual member of the executive to the executive as a whole.[9] The executive was responsi-

[8] Article 48. The idea of collegial responsibility was not mentioned in that article, but was elaborated in the clarification appended to the law.

[9] There is some ambiguity in the term. At times the word "collegial" has been used as though it simply referred to collective responsibility. (For this and other meanings see G. S. Maryanov, *Decentralization in Indonesia as a Political Problem* [Cornell Modern Indonesia Project, Interim Reports Series; Ithaca, 1958], p. 81). But the clarification of Law 1, which suggests the interpretation given above, seems straightforward.

ble for the allocation of duties among its members, and it could hold individual members to account for the fulfillment of their duties and could reallot portfolios if it so desired. From this it was natural that the responsibility of the executive to the representative council should be a collective one.[10] In view of the "collegial" character of the DPD and its collective responsibility to the DPRD, it might have been a more suitable arrangement had the former been the preserve of the majority party (or coalition of parties) in the latter. Instead, it was a matter of firm policy, included in both the provisional and the permanent basic laws, that the executive should be in proportion (*berimbang*) to the representative council. The system of proportional representation, already established as the proper method of electing the representative council, was used also in the selection of the executive in order to ensure that the executive reflected the party composition of the legislature as the latter did of the electorate.[11]

[10] In this respect the 1957 law represented a change from that of 1948. The earlier law allowed the possibility of individual as well as collective responsibility of members of the DPD to the DPRD (Law 22 of 1958, Article 34).

[11] There were a variety of methods of applying the proportional principle. During the currency of the transitional councils a ministerial regulation (*Peraturan Menteri Dalam Negeri* 17 of 1956) laid down the procedure to be used for the selection of the DPD. Under this there was no real election. Instead, the party composition of the DPD was to be calculated in advance by simply applying the principles of proportional representation to the party distribution in the DPRD. This was a straightforward calculation on paper. Each party whose strength entitled it to membership of the DPD put forward two candidates for each seat to which it was entitled. The DPRD was then to choose between the two by a straight vote. It is obvious that this procedure might well yield a

This inevitably made for weak government. The mere fact of a multiparty system in the first place made it difficult for any one party to secure a majority of seats in the representative assembly of a locality. The fact that, even when one party did emerge with an absolute majority, it could not control the executive further accentuated the tendency. The idea was already well established in Indonesia. De Kat Angelino gave a justification of this type of executive when speaking of prewar councils:

The selection of an executive by all the members of the Council has a much more business-like aspect than the representation by a few ministers of the strongest party in the Council or of a combination of parties, when one considers that local development is still very far from the most fundamental premises for a healthy party system, and for the parliamentarism that goes with it. The latter system could in the Indies only

---

different result from that which might be obtained were a ballot held, still on the basis of proportional representation. A ballot would enable the DPD to reflect coalitions or other interparty agreements in the DPRD. Instead, the DPD automatically reflected the *actual* party distribution in the DPRD. For the consequences of this procedure, see the author's interim report *Problems of Regional Autonomy in Contemporary Indonesia* (Cornell Modern Indonesia Project, Interim Reports Series; Ithaca, 1957), pp. 28–29.

The procedure was changed after Law 1 came into operation. The law provided that the procedure to be used in electing the DPD would be laid down in a government regulation, and this was eventually done in Government Regulation 32/57. The regulation provided for parties within the DPRD ("groups of at least 5 members in the case of first-level councils and of at least 3 members in the case of second-level councils") to put forward lists of candidates for election, and these lists formed the subject of a ballot according to proportional principles. This enabled party agreements to be reflected in the composition of the executive.

promote unsteadiness, infinite intrigue, and a weak executive, probably incapable of managing practical affairs.[12]

However, he was clearly thinking of a situation of tutelage, where the paternal advice and supervision of officials were intended to curb and educate local representatives, and his arguments would hardly apply to the contemporary scene. It is true that at the level of immediate local politics (the second and third levels of autonomy) where executive tasks are relatively simple and where the issues involved are of a "parish pump" variety rather than of a profound political nature easy co-operation between members of widely differing political parties may be not so difficult to achieve. At the provincial level the disadvantages should be more apparent, and the creation of unwieldly coalitions might be expected to limit executive programs to the lowest common denominator. For this reason it would appear that the desire to ensure that all major political groups are represented could be adequately satisfied by providing for such representation on the legislative council, leaving the DPD as an executive depending for its existence on its ability to retain the confidence of the legislature. This was not, however, the choice which was made.

The idea of a proportionally elected executive was consciously linked with what appears to be an established characteristic of Indonesian political procedures—the idea of decision by general consensus. The Indonesian term is *mufakat,* which is difficult to translate precisely, but it embodies the notion of discussion until a general agreement emerges, and it thus excludes the idea of majority

[12] De Kat Angelino, *op. cit.,* II, 402.

decisions being imposed on minorities. It is a common feature of contemporary Indonesian political thought that this method, which, it is argued, may be seen operating in its purest form at the level of the village assembly, is held to offer a model for the higher reaches of political life also. Such a view, for example, was an essential element of Soekarno's guided democracy proposals, where he has sought a broad basis of functional representation, constituted so as to reflect the nation as a whole and able to reconcile opposing views and to reach a harmonious agreement which would be universally acceptable.

It is extremely doubtful whether the model, even if it accurately represents what happens at the village level, is really suitable for application above the village. One obvious defect is that it might result in the putting aside of problems where general agreement cannot be reached. But whatever its merits or faults, the ideal of *mufakat* has conditioned behavior in both representative and executive councils—and, for that matter, in Parliament itself. One consequence has been the dislike of a straight vote on unresolved questions. Votes are avoided because they force members to take up public positions from which it is then difficult for them to retreat. If such concrete expressions of attitude are avoided, there may still be room for quiet negotiation and for some adjustment of opposing views behind the scenes where the real political maneuvers occur. This perhaps allows for a greater flexibility in party negotiations. But it has meant that councils tended to become the scene merely of formal proceedings, the recording of decisions already reached elsewhere. The foreign observer is likely to be puzzled by the number of decisions for which no vote is recorded, but which are said to have been made by "acclamation." And, indeed, it is difficult in discussions with council members to get any picture of "divisions" of the assembly. It is insisted that there is rarely such a thing. In fact, the common procedure has been for controversial issues to be withdrawn from debate until some formula acceptable to all major parties has been worked out.

Something of the same process occurred with the filling of the major elective offices of a region: the regional head, the chairman of the DPD, and the chairman and vice-chairman of the DPRD. The law provided for the straight-out election of these officials (by the DPRD except in the case of the vice-chairman of the DPD, who was chosen by that body) and thus allowed the possibility that a majority party could keep them all in its own hands. In practice there frequently (though not universally) appeared to be an agreement to distribute these positions among the main parties so that a representative of one would be elected unopposed to the position of *kepala daerah,* a representative of another to that of chairman of the DPRD, and so on.[13] A significant number (well over one-third of the total) of *kepala daerah* was elected by "acclamation."

These established patterns of Indonesian political life may perhaps be overstressed. While noting their existence

[13] As an example may be cited the case of Probolinggo in East Java, where NU secured 19 seats out of a total of 35—a clear absolute majority. PNI secured 8 seats, PKI 3, PSI 2, and Masjumi, PSII (*Partai Sarikat Islam Indonesia*), and Murba 1 each. NU naturally appropriated the positions of *kepala daerah* and chairman of the DPRD. The position of vice-chairman, however, went to PNI, and the DPD was composed of 3 NU members together with 1 PNI and 1 PSII.

one may wonder whether they are, after all, specifically Indonesian. Other societies, too, have their backstairs negotiations, and the idea of securing a feeling of the meeting is not an uncommon one. What is different here is the elevation of such procedures to the level of principle, so that they are consciously allowed to condition the construction of political institutions.

POLITICAL ALIGNMENTS

Party relationships in the regions were naturally molded by the series of electoral arrangements which were adopted. The major national parties operated at the local level from the establishment of the Republic and reproduced there the same multiplicity of organizations as was to be found at the centre. The old Government Regulation 39 of 1950 under which the first councils were created accepted this fact and sought to accommodate all comers. As already noted, it enabled any party with an organization extending to the *kabupaten* level in at least three *kabupatens* in a province and possessing *ketjamatan* branches in those *kabupatens* to secure council representation.[14] But this provision not merely recognized the presence of a number of parties: it gave positive encouragement to the formation of new organizations. Reference has already been made to its use by Masjumi which aroused PNI hostility and led to the Hadikusumo motion of 1951.

Since a large number of parties were already in existence, it was a foregone conclusion that the system of proportional representation should be adopted for local as well as for national elections. The history of electoral

[14] See above, Chapter II, "Application."

legislation has already been outlined briefly. A regional electoral law had been enacted as early as 1950 (Law 7/50). It provided for a rather complicated system of indirect elections and was, in fact, used only once—in the elections for the DPRD of the Special Region of Jogjakarta. It was replaced in 1956 by a new measure (Law 19/56) which adopted a system of direct elections on the model of an electoral regulation of Daerah Minahasa. The two laws were agreed, however, in prescribing a proportional system.

Although the system makes possible the survival of a large number of parties, it is significant that the first application of it in Indonesia should have rationalized the existing situation considerably. At the level of local politics the elective principle was first introduced in a substitute form—the use of general election returns to determine the composition of local councils for the transitional period 1956–1957—and the result was a drastic reduction in the number of parties strong enough to secure local representation. Whereas there were often up to ten parties represented on the old "temporary" local councils in Java, there were usually only from four to six parties represented on the new "transitional" councils. The major ones in all cases were the NU, PKI, PNI, and Masjumi. The other parties which still managed to keep a foot in the door included the two Christian parties, Katholik and Parkindo, but they were to be found in far fewer councils and, where they were represented, in far fewer numbers than the big four. In general, it may be said that while Government Regulation 39 encouraged the mushroom growth of parties, since all organized parties could claim representation merely on the grounds of their existence, the 1955 general election eliminated the less hardy growths, though proportional voting still allowed a multiparty system. The first regional elections in Java in 1957, under Law 19/56, altered the balance of party strength, but they did not appreciably affect this picture.

This change in party strengths on councils accompanied a change in the character and composition of the parties themselves, and it is necessary to look at local party politics against the wider background of national party organization.

The activity of the national political parties in the local arena was, perhaps, an artificial rather than a spontaneous development at first. It would not have been true, during the first few years of the Republic's existence, to say that local politics provided a training ground for national politics, for it was not until the 1955 elections that local leaders secured an opportunity of graduating through service at the *kabupaten* or municipal level to the broader stage of the province or the national parliament.[15] The converse was true, however: the electoral needs of the parties led them to more activity at the local level. The general elections showed how important grass-roots organization could be, and above the village, too, it was necessary for parties to seek a firmer basis of support among the population of small municipalities or *kabupaten* towns. The organization in the medium-sized and

[15] Many did graduate in this way. For example, in Kabupaten Malang (East Java) in 1955 and 1956 all but three members of the old temporary DPRD were elected to Parliament, the Constituent Assembly, or the provincial DPRD, leaving only a remnant of experienced members to serve on the transitional DPRD in the *kabupaten*.

small towns was, in any case, the best instrument for supervising the proselytizing activities in the village. For these reasons most parties had evolved a national organization on pyramidal lines with a national executive appointed by national congress and drawing its authority, at least in theory, from a descending series of levels extending down to the village. A typical pattern is for the national congress to have its counterpart at the provincial level in a provincial conference, which, again, elects a provincial executive. Both national and provincial conferences are normally composed of delegates from *kabupaten* branches where the elected conference and the executive is again to be found. (In the villages the branches appoint their own leaders, but not all parties may be represented at this level. Individual parties may attempt, by gaining prestige through such methods as winning the support of village officials and traditional leaders, to establish for themselves a virtual monopoly in particular villages.)

The efforts to secure and consolidate bases of popular support coincided with, and contributed to, changes in the nature of the parties themselves. In the early days of independence considerable power lay with the elite which had led the struggle for independence and, in spite of the distribution of that leadership through many parties, there was a broad essential agreement about basic questions of policy. Within the operations of a parliamentary system not only did this solidarity tend to collapse but the intellectual leadership tended to lose its power, and other sources of political strength began to emerge. One observer has noted three main periods in the Republic's history.[16] Up till 1953 the intellectual leaders of the revolution were still politically powerful and substantially united on fundamentals; and parliamentary leadership was itself still of prime importance. The next three years saw, among other factors, the growth in importance of the mass party, the decline in the power of the old elite, and the loss of its underlying unity. At the same time extra parliamentary forces—President and Army—were becoming of greater importance. The years 1956 and 1957, with the outbreak of regional resistance to the centre, saw a further deterioration of the situation and a decline in the importance of Parliament and, in consequence, of parties.[17]

Although preparations for the general elections helped in this process of weakening the earlier national leadership, the results of the elections naturally threw into sharper relief the difference in party strengths from area to area—a difference which was, of course, reflected in the "transitional" councils when they were set up in 1956. In West Sumatra, for instance, the Masjumi Party was very much stronger than it was in Indonesia as a whole and was able to obtain, in many areas, an absolute majority on DPRD's, despite the difficulty of doing so under a proportional system. Similarly, in East Java the NU and

[16] Feith, *The Wilopo Cabinet, 1952–1953,* pp. 210–211.

[17] At the same time one might possibly note an increase in party potential in that the development of mass organization must help in time to widen the country's political leadership. The image of a very narrow leadership and a vast mass base may be correct enough in general, but the growth in each small country town of active party functionaries whose existence must at least be recognized by central party authorities could be increasingly important. (Cf. also Guy J. Pauker, "The Role of Political Organizations in Indonesia," *Far Eastern Survey,* Sept. 1958.)

the PKI secured a greater strength than either of them possessed in other areas, or at the national level, and each of them was able to win absolute majorities in that province.[18] These variations tended to accentuate party confusion for they were likely to lead, in any particular region, to interparty alignments and adjustments which ran counter to the national policies of the parties concerned. Although party discipline was not strong and voting might not always follow rigid party lines, it was broadly true that, in areas where the NU predominated, Masjumi tended to oppose NU-PNI coalitions. This often placed it in the position of supporting PKI members on general issues. In areas where the PKI was strong, on the other hand, the remaining major parties formed a united opposition. More seriously, the sharpness of these regional differences was unfortunate in that it gave to normal political competition a regional flavor, and this helped to accentuate the regional crisis of 1956–1958. Against this background of party confusion the first regional elections held in Java in 1957 are difficult to interpret.

The most dramatic result of the election was the improvement in the position of the PKI since the general election of 1955 (see Table 2). In the whole of Java the party received 6,635,990 votes in elections for provincial councils as compared with 5,477,707 obtained in 1955. (The former figure excludes the Special Region of Jogjakarta, which was included as part of Central Java in the parliamentary election figures.) The increase was felt

[18] The Communist Party was not represented in the "temporary" councils, but by 1956 it had made up much of the ground that it had lost as a result of the Madiun affair of 1948.

primarily in Central and East Java, as may be seen from Table 2. In Central Java the PKI led the field by some 470,000 votes over its nearest rival PNI. (PNI had had a comfortable lead in that electoral district in 1955.) In East Java it was outdistanced by NU, but by a very much narrower margin than had been the case in the general election. In West Java, Masjumi remained in the lead, as had been the case in 1955, but the PKI moved up from third to second place, displacing PNI from that position. In Djakarta the PKI moved from fourth to second place. The main centres of PKI strength were revealed in the elections for second-level councils. In a number of regions the PKI secured absolute majorities. This was not surprising in such centres as the municipalities of Semarang, Surakarta, Madiun, and Surabaja, but its successes were not confined to urban concentrations: a similar result was obtained in a number of *kabupatens* such as those of Blitar, Semarang, Magetan, and Sukohardjo. (Space does not permit figures to be given for all the second-level regions in Java; however, the distribution of council seats as shown in Appendix A indicates in general terms the order of the electoral strength of each party.)

Although the dimensions of the Communist successes were considerable, certain qualifications need to be made. Their victory would appear in general to have been at the expense of the PNI rather than at the expense equally of all parties. And in itself it may easily be exaggerated. Total figures of voting for the provincial councils do not necessarily indicate the real effect for individual second-level councils. Only in approximately a third of the councils did this increase in voting strength appreciably alter

Table 2. Comparison of votes cast for the four main parties in the General Election of 1955 and the elections for first-level (= provincial) councils in Java and South Sumatra in 1957

	Greater Djakarta		West Java		Central Java		East Java		South Sumatra	
	Parlia- ment 1955	Prov- ince 1957	Parlia- ment 1955	Prov- ince 1957	Parlia- ment * 1955	Prov- ince 1957	Parlia- ment 1955	Prov- ince 1957	Parlia- ment 1955	Prov- ince 1957
PNI	152,031	124,955	1,541,927	1,055,801	3,019,568	2,235,714	2,251,069	1,899,782	213,766	187,042
Mas- jumi	200,460	153,709	1,844,442	1,841,030	902,387	714,722	1,109,742	977,443	628,386	553,276
NU	120,667	104,892	673,552	597,356	1,772,306	1,771,556	3,370,554	2,999,785	115,938	113,888
PKI	96,363	137,305	755,634	1,087,269	2,326,108	2,706,893	2,299,602	2,704,523	176,900	228,965

* The general election figures for the electoral district of Central Java include returns from the Special Region of Jogjakarta. The returns for the provincial election do not.

the balance of political color of the councils.[19] (For the purpose of this statement, the test of "appreciable" change has been taken arbitrarily as an increase from below a fifth of DPRD seats to a fifth or more.)

The nature of local issues and the fact that local councils barely had time to assume responsibility for the wider range of functions permitted to them under Law 1 make it difficult to assess the practical effect of changes in council composition. One point needs to be made clearly. It is quite a common belief in Indonesia that during this first period of fully elected local assemblies the Communist Party has studiously avoided responsibility, being content rather to sit back and allow other parties, by accepting office, to accept also the blame for the inevitably disappointing results of fuller autonomy. This was not generally true. A convenient test of the belief may be found in elections to the most important regional office, that of regional head. It is true that there were cases where the PKI, in a majority, preferred to leave this position to a member of another party. This would seem to have been the case in the second-level region of Karanganjar (Central Java) where 16 PKI representatives together with 2 independent left-wing representatives chose not to carry the day, but to concur instead in the election of a PNI regional head, by acclamation. In a few other cases (e.g., Grobogan, Central Java) the PKI preferred to support fellow-traveling candidates rather than to accept office formally themselves. But in the great majority of cases where the party was in a majority (13 second-level

[19] See Appendix A. Note that the figures on party seats for 1957 are not strictly comparable, as they stand, with those of 1956, since the size of councils had been increased by Law 1/57.

swatantras out of 18 [20]) it successfully sought the position of *kepala daerah.* In 8 of these the election was contested.

Where the party was in a minority, it participated in the normal pattern of bargaining and interparty adjustment. Major offices at the disposal of the DPRD tended to be divided up on a basis of general agreement. If the position of *kepala daerah* went to one, that of chairman of the DPRD would go to another, and that of vice-chairman of the DPD to a third. In all of this it is impossible to detect any clear and regular party alignments. An examination of *kepala daerah* elections, for example, would seem to show the presence of almost every possible kind of alliance. There were cases where PKI supported PNI candidates in a contested election,[21] and cases where it opposed PNI candidates; [22] there were cases where it supported NU candidates in a contested election,[23] and others where it opposed NU.[24] And there were many instances where PNI, Masjumi, or NU candidates for *kepala daerah* were elected by acclamation, presumably with PKI consent.[25] There were also cases where all other parties boycotted elections

[20] The party possessed a majority or a virtual majority in the following DPRD's: the municipalities of Semarang, Surakarta, Madiun, Salatiga, Blitar, and Surabaja and the *kabupatens* of Semarang, Sukohardjo, Bojolali, Tjilatjap, Klaten, Madiun, Magetan, Ngawi, Ponorogo, Blitar, Grobogan, and Karanganjar. In the first 3 of the municipalities listed and in the first 10 of the *kabupatens,* it secured the position of *kepala daerah.*

[21] E.g., Kota Kediri, Kabupaten Temanggung, Kabupaten Purwakarta.

[22] E.g., Kota Tjirebon, Kabupaten Wonogiri.

[23] E.g., Kabupaten Blora, Kabupaten Pemalang, Kota Tjirebon.

[24] E.g., Kabupaten Sidoardjo, Kabupaten Temanggung.

[25] E.g., Kabupaten Tjirebon (NU), Kabupaten Garut (PNI), Kabupaten Tasikmalaja (Masjumi).

of *kepala daerah* because PKI controlled a majority of DPRD seats.[26] But boycotts were not confined to that type of situation. In at least two *kabupatens* (Kendal and Magelang) an NU boycott of a *kepala daerah* election was directed against the PNI.

In these circumstances it is not possible to draw any clear conclusions about party policies of alignment. They would appear to have been almost as varied as local situations. This was perhaps partly due to the essentially different character of local as distinct from national politics. Or it might have been due to the fact that party strategy at the second level of autonomy was still very much in an experimental stage.

In general the creation of the local government system provided an important arena for party training and development. The occupational distribution of council membership may have been limited, but the requirements of the competition for power as laid down in the electoral system were bound to encourage a rapid growth of political sophistication. This process, though not completely blocked, was to be thrown radically out of gear by the general curtailment of party power which followed the return to the Constitution of 1945 and, more specifically, by the alterations to be made in the local council system by presidential edict.

[26] E.g., Kota Semarang, Kabupaten Magetan, Kabupaten Sukohardjo.

6

Powers

IT proved easier to establish the main institutions of local government in Indonesia than to give them anything of importance to do, and the determination of a suitable sphere of activity for local bodies was a slow process. In retrospect it is not clear why this should have been so, except, perhaps, that from the beginning there was a tendency to define on paper an overelaborate division of powers between centre and regions and between one type of region and another. Difficulties arose in attempting to translate the complex blueprint into everyday reality. Broadly speaking, however, a tendency could be observed, even before the passage of Law 1, toward the introduction of a much simpler (and also more liberal) concept of local powers, and Law 1 itself set the seal upon the trend. It is worth examining in greater detail the provision made in the earlier legislation, and the extensions and simplifications made to it subsequently, before coming to a consideration of the character of local powers themselves.

Law 22, as has been noticed, provided in general terms that local authorities could handle all matters of local concern—their "household affairs." This was to be the field of their "autonomous" activity, as distinct from the administrative co-operation (*medebewind*) which they could give to the central government or to higher local governments. The precise powers summed up in the term "household affairs" were not enumerated in detail in the law, but it was provided that they would be elaborated subsequently in the further establishing legislation which was required actually to create each region as an area of local government under the basic law. In due course the earlier establishing legislation, setting up provinces and *kabupatens* in Java and provinces in Sumatra,[1] listed fifteen general subjects as falling within the field of activity of local governments. (An odd feature of this list, and one which will be discussed below, is the fact that the same general subjects appeared in the establishing legislation for all levels of local government—provinces, municipalities, and *kabupatens*. No attempt was made to allot different fields to different levels. The actual responsibility of the province was not intended, of course, to be the same as that for the *kabupaten* or municipality, and a more exact division of authority was provided in the appendix to each establishing law.)

I. The maintenance of a DPRD and of the general organization which goes with it (*urusan umum*)
II. The execution of laws and regulations passed by that council (*urusan pemerintahan umum*)
III. Control of public lands (*urusan agraria*)
IV. Public works—irrigation, roads, and public buildings (*urusan pengairan, djalan 2, dan gedung 2*)

[1] Laws 2, 10, and 11 of 1950 (provinces in Java), Laws 12, 13, and 14 of 1950 (*kabupatens* in Java), and regulations in place of Laws 3, 4, and 5 of 1950 (provinces in Sumatra).

V. Agriculture, fisheries, and co-operatives (*urusan pertanian, perikanan, dan koperasi*)

VI. Veterinary services (*urusan kehewanan*)

VII. Control of handicrafts, internal trade, and industry (*urusan keradjinan, perdagangan dalam negeri, dan perindustrian*)

VIII. Control of labor (*urusan perburuhan*)

IX. Social welfare (*urusan sosial*)

X. Marketing, distribution, price control, and so on (*urusan pembagian [distribusi]*)

XI. Information (*urusan penerangan*)

XII. Education (*urusan pendidikan, pengadjaran, dan kebudajaan*)

XIII. Health (*urusan kesehatan*)

XIV. Traffic control (*urusan lalu-lintas*)—for province only

XV. Operation of the region's own enterprises (*urusan perusahaan*)

There was a certain ambiguity here, since the basic law had made a general provision that each autonomous government should manage its own "household." It was not clear whether the list of powers set out in the establishing legislation was intended to constitute an exhaustive definition of "household affairs," and thus to indicate the full scope of activity of the local government, or whether the term might have been held to include other matters of clearly local interest which fell outside the list but which could be handled by the local government on its own initiative, subject only to the general provision that such initiative must not infringe the legislation of a higher level. This point was not made clear either in the basic law or in the earlier establishing laws for the provinces in Java and Sumatra, though the statement in the basic law that matters included in the concept of *rumah tangga* would be determined in the establishing legislation for each region [2] suggested the narrower interpretation.[3] So did the fact that the mere listing of the fifteen powers in the establishing legislation did not mean that those powers were immediately possessed by the regions being established. The actual surrender of each power (except the first two, which were implied in the mere establishing of local bodies) required a separate legal instrument—a government regulation. In fact, the actual transfer of power by regulation was very slow.

Changes in the wording in later establishing legislation, however, suggested that the wider interpretation was intended or, at least, that it had since come to be favored. The legislation establishing *kabupatens* and large and small municipalities in Central Sumatra was substantially different from that establishing autonomous governments in Java. Although a list of subjects was included (the same subjects as those already listed for Java), it was

[2] Law 22, Article 23 (2).

[3] Article 1 of Law 22 provided that Indonesia shall be divided into three levels of autonomy which "have the right to regulate and arrange their household affairs themselves." Article 23 (1) provided that the DPRD shall regulate the household affairs of the region. The next paragraph continued: "Matters which are included in the *rumah tangga* mentioned in par. 1 are to be determined in the establishing law for each region." The question would appear to turn on the words "are included" ("hal-hal *jang masuk* urusan rumah tangga"). Article 28, dealing with the legislative powers of DPRD's, empowers the DPRD to legislate for the "interests" of the region, but the general explanation attached to the law, in elaborating this article, equates "interests" with the *rumah tangga* dealt with in Article 23 and thus does not clear up the ambiguity.

further provided that the autonomous governments had the right to concern themselves with matters not dealt with by the central government or by the provincial government until higher legislation decided otherwise.[4] A similar provision was included in the legislation dividing Kalimantan into three provinces [5] and in that creating the Province of Atjeh.[6] These later formulations appeared to indicate a trend in the direction of allowing a greater degree of flexibility in the conferring of powers upon local governments. This trend was eventually confirmed in Law 1 of 1957, whose general statement that a region may deal with those matters not already pre-empted by the centre or by a higher local government removed the ambiguity of Law 22 and the earlier establishing legislation issued under it.

The more general wording of Law 1, it should be noted in passing, was likely to be particularly satisfactory to those areas which had been self-governing principalities under Dutch administration. It has been seen that these states enjoyed all powers not specifically pre-empted by the Indies government—a method which, in fact, allowed greater room for initiative than was the case where specific powers were surrendered by the centre to the regions.[7]

[4] Law 8/56, Article 8; Law 9/56, Article 8; Law 12/56, Article 8. These three laws provided for the transfer to the *kabupaten* or municipality of some of the listed powers by the province, not the central government. This was merely because, in the absence of autonomous governments of the second level, the powers of such governments had been surrendered to the province already.

[5] Law 25 of 1956, Article 81. A roughly similar provision had been included in the law establishing the original Province of Kalimantan (Emergency Law 2 of 1953, Article 75).

[6] Law 24 of 1956, Article 13.

[7] It is worth noting the existence, in the laws establishing second-

Nevertheless it was felt that the general concession of Law 1 needed closer definition. Clearly, the wider interpretation could mean very little if all important fields of local initiative and activity were, in fact, to be pre-empted by a higher authority. To make it abundantly clear that the new law was intended to create a framework within which genuinely extended powers might be enjoyed by local governments, the central government decided to make further specific transfer to the regions of powers which, hitherto, had been exercised by the centre. Up until 1958 only a limited number of the fifteen subjects had actually been relinquished. To provinces, powers had been transferred in only seven fields (public works, agriculture and fisheries, veterinary services, control of small industries, education, and health), and to *kabupatens* and municipalities, powers in only two fields (public works and health) were surrendered. In 1958 the list was extended, and forestry, social welfare, labor, traffic control, and housing were added. (These later transfers were to the first level of autonomy only. By a change in procedure it was now decided that the centre would hand over responsibility only to the first level, leaving it to the authorities of that level to make the further transfers to the lower branches of local government—and, incidentally, to incur the opprobrium of failing to do so if that should be their decision.)

On the face of it, then, it may seem as though, by 1958,

---

level regions in Maluku (Law 23 of 1957), Nusa Tenggara Timur, Nusa Tenggara Barat, and Bali (Law 69 of 1958), of a provision which safeguards existing powers enjoyed formerly by these areas before the operation of the new legislation. And the powers formerly exercised were, in fact, residual powers.

central government generosity had gone as far as it could reasonably be expected to go and as though there was no longer any real ground for the complaint that the regions had been denied a genuine scope for their activity. But certain problems still remained, touching both the character of the powers surrendered and the workability of the division of functions between levels.

An examination of the fifteen fields listed in the earlier establishing legislation (and, in spite of the blanket provision of Law 1, the fifteen fields would still appear to be a correct reflection of both central and local thinking on the question of what things a local government may properly do) must leave one with some feeling of bewilderment. It would seem reasonable to suppose that certain fields of activity are more suited to one level of government than to another, and for this reason alone, quite apart from the advantages of clarity and simplicity which would have followed, it might have been better to make a more exclusive division of functions, earmarking some fields for the centre, others for the first level of autonomy alone, and others again for the second and third levels. There are exceptions to the rule. Public works is one sphere which must be divided among all levels, and no problem arises, for example, in making trunk routes the responsibility of the nation or the province, branch roads that of the *kabupaten,* and so on. Similarly, the field of public health is of such a character as to invite the cooperation of a multiplicity of public authorities. But does the same apply to the duties falling to the Ministry of Agriculture, or Social Welfare, or Labor, or Education? In these cases the idea that all levels of local government have a contribution to make means that there must be a hierarchy of detailed duties within the one broad field, matching the hierarchy of local governments themselves. To split up the field of education, for example, allotting responsibility for curricula, teacher training, and so on to one level and the erection of buildings and provision of equipment to others, may conceivably be convenient, but on the face of it appears to be dictated less by convenience than by the desire to share powers on principle, as though the central government were saying, "If the regions want more power, here is one activity they may take over."

One obvious consequence of dividing up the one field among several levels in hierarchical fashion is that it must affect the reality of the autonomy which is enjoyed by any level. The explanatory appendix attached to the earlier establishing laws made it clear that, in the case of many of the fields listed, the role of the autonomous government was to be merely that of assistant to the central government in the case of provinces and assistant to the province or the centre in the case of *kabupatens*. This limitation was effected partly by the specific classification of many of the powers as *medebewind* rather than as *otonomi*. (*Medebewind*, it will be remembered, referred to the role of local governments in executing tasks delegated by the centre or a higher level of local government. *Otonomi* referred to the right to deal with fields which had been surrendered to the regions and thus fell completely within their competence—their "household affairs.") For example, under the heading VIII, labor, the five activities to be entrusted to the province were all specifically described as *medebewind*. For the most part they comprised the provision of statistical information to the central Ministry of Labor. But even where the powers to be surrendered were not specifically described as *medebewind,* their character was often, in effect, not more than that of giving assistance to the centre. The education power may serve as an example. The duties in this field which were surrendered to provinces were limited to primary schools only, and then were concerned mainly with the erection and care of primary school buildings and the provision of equipment for those schools. (In this task *kabupatens* could be requested to assist.) All other educational matters—the drafting of curricula for all schools, the inspection of all schools, the training of teachers, and so on—remained matters for the central Ministry of Education. It is not intended to suggest that, in these particular fields, full provincial autonomy would be more desirable than central control, that education would be better handled, for instance, on a provincial rather than a national basis. The examples are chosen because they illustrate a general limitation placed on provincial autonomy by the earlier legislation, a limitation to be found not just in the fields of labor and education but in other fields also.

This situation might be summarized very briefly: apart from headings I and II, only two of the fields to be surrendered to the provincial level under the earlier legislation could be described as fields of substantial autonomy, with room for full local initiative and full local control. These were public works and health. All the remainder were, in greater or lesser degree, powers of *medebewind,* whether so described in the explanatory appendix to the establishing act or not. The same comment applied in an even greater degree to the *kabupaten,* to which level, in any case, only public works and health had then been surrendered.

A second consequence is that this division of powers between levels makes the whole task of administration unnecessarily cumbersome, so much so that it gives support to the arguments, already examined elsewhere, that three levels of local government, together with a central government, are altogether too many levels. According to the general plan, a man must be a citizen not merely of his country, but of his immediate neighborhood, of his district, and of his province as well. His need for government might surely be satisfied with less. Apart from the confusion to the individual, there is the inevitable complexity which must arise in devising administrative machinery to secure co-operation between such a multiplicity of governments, in fields where co-operation is necessary. But this is a question which can be better discussed below.[8]

In general, then, the division of powers and the hierarchy of levels provided in the legislation suggest some confusion as to just what local government should be. There is obviously a very big gap between the first level of autonomy and the rest. Provinces, if the term may still be used, are large enough in area and population to merit complex governmental organization. They are units which, though they happen to be established within the framework of a unitary state, could, in other circumstances, adapt themselves to the role of constituent states of a federation. As such, the term "local government" as it is commonly used is hardly applicable to this level. The situation is entirely different with other levels—districts,

[8] See Chapter VII.

village groups, and municipalities, even very large municipalities such as Surabaja. Governments at these levels are more clearly "local governments," and their powers might well be defined accordingly. To put the matter bluntly, local governments, as the term is normally understood, are usually concerned with "domestic" affairs—with drains and such matters. The Indonesian term "household" is a good one. (This does not mean that the lower levels should not also be the arena of normal party competition. But in seeking office at the lower levels, the parties might be expected to concern themselves much more closely with immediate local issues.) To have too many levels, as well as to give all levels the power to participate in many of the same fields of activity, is to cut across this concept. It is also to place a heavy financial strain upon smaller governments, since many of these fields of activity require considerable outlay. Even if the necessary funds were provided by higher levels of government, it might be doubted whether the lower levels of administration would be capable of administering the large budget involved.

These remarks raise the whole question of the "fullness" of local powers. The provisional constitution had promised the regions as full a degree of autonomy as possible (*otonomi seluas-luasnja* [9]). The action on the part of the Ministry of Home Affairs during 1958 to effect further specific transfers was in line with its final concession to regional pressure. A consideration of the functions transferred, however, may leave some doubts as to whether, in their sum total, the additions really constituted a substantial enlargement of the actual autonomy of the governments in question. For that matter, it may be doubted

[9] Provisional Constitution Article 131 (2).

whether, except at the first level of autonomy, it would even be possible to make a very substantial increase, as local governments, by their very nature, are limited in their powers. In Indonesia there has been a tendency to discuss the question as though this were not so—as though units at each level had the capacity to become almost independent states and as though all that was needed to meet local demands was the transfer of more and more functions. In fact, it could be argued, the control of more and more administrative functions does not make a local government unit essentially more powerful.

There is one field, however, in which the substance of power has been genuinely at stake between centre and regions—the field termed "general government," which is a peculiarity arising from the traditional machinery of Indonesian government whereby the special administration corps, organized on a territorial basis, was responsible for peace, order, and co-ordination of all activities of government in each area. The implications for local government of the retention or abolition of the *pamong pradja* have already been examined in some detail, but it is necessary to glance again at the question from a slightly different angle—the question of the disposal of powers formerly exercised by this corps.

In some places steps had already been taken during the provisional period to give local executive councils some experience in the problems of "general government" at the lower levels, on the assumption that this would eventually become part of their work. In East Java, for example, *kabupaten* DPD's were associated with the supervision of *desa* administration. The DPD was given power to approve *desa* regulations, and in the division of duties among

DPD members one member would be entrusted with the "portfolio" of *desa* affairs. The extent to which this member really performed a serious task varied from area to area and depended upon co-operation with the administrative service in each place. Since, strictly speaking, this field of activity did not properly belong to the autonomous *kabupaten,* the arrangement was purely informal. The experiment was conducted on the initiative and authority merely of the Governor of the province. Apart from that local experiment, the central government, when it came to the point, appeared reluctant to relinquish this over-all function; or rather its willingness to do so was intimately connected with its determination to exercise a general official control over local bodies. It was prepared to concede wide powers to regions provided it could retain a firm supervisory machinery. Alternatively, the loss of that machinery could be accepted with equanimity, provided the field of activity surrendered to local governments was comparatively limited. But the ministerial instruction of December 5, 1957, which laid down the three-phase plan for the transfer of *pamong pradja* powers to local governments, reflected a defeat on both fronts. It would seem that regions were, in consequence, to enjoy powers of the widest character.

In accordance with this instruction, legislation was prepared in the course of 1958 to effect the transfer to regional governments of powers falling within the field of "general government." It was passed by Parliament and proclaimed in March 1959 as Law 6 of that year. Before steps had been taken to implement it, its practical effect was negated, as will be seen, by Presidential Edict 6/59.

However, an examination of it will indicate the extent of the victory won, up to July 1959, by the exponents of fuller regional powers. The Act provided that, except for the responsibility of maintaining peace and order, of co-ordinating the work of central agencies with each other or with the work of regional agencies, and of supervising local governments, the tasks of the *pamong pradja* were to be surrendered to local authorities. The power to issue regulations, conferred by a variety of instruments upon governors and Residents, was to be transferred to the representative councils of first-level *swatantras,* and their executive powers, also deriving from a number of enactments, were to pass to executive councils at that level. Similarly, the regulatory and administrative powers of *bupatis* were to be transferred respectively to the DPRD and DPD of second-level *swatantras.* It was also decided that, for the time being, servants of the central government would be attached to regional authorities to assist them in the exercise of these new tasks. Officials hitherto employed in the offices of governors and Residents were to be attached to the first-level region to which they belonged. At the municipal level similar arrangements were to be made, and other second-level *swatantras* were to be assisted by officials of the *kabupaten* office and the offices of *wedanas* and *tjamats* or their equivalents. The respective regions were to be required to accept these assistants and were to refrain from making new appointments to their own services unless these inherited officials were all employed. These officers were to remain national civil servants for the time being, however, and their salaries were to be financed by the centre in the form of subsidies to the regions concerned. But there was to be provision for the actual absorption of these national servants by gradual stages into local services.

This Act, on the face of it, seemed intended, at one move, to yield the citadel: it purported to surrender the bulk of *pamong pradja* power and functions to regional governments. An interesting feature of the bill was its blanket character. The *pamong pradja* did not derive its existence or its character from any single enactment. Its duties had been built up gradually over the years, and a full definition of them was spread over some hundreds of individual enactments and regulations. There were some who argued that to dismember such a complex organism required delicate surgery, not a single blow from a blunt instrument. Specific powers should be transferred step by step and group by group in the form of amendments to specific regulations.[10] It should be noted, of course, that, although the emphasis of the Act appeared to be on the general surrender of all except the three reserved fields, the exceptions were equally important and they, too, were described in the broadest terms: public order, co-ordination, and supervision. Much would depend on how these were interpreted. What is involved in the concept of general government beyond these tasks? It is not easy

[10] This view was held, for example, by the former Governor of East Java, R. Samadikoen. Samadikoen had already, through the Regional Military Authority (*Peperda*) of East Java, postponed the operation of the ministerial instruction of December 5, 1957. By a decision of the same authority (May 27, 1959) the operation of Law 6/59 was also set aside in East Java. Samadikoen's own views on regional administration were developed in an address to the Douane Study Club, Surabaja, under the title *Desentralisasi dan Pelaksanaannja* (Surabaja, 1958).

to say precisely. In cities nobody knows who the local *tjamat* is, and he can be bypassed to a very large extent in the ordinary course of central or municipal administration. But for the village it is different. So long as the *pamong pradja* continued to exist, even if only for the three reserved fields, was it likely that any approach would be made to the village by any first- or second-level government agency except through that channel? Would not the reservation of "co-ordination" alone be sufficient to ensure the primacy of the central official?

The changes of 1959 have so effectively limited the effect of this law that the question is now academic. One can only speculate about the exact significance which Law 6 would have possessed had it been implemented within the environment of Law 1/57. If *pamong pradja* powers of the type prescribed by that law really had been transferred to executive councils, how far would this have gone, after all, toward satisfying local discontent? It is not without importance that, even after the more flexible wording of Law 1 had permitted regions to take up the responsibility of new burdens in fields not pre-empted by higher levels of government, they did not really take advantage of the opportunity. Their slowness to do so may have been partly a matter of financial limitation and partly a matter of inertia. But it is also possible that there was little genuine incentive to extend the duties of the lower levels of local government. Law 1, in permitting regions a wider field of activity and allowing it to be determined to a great extent by the desires of the regions themselves, had, in effect, put local governments on the spot to the extent that their dispute with the centre had really been about the fullness of local powers. The basic law seemed to have provided a central concession. The fact that advantage was not taken of this concession may suggest that the debate has not, after all, really been concerned with powers and that, therefore, the further concessions made by Law 6/59 would not have contributed greatly to solving the problem of regionalism. It will be argued below that this is at least partly true: that much of the "autonomy" debate has not been about powers but about policies in matters which the regions have never suggested should be the responsibility of any but the central government. The appropriateness of central financial policy, for example, was not viewed in the same light from Manado or Medan as it was from Djakarta, and this constituted one type of problem which would not be affected one way or another by an extension of local government powers.

7

Civil Service

EACH autonomous government was to maintain its own civil service, organized, of course, on functional, not regional lines. Regulations governing the recruitment and employment of local services were subject to the prior approval of the next highest executive council. The Ministry of Home Affairs also issued a general guide to regions, in order to secure a degree of uniformity in conditions of service throughout the country, so that the risk of anomalies between the services of different areas, or between all of them and the centre, might be reduced to a minimum.

The provision of staff for local administration was bound to become increasingly difficult as local governments were established on a more thoroughgoing basis and as they assumed wider and wider powers. Adequately trained administrators and technical staff are in short supply in the country as a whole, and the lower levels of the hierarchy have to compete with the higher levels for efficient people. It is, perhaps, one of the severest indictments which can be leveled against Dutch colonial administration that it left such an inadequate supply of qualified Indonesian doctors, engineers, agriculturalists, or administrators for the service of the young Republic. During the provisional period the problem was disguised for three reasons. The limited powers assigned to local authorities meant that their need was a limited one. In those fields where they did operate they were able to rely comfortably for technical staff on the assistance provided by central ministries. Local departments of health, at provincial or *kabupaten* levels, were staffed, with isolated exceptions, by doctors employed by the Ministry of Health. Provincial departments of agriculture were similarly assisted, and so on. These technical assistants remained the servants of the central government, though their salaries were paid by the local government. Thirdly, the continued presence of the *pamong pradja,* particularly of Governor, *bupati,* and *wali kota,* who filled at their respective levels the office of *kepala daerah,* provided general administrative experience and leadership which could secure the co-ordination of central and local tasks. The passage of Law 1, with its enlargement of local powers and with its consequent limitation upon the role of the *pamong pradja,* stripped away the disguises and exposed the outlines of the problem in unambiguous terms.

The arrangements of the provisional period, although they enabled a beginning to be made in the development of local responsibility for local services, reflected the peculiarity of the Indonesian method of dividing powers. The role of local governments as assistants to the centre in certain fields and the need of local government, in any case, to rely upon the services of central officials meant a close interlocking of local government machinery with that of the several government departments concerned and made for unnecessarily complicated machinery. The field of education may provide an illustration of this problem. Attention has already been drawn to the subordinate role of local governments in the educational field. The province was entrusted with the maintenance of primary schools and the supply of equipment, and the remaining responsibility rested with the Ministry of Education. Each province had its own Education Office for the administration of its allotted responsibility. It also maintained branches of that office in the *kabupatens.* But the Ministry of Education, too, maintained its own provincial offices and *kabupaten* offices for the primary school inspectorate, its separate provincial offices for the supervision and inspection of lower secondary schools (Sekolah Menengah Pertama—SMP) in the province, and a separate office for the administration of mass education programs. (The inspectorate for the higher secondary schools [Sekolah Menengah Atas—SMA] was established in Djakarta, not in each province.) Thus the general field of education in each province was divided among a number of separate offices,[1] though the nature of their work made close cooperation imperative. That was particularly true in such *kabupatens* as Pasuruan, where an experiment in compulsory education was initiated. The experiment was financed by the Ministry, but supervised by the autonomous province.

Even in fields where local control was comparatively full, the fact that the same power was surrendered to all levels had its peculiar consequences from the point of

[1] In West Sumatra, for example, there have been three offices of the central Ministry in Padang (inspectorate of SMP and of foreign schools and the office of mass education) and three in Bukittinggi (inspectorate of primary schools [Sekolah Rakjat—SR], of technical education, and of religious education).

view of staffing, particularly when a technical staff was required. The field of health was a case in point. The province had power to establish and maintain its own hospitals, and it paid and controlled its own staff. It also had educational responsibilities in the training of orderlies and midwives. The *kabupaten* had similar powers. The fact that medical services were in any case inadequate and doctors in appallingly short supply removed any danger of overlapping between the two levels. But the Ministry of Health also operated directly in the local field, supervising local health services in technical matters, maintaining its own hospitals, and running a number of national campaigns against malaria, frambesia, and tuberculosis. Any *kabupaten* doctor was expected to assist in the execution of the central campaigns as well as performing his own duties for the autonomous local government which employed him. In fact, also, because of the shortage of doctors, most of those employed by *kabupatens* and provinces were supplied by the Ministry and could be transferred by the Ministry, although they were paid by the local authority. (There are rare cases where a *kabupaten* has actually appointed its own doctor, and in these cases it retains full control over him. The Ministry of Health is still his ultimate superior for technical matters. But it cannot transfer him. These are exceptions, however. For the most part official doctors are not merely under the Ministry for technical supervision. They belong to the Ministry and are simply on supply to the local government.)

In this situation there should be, ideally, in each province (1) an inspectorate of the Ministry of Health (i.e., a branch office of the Ministry) to control the direct activities of the Ministry in the province and to exercise technical supervision of the professional servants of the local governments and (2) an office of the provincial health service, controlled (except in technical matters) and financed by the autonomous provincial government. In actual fact the chronic staff shortage decreed otherwise. In most cases the two offices were combined in a single building and under a single head. A description of the organization of health services in the Province of East Java and in one *kabupaten* in the province will illustrate the complexity of the situation.

The chief health officer in the Province of East Java, though paid by the province, was both provincial inspector of health—for the Ministry of Health—and head of the province's own health service. (He also happened to be an inspector general of the Ministry of Health, a special advisory position, and the World Health Organization officer in the province.) As inspector he was responsible for the conduct in the province of the campaigns conducted by the Ministry against malaria, frambesia, and typhus. He was responsible, too, for the technical supervision of *kabupaten* health services. He was not responsible, however, for a central government hospital and a venereal disease institute which happened to be situated in the province. These were directly under the Ministry of Health. Secondly, as chief health officer in charge of the provincial health service, he was responsible for all the strictly provincial activities in the field, including the operation of two hospitals (at Malang and Madiun); an antimalarial campaign run by the province in addition to the central campaign and financed from a section of the provincial budget which allows for measures to combat "epidemic and endemic diseases"; and the training of medical auxiliaries for the province. In his two capacities he was responsible for two budgets—one relating to his administration of the central funds which were allotted to the provincial office in its capacity as provincial branch of the Ministry and one relating to his administration of the health services of the autonomous province. The divided responsibility of this officer will be clear from Chart 1.

Something of a similar duplication occurred at the *kabupaten* level. In the *kabupaten* of Pasuruan, for example, one hospital was maintained by the autonomous *kabupaten*, and another was maintained by the autonomous municipality of Pasuruan. The *kabupaten* doctor was responsible to the DPD of the *kabupaten* for all *kabupaten* health services, including the hospital and the polyclinics in the area. He was also technically responsible, through the subinspectorate of Malang Residency, to the provincial inspectorate in Surabaja and ultimately, of course, to the Ministry. He was expected to assist in the conduct of central campaigns in the *kabupaten*. And he was responsible for the supply of statistical information to the Ministry. Further, since he was originally supplied by the Ministry and was merely on loan to the *kabupaten*, he was responsible to the provincial inspectorate in more than a technical sense. The provincial inspector could transfer him within the province. And the Ministry could transfer him beyond the province. Finally, as an added complication in Pasuruan, is the fact that the staff shortage again forced a combination of positions, and one man served as both *kabupaten* doctor and municipal doctor.

This duality of character of health services at all levels

Chart 1. Organization of health services in the Province of East Java

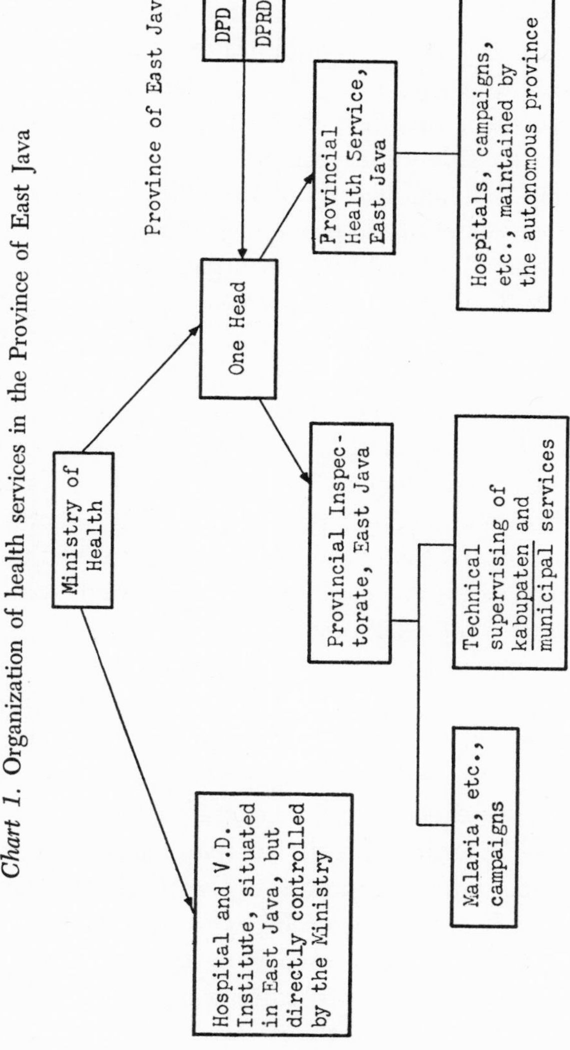

is not necessarily a disadvantage. Indeed, at the provincial level, it could be a positive advantage for an administrator who knew what he wanted and who could bend to his purposes whatever organizational devices happened to exist. Ultimately, it might be possible for all the executive tasks in a province to be the responsibility of the province considered as an autonomous region. In the meantime the combination of the offices of provincial inspector and chief of the provincial health service has been perhaps more rational than an organizational plan which attempted to define the two areas of responsibility more sharply and to divide those areas between two officials.

While these difficulties confronted the services for which local governments were themselves responsible, the continuance of the *pamong pradja* and the close connection which was maintained between central administration and autonomous affairs produced further organizational complexities by giving a dualistic character to the central secretariat of province, *kabupaten,* and municipality. Departments of the autonomous governments were generally housed under the same roof as the central secretarial staff in the region (i.e., in the office of Governor, *bupati,* or *wali kota*), and the dual function of these officials—as *pamong pradja* and as head of the autonomous governments—was reflected in the general office organization. If portrayed diagrammatically, a reasonably clear division of functions was apparent between those sections of the office which were concerned with central matters and those which were concerned with local government matters. In practice, the two sides were apt to interlock, a fact which was not without its advantages for general efficiency. Chart 2 is based on the organization of the

Chart 2. Organization of the office of *bupati/kepala daerah* in Kabupaten Malang, East Java, before passage of Law 1 of 1957

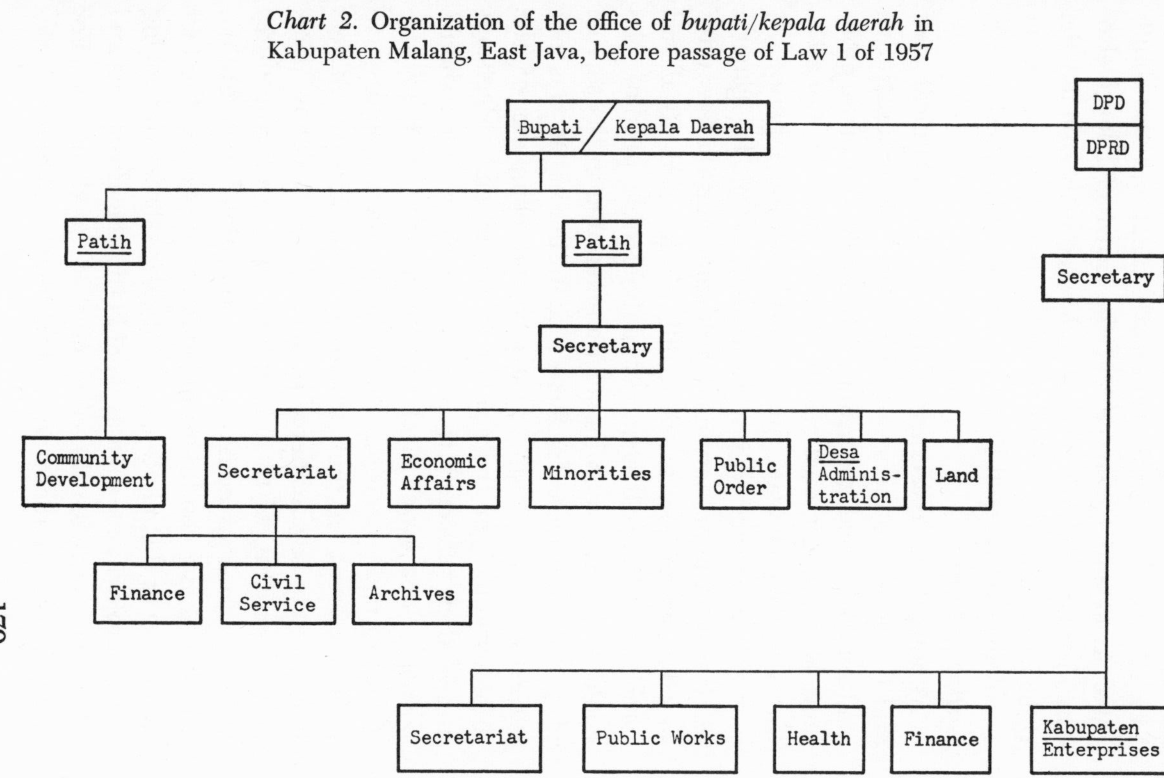

kabupaten in Malang as it was under the operations of Law 22, but the organization was typical and was duplicated in essential character at the provincial level also. The election of the *kepala daerah* effectively divided the right-hand side of the chart from the left, but more recent developments, as will be shown, will tend to restore the earlier pattern.

Although the assistance of the central technical staff and the general supervision of the central administrative staff enabled local governments to avoid the main problems of creating a civil service, their difficulties nonetheless were acute, even during the provisional period. It was still necessary to rely to a great extent for general clerical work upon untrained personnel, and the low rates of civil service pay made it difficult for both local and national services to attract and hold able people, who could command much higher remuneration in the service of private business. In these circumstances, it was not surprising that senior officials should complain of the dubious ability of their subordinates to make decisions and of their tendency to pass on decisions which should be made at a lower level or, alternatively, of their proclivity to make decisions on matters which should go to a higher level, of their slowness in passing on matters which had to be considered by several sections of an office, and, in general, of their ignorance of proper procedures and their lack of administrative traditions. In addition, the poor living conditions of public servants and the fact that many of them had to eke out their salaries by seeking other employment, such as teaching in the afternoons and evenings, were hardly conducive to good service. For reasons such as these any communications between departments, between lower and higher levels of local government, or between local governments and the Ministry of Home Affairs were apt to be interminably slow and productive of great frustration for civil servants and local governments alike.

A start has been made in the direction of providing a core of trained officials at least for the provincial level. Through the assistance of the Ministry of Home Affairs a number of men from each province have been sent each year for training in public administration and related fields at the Gadja Mada University, Jogjakarta. These men are now beginning to filter back to their respective provinces, and some are employed on the autonomous side.

With the passage of Law 1 these problems were bound to be greatly accentuated. The law followed the general lines of its predecessors in empowering local authorities to make their own regulations to govern recruitment, terms of employment, and remuneration,[2] but there were safeguards to ensure a reasonable degree of uniformity throughout the country among governments of the same level. Regulations concerning civil service recruitment, employment, and dismissal were included with those which had to await approval of the DPD of the next highest level before coming into effect,[3] and such regulations were to follow as far as possible the lines laid down by the central government for the control of state civil servants. As before, there was provision, too, for regions to receive assistance from state civil servants or from civil servants of a higher level of local government. These would be attached to a region and would be paid by it.

[2] Article 53 (1). [3] Article 53 (27).

But this was envisaged as a temporary necessity and left unsolved the permanent problem of shortage.

For the lower levels of autonomy the chances of being able to build up reasonably efficient services would seem to be particularly difficult, since the avenues of promotion were inevitably limited. Able people were hardly likely to enlist in the service of a lower level *swatantra,* where the office of regional secretary represented the peak of possible attainment. It would, no doubt, be possible to develop civil service arrangements on a wider basis so that a man could transfer from the service of one region to that of another, carrying his status, seniority, and pension and other rights with him, but so far no such broad approach to the problem has been adopted.

An important question which was not decided in the basic law, and which presumably could be answered only in practice, was whether a career system or a spoils system was to be adopted in civil service appointments. The provision requiring higher approval before civil service regulations come into operation in a particular region has been a check on the possible development of the latter. But, in fact, there have already been some signs of the practical emergence of the spoils system, at least in the higher ranks. The office of regional secretary is a pivotal position which requires experience and ability, and hence the centre expected that the loan of its own servants would be necessary to tide local governments over the interim period. The Ministry of Home Affairs made a general offer of the secretaries of governors' offices for the use of first-level regions. Not surprisingly, however, the position of secretary was the very position which local governments were determined to fill themselves. The procedure for the selection of the secretary was laid down in the basic law. He was to be elected by the representative council from candidates nominated by the executive council and in a manner prescribed by regional regulations.[4] In the case of this office, the DPD, if it wishes, could select its secretary for such reasons as that of party loyalty.

It is difficult to predict the effect, for civil service development, of the application of guided democracy to the regions. The closer integration of local government with the system of central control may restore the situation as it existed before the passage of Law 1. But at most this will merely disguise for a time the very real shortage of administrators available at the local level.

[4] Article 52. An example of the kind of application of this general provision is the East Java regulation which provides that the DPD shall bring forward, at the most, three names for the consideration of the DPRD, but it is open to the DPD to advance one name only (as was, in fact, done)—a procedure which is thus tantamount to giving the DPD power to appoint the secretary.

8

Finance

IT goes without saying that, whatever formal machinery may be evolved for the devolution of authority and whatever powers may be surrendered, no local government can exercise genuine independence and initiative unless it is founded on a satisfactory financial basis. Finance and responsibility are closely linked. Although it is possible for grants to be made without strings, control of the purse normally involves at least some control over the way money is spent, and a local authority entirely dependent for its revenue upon the bounty of a central government subsidy is bound to be severely restricted in its freedom of movement. It is important, therefore, that there should be at least some clear agreement as to areas of taxation which are to be shared between centre and regions or which may be left free by the centre as fields specifically intended to provide funds for local purposes. A further principle is involved also. It is probably desirable that whoever has the task of spending the money should also have the responsibility of collecting it. Only in that way can a proper sense of perspective be developed with regard to the feasibility of projected developmental plans on the part of a local council. A good deal of regional resentment in recent years has sprung from dissatisfaction with the amount spent by the central government on capital works in particular areas. But demands of this kind, reflecting a preparedness to rely on central handouts, are hardly consistent with the simultaneous demands for autonomy.[1]

These principles were not in effective operation in Indonesia during the provisional period of local government planning. In the case of some central taxes, certainly, it had become an established practice to return a percentage to the regions, and the latter had, in addition, the power to levy a number of rates and charges. These, however, amounted to a minor proportion of the total cost of local government. For the rest it was necessary to rely on a straight-out grant-in-aid made through the Ministry of Home Affairs by the Ministry of Finance. (The situation was more serious in Java than in the regions outside, for in the latter some extra sources of local revenue had been left in local hands. Nevertheless a substantial grant from the centre was an essential part of the pattern and formed the bulk of local budgets.[2]) For the lower levels of local government—*kabupatens* and municipalities[3]—the main

[1] This point does not apply, of course, where regions are performing functions delegated by a higher authority (*medebewind*) and receive a special grant for that purpose.

[2] Douglas S. Paauw, "The Role of Local Finance in Indonesian Economic Development," *Ekonomi dan Keuangan Indonesia,* Jan. 1955, p. 2.

[3] Although there were no autonomous governments of the third level, something should be said here about the financial resources of the village. These also varied from area to area and were determined to some extent by the character of the village itself—also a very variable factor. The main resource of the village was the principle of mutual help (*gotong rojong*) or the ability to call upon the labor services of its members. This principle has, perhaps, been

revenue sources available were roughly of four types: (1) taxes levied by the local government itself, e.g., the bicycle tax, entertainment tax, dog tax, vehicle tax; (2) the reversion of a certain proportion of taxes collected by the central government from the regions concerned, e.g., the household tax, 5 per cent of which was returned to the province and 15 per cent to *kabupatens;* (3) returns from services provided by the local government, e.g., water rates, hospital charges, charges for the use of space in markets; (4) returns from enterprises operated by the local authority, e.g., swimming baths and, in some in-

idealized in much contemporary Indonesian political thinking. The President himself has frequently referred to the idea of community activity as being basic to the Indonesian way of life. In developing his idea of guided democracy, for example, he called for the establishment of a *gotong rojong* cabinet and a more general application of this principle in national life. It is not necessary to consider whether the symbolic use of this term is really justified by the actual practice at village level. But it is certainly the case that labor is called on by the village authorities for many purposes, such as the maintenance of village roads. One example observed by the author was the construction of schools in *desas* in Kabupaten Pasuruan (East Java) as part of a pilot experiment in compulsory education. But *gotong rojong* does not represent the only means by which the village can maintain its services. In West Sumatra the *negeri,* rather than the *kabupaten,* is responsible for the administration of markets. A group of *negeri* may control one market, and the returns from market charges form part of their revenue. Reference has already been made above to the *marga* of South Sumatra which is often able to mobilize quite considerable resources, through, for example, a tax on the sale of fish. The budget of Kajuagung, admittedly a wealthy example, in 1957 ran into six figures. For a case study of the financial resources of a Javanese village, see Widjojo Nitisastro and J. E. Ismael, *The Government, Economy, and Taxes of a Central Javanese Village,* translated by Norbert Ward (Cornell Modern Indonesia Project, Monograph Series; Ithaca, 1959).

stances, cinemas. Of these sources by far the most important in the case of *kabupatens* has been the return from the administration of markets. For municipalities water supply and markets formed the major source of income. There was a closer approach to self-sufficiency in the case of municipalities, for their functions and character had been more fully developed during the colonial period. But for *kabupatens* the central subsidy provided the major share of the annual budget. Although the total budget and the exact proportion of it which was borne by the central government varied from area to area, a fairly representative example may be quoted. The *kabupaten* of Probolinggo in East Java budgeted in 1956 for a total expenditure of over Rp.8,000,000. It was estimated that local resources (including the reversion of the usual percentage of particular central taxes) would contribute only a little over Rp.4,000,000. For the remainder a central subsidy was required. Provinces were in a much worse position, for the funds available to them did not match their greater commitments. In 1956 the Province of East Java, for example, required an estimated subsidy of Rp.369,000,000 from the central government in a total budget of Rp.412,000,000. Only a little over Rp.7,000,000 was expected from provincial taxes and charges. (The remainder represented the balance from the preceding year's grant.)

This financial dependence of regional governments meant an accompanying limitation upon their freedom to spend. Supervision in financial matters has been conducted through the ordinary supervisory machinery. The budgets of local governments were approved in the first instance by the DPD of the next highest level. *Kabupaten* budgets, that is to say, were considered by the DPD of the province whose task was to compare and balance the demands of *kabupatens* of the whole province before making a recommendation to the Ministry of Home Affairs. Provincial budgets were approved by the Ministry itself. A final allocation as among local authorities was determined by the Ministry, which had to act, of course, within the general limits set for it by the Ministry of Finance. The final allocation for each area included provision for the technical departments—health, agriculture, etc.—maintained by the local authority. These were not financed directly by the central Ministry within whose field they fell. A local government could also receive special assistance for a particular task to be performed for a central Ministry. The several pilot experiments at present being conducted in compulsory education offer one example. In cases such as this the Ministry of Finance has made a special allowance for the project, but the actual disbursement was still made through the Ministry of Home Affairs.

Local governments have also been able to borrow from the central government for particular purposes, and again the projects had to pass the scrutiny of a higher authority. The object of the loan and the exact details of its application were first to be approved by the Ministry of Home Affairs and the Ministry of Finance and, in the case of the lower levels of autonomy, by the province also. The provincial DPD again acted as an initial filter for such proposals, considering in detail the nature of the works to be financed from the loan, the validity of the estimates of costs, and so on, and it had to balance each request against others from within the province. It then passed on the request together with its recommendation to the Ministry.

The justice of regional complaints about their financial dependence was recognized, and it was intended from the beginning that the passage of a permanent basic law would be associated with more appropriate financial arrangements. The whole question of regional finance had been the subject of investigation some years earlier by a special committee under the chairmanship of Mr. M. Nasroen, formerly head of the Autonomy Division of the Ministry of Home Affairs, and the substance of the recommendations of the Nasroen Committee was embodied in Law 32 of 1956 concerning the financial equilibrium between the state and the autonomous regions (gazetted as the Financial Equilibrium Act). The Act provided that, to the comparatively insignificant sources—dog tax, entertainment tax, and the like—already at the disposal of regional governments, were to be added three distinct types of revenue.

(1) Certain specified state taxes were to be transferred entirely to the regions and were to become regional taxes (Article 3). Eight taxes were listed: the urban land tax (*padjak verponding*), the "Indonesian land tax" (*padjak verponding Indonesia,* levied in some rural areas), the household tax (*padjak rumah tangga*), the motor vehicle tax (*padjak kendaraan bermotor*), the road tax (*padjak djalan,* a tax on adult males resembling a head tax),[4] the slaughter tax (*padjak potong,* an indirect consumer tax), the copra tax (*padjak kopra*), and the development or reconstruction tax (*padjak pembangunan,* a postwar tax levied on restaurant charges).

(2) The returns from several other state taxes were to

[4] *Ekonomi dan Keuangan Indonesia,* Aug.–Sept. 1958, p. 515

be divided, according to proportions to be determined, between centre and regions. In this category were, first of all, the income tax (termed "transitional" tax—*padjak peralihan*), wages tax (*padjak upah*), and stamp duties (*padjak meterai*). Regional governments were to receive between 75 and 90 per cent of the returns from these.[5] Secondly, they were to receive varying proportions, to be fixed year by year, of the property tax (*padjak kekajaan*) and company tax (*padjak perseroan*).[6] Thirdly, import, export, and excise duties were to be similarly divided.[7] And, finally, it was provided that regions could receive the proceeds from extra duties levied on the products produced within their boundaries.[8]

(3) It was recognized that the additional funds from these sources would still be insufficient to cover all the costs of local government, and provision was made for direct financial assistance from the centre for special purposes or to make up the budget deficiencies of poorer regions. Three types of grant were specified: "payments" (*gandjaran*) could be made by the centre to regions for special programs to be undertaken by the latter (a category which would include tasks performed by the regions on behalf of the centre—*medebewind*); "subsidies" (*subsidi*) could be requested by the regions to meet exceptional needs; and "contributions" or grants-in-aid (*sumbangan*) could be made by the centre to assist regions which were unable to pay their way in performing the ordinary tasks of local government.

Apart from these donations, subsidies, and grants from

[5] Article 4 (1). [6] Article 4 (2). [7] Article 5 (1).
[8] Article 5 (2).

the centre, the new classes of taxation revenue to be made available to regions under the Act constituted a substantial financial basis for their operations. Admittedly the taxes in the first category, which were to be transferred completely to the regions, were not so very important, as may be seen from Table 3 based on the year 1955. The most important of these taxes, the development tax levied on restaurant receipts, yielded slightly over Rp.25,000,000. The household tax came next with a total of Rp.18,900,-000, and the slaughter tax produced Rp.14,000,000. Out of a total revenue from taxation in that year of Rp.7,686,-500,000 the total of the eight taxes combined amounted to a little over Rp.70,000,000. In the same year the expenses of local government, even though they were then far from fully developed, were in the neighborhood of Rp.2,700,-000,000. However, the taxes under the second heading, which were to be shared between centre and regions, were of a very much more important character. As may be seen from Table 3, the really important revenue producers in Indonesia are the company tax (Rp.1,807,400,000 in 1955), import and export duties (Rp.1,860,100,000),[9] and excise (Rp.1,831,700,000). Quite a way behind is the so-called "transitional" tax on incomes (Rp.928,900,000). These were all included in the taxes whose revenues were to be shared. Much would depend on the exact amount to be set aside for the regions, but in the case of the income tax the law itself fixed a 75 per cent minimum. As

[9] Export duties were replaced in July 1957 by a tax of 20 per cent of the proceeds from the sale of export certificates (*bukti ekspor*). Since these certificates represented foreign currency, the tax was still a tax on the proceeds of exports.

Table 3. Taxation revenue, 1955 * (in millions of rupiahs)

Assessed taxes		Nonassessed taxes		Customs and excise	
Income tax [b]	928.9	Wages [b]	303.9	Duties [c]	
Property tax [c]	11.4	Free-sale profits	10.2	Import	1,105.6
Company tax [c]	1,807.4	Development [a]	25.6	Export	754.5
Household tax [a]	18.9	Sales	653.9	Statistics	40
Road tax [a]	1.2	Radio licenses	29.0	Excise [c]	
Motor vehicle tax [a]	5.4	Slaughter tax [a]	14.0	Petroleum, motor spirit, etc.	597.6
Urban real estate [a]	8.5	Stamp duties [b]	63.5	Tobacco	1,029.0
Miscellaneous, incl. others [a] (as Indonesian land tax) not separately listed	3.7	Property-transfer duties	14.3	Alcoholic liquors	23
		Miscellaneous (lottery, public-auction duties, etc.)	26.8	Beer	23.4
				Sugar	158.7
				Other	28.1
Total	2,785.4		1,141.2		3,759.9
Total, all taxes					7,686.5

* These figures are taken from Biro Pusat Statistik, *Statistical Pocket-Book of Indonesia, 1957*. At the time of its publication the figures for 1956 were not complete. The 1955 figures, however, give an indication of the proportionate contribution of each tax. The table does not include two important sources of central revenue, the duties on the purchase of foreign currency for imports (TPI) and the duties on the purchase of foreign currency intended for transfers (TPT). In 1955 these duties realized Rp.1,100,000,000, and Rp.400,000,000 respectively (Bank of Indonesia Report, 1955–1956).

[a] Taxes to be transferred to regions under Article 3 of Law 32/56.

[b] Taxes of which between 75 and 90 per cent are to be returned to regions under Article 4 (1).

[c] Taxes of which a percentage, to be decided annually, is to be returned to regions under Article 4 (2) and Article 5 (1).

will be seen below, the discretion allowed to the government in dividing the company tax year by year was, in fact, to be exercised in a generous fashion.

The inclusion of customs and excise duties among taxes to be shared was particularly important because of the connection of these taxes with the grievances felt by the export-producing areas of Indonesia. The standard complaint of the outer islands, particularly Sumatra and Sulawesi, was that though they were major producers of Indonesia's wealth they were neglected by the central government. It will be necessary to examine more closely the character of this complaint, but it should be noted here that it related to two distinct issues. As producers of export commodities the outer islands were both revenue earners and foreign currency earners. They were demanding, therefore, a greater share of central government expenditure (or a greater share of grants to their local governments) and also a greater share of imports. The former demand is relevant here. The return of a part of the revenue derived from duties might help to reduce their feeling that their export earnings were devoted merely to the support of parasitic Java.

Unfortunately, the implementation of the Financial Equilibrium Act has been slow. The Act merely defined the main outlines of the future financial relationship. It remained to fill in the details by government regulation. In particular, where the Act had assigned certain taxes to the regions, it was necessary to distribute these tax sources among the two existing levels of local government; and where taxes were to be shared, it was also necessary to fix the exact proportions. Government Regulation 3 of 1957 accomplished the first of these tasks. The household tax, the motor vehicle tax, and the urban land tax were to be surrendered to first-level *swatantras*. The remaining five taxes were to be surrendered to second-level *swatantras*. However, the actual transfer depended upon the preparedness of the regions to accept the responsibilities of collection. It was to be effected by a joint decision of the Minister of Home Affairs and the Minister of Finance after regions had enacted suitable taxation ordinances and had established the necessary staff to execute them. Until then, under the general act, the centre was to continue to collect the taxes and was to retain 10 per cent for administrative costs, leaving 90 per cent to be returned to local governments. This interim arrangement remained in force for two years.

For the shared taxes—income tax, wages tax, stamp tax, property tax, company tax, and customs and excise duties—the question was rather more complicated. The Nasroen Committee had proposed that the portions of these state taxes earmarked for the regions should be paid into one general fund for the support of regional governments. The actual allocation among provinces of revenues from this fund was to be based upon a consideration of eight factors: the extent of each province, its population, its economic potential, the educational level of its population, the cost of living in the province, the length of roads maintained by it, the length of canals in its irrigation system, and its geographical character (e.g., whether it was an island or a group of islands). The Committee proposed a complex formula for the weighting of each of these factors in calculating a region's entitlement.[10] The un-

[10] For a discussion of the details of the formula see Paauw, *op. cit.*, p. 18, and also articles by J. de Bruine in *Ekonomi dan Keuangan Indonesia*, Feb., March 1954, pp. 53, 128.

wieldy and perhaps artificial character of the proposed formula was likely to make it very difficult to apply, and it is doubtful whether there was really any intention to apply it as it stood. The proposal was not embodied in the Act. That in itself was not surprising, since the Act, after all, was intended to deal only in general terms. It was provided merely that the principles of distribution should be laid down in a government regulation "having regard to the factors influencing the situation of a region." The eight factors were then listed, but rather, it would seem, as examples of what was meant than as an exclusive list to be applied strictly according to the Nasroen formula. There remained also the problem of dividing the fund between the various levels of government in the one area. The Nasroen proposals had not attempted to cover that question, but had been concerned only with distribution between provinces.

By 1958 there had still been no government regulation to deal with these two questions. In these circumstances it was proposed, as an interim measure, to make a straightforward allocation to regions not on the basis of their general situation at all, but merely on the basis of the amounts collected in each area up to the amount of the 1957 grant. And these returns were to be divided between levels according to fixed proportions. From the tax on incomes above Rp.5,000, 60 per cent of the amount collected in each first-level *swatantra* was to go to the government of that *swatantra,* 30 per cent of the amount collected in each second-level *swatantra* was to go to the government of that *swatantra,* and 10 per cent of the amount collected in Greater Djakarta was to go to the municipality. For the tax on incomes under Rp.5,000, 90 per cent of receipts were to go to the second-level region within which they were collected. And similar arrangements were made for the other taxes: first-level regions (except Greater Djakarta) were to receive 90 per cent of the stamp tax collected within their boundaries, 75 per cent of the property and company taxes, and 50 per cent of the import and export duties. Djakarta, listed as a special case, was to receive 20 per cent of the receipts from the wages tax. And second-level regions were to receive 90 per cent of the returns from the wages tax. A summary statement of the proportions of all taxes available to the regions is given in Table 4.

It is still too early to judge the real effectiveness of the new revenue system. It was not enough for the regions to be receiving a more substantial revenue as of right instead of their earlier dependence on the bounty of the central government. Not until they actually shouldered the task of collection would they really be financially responsible, and this they began to do only in 1959. Indeed, the blueprint laid down in Law 32/56 must itself be judged not only in terms of the absolute contribution it makes to regional finances, but also in terms of its handling of the task of collection. Has it assigned to the regions those taxes which may be most efficiently collected at the regional level? And are the taxes themselves the most suitable revenue producers?

One peculiarity of the Indonesian taxation system is the high proportion of indirect to direct taxes. The latter account for approximately 60 per cent of the total receipts from taxation. This is in part a reflection of the special problems of Indonesia—the size of the population and the lack of accurate census figures, the high degree of illiteracy which affects the ability to make returns, the

Table 4. Distribution of central taxes among regions, 1958 *

Tax	Percentage surrendered to		
	First-level regions	Greater Djakarta	Second-level regions
I State taxes transferred to regions	%	%	%
Urban real estate tax	90	90	
Household tax	90	90	
Motor vehicle tax	90	90	
Road tax			90
Slaughter tax		90	90
Copra tax			90
Development tax		90	90
II Taxes to be divided between centre and regions			
Income tax: large incomes	60	10	30
Income tax: small incomes			90
Wages tax		20	90
Stamp tax	90		
Property tax	75		
Company tax	75		
Import duties	50		
Export duties	50		
Total estimated returns for 1958–1959	Rp.1,640,-000,000	62,130,-000	713,000,-000
Total estimated costs of local government for 1958–1959	Rp.2,528,-000,000	63,914,-000	1,077,000,-000
Difference to be met by subsidy or grants-in-aid	Rp.888,-000,000	1,784,-000	364,000,-000

* These figures are given as an example only. They were revised in some detail in the following year (Government Regulation 14/1959). The taxes under heading I were by this time collected by the regions themselves.

shortage of trained administrative staff, and the existence of a vast number of very small enterprises. Although some indirect taxes, because of their local character, may be more efficiently collected by local authorities—the slaughter tax, for example—the existence of these special difficulties suggests that local administration may offer particular advantages in the collection of direct taxes. Paauw [11] cites the example of the tax on small incomes (*padjak peralihan ketjil*), which applies mainly to the rural sector of the economy.[12] For this reason it would appear most likely to produce maximum revenues if assigned to local authorities as one of their own taxes. In fact, under the Act it has been retained as a central tax, though the bulk of its proceeds is to be earmarked for local purposes.

A related problem is the need for a simplification of the whole Indonesian taxation structure. The 1956 Act is concerned with the distribution of the revenues from existing taxes, and these have been developed gradually over the years, both during and since the colonial period, in a more or less *ad hoc* fashion. The existence of gaps in many areas of taxation and of duplication in others is pointed out in an analysis of the whole taxation system prepared for the Government of Indonesia by an expert appointed by the United Nations Technical Assistance Administration.[13] For example, the two land taxes—the urban real

[11] *Op. cit.*, p. 20.

[12] The income tax (*padjak peralihan*) is divided into two parts according to the size of the income and the mode of collection. The *padjak peralihan besar* applies to incomes of over Rp.5,000 and is collected by a central official. The *padjak peralihan ketjil* applies to incomes of between Rp.600 and Rp.5,000 and is collected by the *lurah*.

[13] M. D. Dris, "Taxation in Indonesia," published in *Ekonomi dan Keuangan Indonesia,* Aug.–Sept. 1958.

estate tax (*verponding*) and the rural land tax (*verponding Indonesia*)—do not cover all categories of landed property. It was suggested that a new tax on landed property, applying to all immovable property, should replace these two taxes and eliminate, at the same time, the need for the existing road tax which duplicates, in some respects, the functions of the other two.[14] Similarly, the income tax (*padjak peralihan*) and the tax on wages are two distinct taxes which overlap in their functions. The abolition of the latter and the bringing of all wages under the operation of the former would remove unnecessary duplication.[15] This type of simplification would conceivably make easier the division of fiscal functions as well as the division of revenues between centre and regions.

Even if this were effected, however, it may be wondered whether the type of division contemplated in Law 32 is really necessary. The basic local government law provided machinery for the supervision of lower by higher local governments and of first-level governments by the centre, and this supervision was particularly strong in the field of finance. That being so, it is at least arguable that an allocation of taxes in detail between levels is unnecessarily complex. Provided the centre is willing to vacate certain tax fields, could it not be left to local governments to enter such vacant areas at their own discretion—to introduce new taxes of whatever kind in fields not exclusively reserved for the centre or for higher levels of local government? Such a solution would be in line with the greater flexibility which, as has been noted, was introduced by Law 1/57 into the question of division of powers (other than financial powers) between centre and regions. It is now open to regions to deal with matters not

[14] *Ibid.*, pp. 490, 516. [15] *Ibid.*, p. 452.

pre-empted by a higher authority, whether or not they have been specifically assigned.

It may be, however, that such an open solution would depend upon greater experience and maturity than regions at present possess. If that is so, Law 32 may be seen as providing, in the field of finance, a compromise solution. It places the regions, in absolute terms, on a much sounder financial footing than they ever possessed before. In doing so it could go some distance toward conferring the type of autonomy they have demanded. But it imposes greater restrictions than those imposed with regard to other powers which local governments may properly exercise.

Whether, if these restrictions had not been imposed, the Act would really have gone very far toward conferring the type of financial autonomy the regions were demanding is another matter. It was particularly important in regional eyes, not merely that they should have command of greater resources, but that they should have control of certain specific resources, notably the revenue from customs duties. And these duties were not likely to be among those over which the centre would willingly relax its control.

9

The Retreat from Autonomy

LAW 1 of 1957 was intended to provide a legal "basis," a "foundation" on which a system of actual institutions would be established, a "framework" within which actual procedures would be developed. Metaphors of this kind are not always helpful. At best such a legislative provision is likely to bear only a rough relationship to the reality which it is said to create. This was particularly so in the present instance. Law 1 was undoubtedly important, as the vigor of the controversy surrounding it suggested. As finally passed, it reflected the balance of parliamentary opinion, and up to a point it helped to determine reality. Its terms were given substance in local councils and local offices and in the relationships between central and regional governments. But any consideration of this legislation must take into account the general environment in which the law was drafted and in which it began to function. Even at the time of its proclamation there were present many factors which were bound, in some degree, to distort the operation of the law. As a general statement it may be said that the ultimate passage of Law 1 and the early steps in its implementation coincided with a decline in the power and influence of Parliament and of the parties of which it was composed. Even while the regions were gaining further concessions, there was counterpressure for a strengthening of central control and, in the regions themselves, a growth in military influence.

Political crisis had begun to make itself apparent well before the last months of the second Ali Sastroamidjojo government, which had been responsible for the final passage of the law. On November 16, 1956, Col. Zulkifli Lubis, Deputy Chief of Staff, attempted to bring about a *coup d'état* in Djakarta by seizing control of the city and overthrowing the Ali Sastroamidjojo government. The plot was discovered in advance and frustrated. In the following month, however, Lieutenant Colonel Husein, regimental commander in Padang, staged a successful coup in the Province of Central Sumatra. Although protesting his loyalty to the President and the Republic, Husein rejected the authority of the Ali government, and, on December 20, he overthrew the existing civil administration of the province and transferred power to the Banteng (Buffalo) Council, which had been formed under his chairmanship at a reunion during the previous month of the old Banteng Division of the revolutionary era. In Medan, the capital of North Sumatra, an attempt was made to follow Husein's example. Colonel Simbolon, commander of Military Region I (North and Central Sumatra), similarly renounced the authority of Djakarta. In this case, however, the coup was short-lived, for Simbolon's second-in-command, Lt. Col. Djamin Gintings, was immediately appointed to succeed him, and within a few days Gintings had managed to carry through a countercoup which recovered control of Medan for the central government.

The Sumatran developments had revealed the serious nature of the widespread feeling against the government, and it was followed by the withdrawal of the five Masjumi Party members from the Cabinet. These events formed the background for Soekarno's plan for guided democracy involving two main points—the idea of a "four-legged" government, composed of the four major parties, and the idea of a national council based on functional representation.[1] Soekarno felt that liberal democracy had failed, that political parties who pursued their own selfish interests were not really representative of the nation, and that a council composed of functional representatives—representatives of workers, peasants, religious groups, women, youth, citizens of foreign descent, the various regions of the country and other major interests—would enable the emergence of a common will. Such a council would follow the principles of discussion which, the President argued, were to be found in their ideal form at the level of the village. The proposal triggered off a further series of regional revolts. In Sulawesi, Lieutenant Colonel Sumual, commander of the East Indonesian Military Region (comprising Sulawesi, the Moluccas, and Nusa Tenggara) assumed control of the administration of these provinces on March 2. A few days later similar developments occurred in Kalimantan and South Sumatra. Finally, on March 14, the Ali government resigned, and the President proclaimed a "state of siege and war," thus legalizing the *de facto* control of the provinces by their military commanders.

The task of forming a new government proved difficult. The political vacuum was eventually filled by the "Karya" (working) Cabinet of Dr. Djuanda, formerly Minister of Planning in the Ali Cabinet. It was a nonparty Cabinet,

[1] For a fuller discussion of this period see G. McT. Kahin, ed., *Major Governments of Asia* (Ithaca, 1958), pp. 563 ff.

though most of its members bore party labels. Masjumi, however, boycotted it, and the Cabinet fell far short of the President's conception. So did the National Council (*Dewan Nasional*) which was set up by the new government, but which was obviously less powerful than the President had intended. It owed its creation to an emergency act of Parliament, a method which was quite consistent with existing constitutional procedures—the procedures of "ordinary" as distinct from "guided" democracy. And the law which created it also limited its powers. It could give advice, solicited or unsolicited, and it could thus form, perhaps, a useful forum for the kind of discussion which party rivalry in Parliament precluded. But that was the extent of its formal power. It was a sounding board for the views of the President himself, and behind the scenes it could exercise considerable influence—how considerable it is not easy to say, since neither the records nor the decisions of the Council have been made public. The Council attempted to work on the principle of consensus, and it avoided the taking of a formal vote. For this reason the extent to which its deliberations were able to resolve major differences of opinion is not known. It is an open secret that a number of its recommendations were unacceptable to the government, or to Parliament, or to both.

The remainder of 1957 saw a number of attempts to restore unity. A reorganization of the East Indonesian Military Region restored the greater part of that area to central control (though North Sulawesi remained in effective opposition), and a series of consultations with other military commanders secured a measure of formal agreement between them and the Chief of Staff. Central

Sumatra, however, remained outside the fold and under the administration of its own Banteng Council. In September a national conference under the chairmanship of the Prime Minister and attended by about 200 of the country's civil and military leaders attempted to find a basis of agreement and produced a number of very general recommendations to the government (e.g., that it move rapidly to extend the power of local governments and to determine a just financial relationship between the regions and the centre). In February 1958, however, in the aftermath of the economic crisis accentuated by the stepping up of the campaign for the "liberation of West Irian," there came the proclamation in Padang of the "Revolutionary Government of the Republic of Indonesia." The institution of forceful measures to meet the revolution enabled government control to be restored formally to most of the rebel areas, but the wiping out of all pockets of resistance in West Sumatra and Tapanuli and also in northern Sulawesi proved to be a prolonged business, and at the end of 1958 Parliament renewed for the second time the "state of emergency." [2]

The operation of the emergency law naturally constituted a limitation upon the freedom of local authorities. In the regions civil authority under the emergency act rested with a committee—*Penguasa Perang Daerah* (*Peperda*)—composed of the *kepala daerah*, the members of the DPD, and the regional chief of police, under the chairmanship of the regional commander. How much this

[2] In December 1957 Parliament repealed the old Dutch measure "Regeling op de Staat van Oorlog en van Beleg" (usually abbreviated to SOB), under which Soekarno had declared the emergency in the preceding Parliament, and replaced it by a new measure (Law 74/1957).

meant in practice varied from area to area and depended on the local situation and upon the regional commander himself. Although ultimate decisions may have belonged to the military authorities, there were many matters with which they did not bother to concern themselves and others on which they refrained from testing their power. The Army was not, in any case, a monolithic structure. The Chief of Staff was not able to rely with certainty upon the obedience of his regional commanders, and his own position involved the need to compromise with and conciliate subordinates. There was a more restricted limit in fact than there was in theory to the emergency powers of the Army, and there was no detailed military intervention in daily civil administration. But still the terms of the emergency legislation did affect the implementation of Law 1. The concessions obtained by the regions during 1957 and 1958 were largely paper concessions, whose real substance was withheld during the prolonged crisis.

Toward the end of 1958 the President returned to the idea of guided democracy, but in a new form. His Independence Day speech appealed for a new electoral law to control party activity and to "simplify the party system." In the following month a speech by Roeslan Abdulgani, Vice-President of the National Council, added a further point to the plan by suggesting that the principle of functional representation should be introduced into Parliament itself.[3] In January 1959 a series of "open talks" were held between the President and the Cabinet, at which were discussed procedures for modifying Parliament's composition. At the same time, the idea of a return to the Constitution of 1945 was canvassed as one means of securing

[3] *Pos Indonesia,* Sept. 15, 1958.

such a modification. The 1945 Constitution was more flexible in character than the provisional constitution. One of its more important features was that it provided for a presidential Cabinet—i.e., a Cabinet formed by the President and responsible to him, though possibly with a separate Premier. (The relevant clause stated that the President would be assisted by Ministers of State.) Such a Cabinet could not be displaced by a simple parliamentary vote of no confidence.[4] Finally, on February 19, the Cabinet decided to adopt the idea of a return to the 1945 Constitution and of an amendment to the electoral law to allow functional representation in Parliament.

Although the Cabinet had committed itself by this decision and although leaders of the major parties had appeared to agree "in principle" to accept the Cabinet plan, the Constituent Assembly, when it came to the point, failed to adopt the proposal to return to the 1945 Constitution by the required two-thirds majority. Soekarno, on his return from abroad in July, dissolved the Constituent Assembly and introduced the 1945 Constitution by decree.

The method by which the Constitution of 1945 was in-

[4] The Constitution, in addition to provision for a Parliament, Cabinet, President, and so on, provided also for two additional bodies: a general consultative assembly (*Madjelis Permusjawaratan Rakjat*), composed of members of Parliament and representatives of regions and groups, and a Supreme Advisory Council (*Dewan Pertimbangan Agung*). The former—the MPR—had power to choose the President and Vice-President and to determine the main lines of state policy. The latter—the DPA—had power to give advice to the President. The MPR was described in the Constitution as an executor of the people's sovereignty and was presumably expected to carry more prestige than Parliament itself. In drawing his authority from this body, the President would have a separate mandate distinct from that on which parliamentary authority rested.

troduced—by presidential decree following upon the failure of the Constituent Assembly to accept the proposal —was itself a reflection of the decline which had occurred in the power of political parties. The terms of the Constitution confirmed their reduced role. Party representatives were included in the Provisional Supreme Advisory Council (*Dewan Pertimbangan Agung Sementara*) appointed by the President in July, but they were in a minority there (12 party representatives in a total membership of 45). And members of Parliament were, by the Constitution, to be included in the People's Deliberative Assembly (*Madjelis Permusjawaratan Rakjat*), the supreme body which was to elect the President and to determine the main direction of state policy. But here also parliamentary representatives were to be balanced by those of regions and of functional groups.[5] Although the government was no longer to be responsible to Parliament, Parliament's consent, of course, was still required for normal legislation, but it was soon proved possible for the government to legislate in effect by presidential edicts or presidential regulations.

It would be misleading to see this as part of an inevitable trend toward a presidential dictatorship. Parliament was never, in any case, the only source of authority in the country. Power in Indonesia, in fact, has been spread very widely between a number of forces—the President, the government, Parliament, the parties (these with their own social sources of strength), the Army, the regions. The exact relationship between these forces has never been clearly defined, and it has so far been worked out by a

[5] The MPR was to consist of the members of Parliament (about 270), 94 representatives of regions, and 200 representatives of functional groups (Presidential Regulation 12/59)

series of adjustments in practice. There have been things the President cannot do and things the Army cannot do. Each has depended upon the other, as they have done also upon a degree of agreement with political leaders. Indonesia's provisional constitution bore only a loose relationship to the actual way in which power was exercised, and the formal increase in presidential authority under the new Constitution may not alter that situation very much.

Nonetheless, guided democracy had serious implications for the regions. The system of local government established by Law 1 presupposed political party activity of a liberal kind. Even without any formal changes the return to the 1945 Constitution was bound to have repercussions for the parties at the regional level as well as at the centre. And, in fact, there were to be formal changes which made this much more explicit, by carrying the idea of guided democracy into the regional sphere also.

PRESIDENTIAL EDICT NO. 6

The appointment of Ipik Gandamana as Minister of Home Affairs in Soekarno's first presidential Cabinet under the 1945 Constitution suggested the possibility of an official rather than a political approach to the question of local government. Ipik had formerly been Governor of West Java and could be expected at least to understand the *pamong pradja* point of view. But the policy that he implemented bore the signs of the strong personal influence of the President himself.

The expected revision of existing arrangements came about in September 1959, when Presidential Edict (*Penetapan Presiden*) no. 6 suspended the provisions of Law 1/57 relating to the election of *kepala daerah* and reverted to the principle of appointment. In doing so, it reversed the trend expressed in the ministerial instruction of December 5, 1957, and any subsequent planning, and it ended, at least for the time being, the whole experiment in fuller autonomy based on Law 1/57.

The instrument by which the change was made was the subject of some controversy. Critics of the measure argued that a law could not be changed by a presidential edict and that action of this kind required the approval of Parliament. According to the government view, on the other hand, no such approval was necessary, since the measure was merely designed to implement the presidential decree of July 5 by which the 1945 Constitution had been adopted.[6] Unsuccessful attempts were made to initiate a parliamentary debate.[7]

In its provisions concerning the office of *kepala daerah,*

[6] Statement by Ipik Gandamana, *Pos Indonesia,* Sept. 10, 1959. The Minister of Information had already issued a statement concerning the rather complex hierarchy of measures which were to be issued under the 1945 Constitution. Under the 1950 Constitution there were four common forms of enactment and regulation: laws, emergency laws, ordinances in place of laws, and government regulations. The first three required parliamentary approval. (In the case of emergency laws this approval was subsequent to the enactment.) The fourth type was issued under the authority of an act. Apart from these there were now to be two important types of presidential actions: "edicts" (*penetapan presiden*), the purpose of which was to implement the decree of July 5, and "regulations" (*peraturan presiden*), for the purpose of implementing edicts. *Peraturan presiden* could also be issued under Article 4 (1) of the Constitution, which vested in the President the power of government under the Constitution. There were also to be presidential "orders"—for the purpose of making appointments—as well as a range of ministerial instructions and orders.

[7] E.g., M. Ardiwinangun, in September, argued that the decree of July 5, having reintroduced the 1945 Constitution, had completed its function. The single source of legislation should now be the Constitution itself. The President could only exercise legislative powers if his actions secured parliamentary approval.

Edict 6 brought the wheel almost full circle. The old "official" view, having lost the first series of engagements, succeeded, after all, in winning the last battle. The edict provided that the regional heads of first-level regions were to be appointed by the President, and the heads of second-level regions were to be appointed by the Minister of Home Affairs ("with the agreement of the President"). Appointments in each case were to be based on qualifications of education, ability, and loyalty, to be determined by a subsequent presidential regulation. (Presidential Regulation 4 of 1959 subsequently laid down the qualifications.[8]) There was provision for some expression of opinion on the part of the regions themselves. Regional representative councils were permitted to submit names of candidates for the position of *kepala daerah.* But a loophole for the exercise of central government discretion was specifically included. It was provided that, if the candidates nominated by local representative councils failed to fulfill the required conditions, a second list of candidates might be submitted. But if the names on the second list also failed to fulfill the requirements, the President or the Minister was empowered to make appointments from outside the list of nominations.

This provision was included in a "perfected" version of

[8] This measure was a presidential *regulation* to realize the Presidential *Edict* no. 6/59, which in turn was designed to implement aspects of the *decree* of July 5. The regulation limited candidates for the office to those who were Indonesian citizens, who had never opposed the Indonesian struggle for independence, who were "ready and able to develop regional government in execution of the Government's program." For first-level regional heads education up to higher secondary school standard was required, plus ability and experience in government. For second-level regional heads education up to lower secondary school level was required, as well as ability and experience in government.

the edict, which was issued by the President in November 1959 after the question had been discussed by the *Dewan Pertimbangan Agung* (Supreme Advisory Council). The original version provided only for the submission of one list of candidates by the local councils. The fact that a revised version was issued in these terms possibly suggested an intention on the part of the government to take notice of local wishes where possible. And, indeed, the wording of the edict—that where the list of nominees did not include candidates "who fulfill the conditions for appointment as *kepala daerah*" the President or the Minister could appoint from beyond the list of nominees—would appear to put the onus on the representative council to select men who fitted the description given in Presidential Regulation 4/59 and to suggest that only their failure to do so would lead the government to look for its own candidate. But some of the conditions laid down in the regulation were so vague—"ability," "experience in government"—that the centre in actual fact was not subject to any very clear limitation. In fact, among the first appointments made to first-level regions, there were a number which were made directly by the President after the rejection of the two lists of DPRD nominees.

With the return to the principle of appointment came the natural corollary—the restoration of the *kepala daerah*'s functions, both as representative of the centre and as a genuine chief executive of the region, with the emphasis, however, on the former. The edict described him as a state civil servant. He could not be dismissed by the regional representative council, but only by the authority—the President or the Minister—which had appointed him. The edict referred, in its explanatory appendix, to the old concept of dualism: on the one hand there was the field of general government, which was the responsibility of the *pamong pradja,* and on the other was the field of autonomy, which was the responsibility of the local authorities. The edict aimed to vest the leadership of both these fields in the one person, that of the *kepala daerah.* For his handling of local matters he was in some sense, not clearly defined, said to be "responsible" to the DPRD, though the nature of the responsibility was clearly limited since he could not be dismissed by that body. But at least it was clear that he was intended to be the chief executive officer for the region in respect to these matters. As an agent of the centre he was to be charged with the old functions of maintenance of order and co-ordination of the tasks of central and local departments. He was again to be the link in the *pamong pradja* chain. The lower and intermediate *pamong pradja* ranks—the *wedana* and *tjamat* below the second level and the Resident below the first level—whose disappearance or transference to the control of autonomous governments had been foreshadowed two years earlier, were now to be retained in a position of responsibility to the *kepala daerah* in his capacity as a central government representative.

With all of this it was natural that the *kepala daerah* would also, on behalf of the centre, exercise the same powers of supervision as had belonged to the office under the old Law 22. The edict, using practically the same words as had been used in Law 22, empowered him to delay the decisions of his DPRD "when, in his opinion, they conflicted with the main features of State policy, with the general interest or with higher legislation" (the reference to the main features of state policy was an addition to the old clause). In addition, the *kepala daerah* of a first-level region could impose a delay in similar circumstances upon the decisions of second-level governments within his region.

It will have been apparent from earlier discussions in these pages that there was much in Indonesia's social situation to justify the continuance of central government machinery in the regions and to use it also to supervise the workings of local authorities. The restoration of the close connection between the autonomous system and the *pamong pradja* was warmly welcomed in many quarters. The SSKDN, as the profession organization of the *pamong pradja,* was naturally pleased by this aspect of the measure, as were officials of the Ministry itself. If this had been all, the edict would have fitted into the existing discussion from which even Law 1 had emerged. It would have represented a retrograde step in the eyes of the parties, no doubt. But it would have left the regions in possession of other important advantages they had gained—their wider powers, for example. In general it would merely have modified the system of Law 1, though admittedly in a very important respect. However, the edict went far beyond any earlier proposals for retaining firm central control of development of local government. The changes it produced were related not merely to the position of *kepala daerah,* but to the very character of the regional executive.

It was the President's intention that the changes in the relationship between government and Parliament at the centre should have its counterpart in regional government also. Edict 6 left the regional representative council untouched: for the time being it was still to be an elected body, and existing DPRD's were to remain in office provided they were willing to be sworn in afresh, according to a new oath which included acceptance of the 1945 Constitution.[9] But the DPRD was no longer to elect, from its own members, an executive responsible to it. Instead, the old DPD was to be replaced by a new executive body —*Badan Pemerintah Harian* (Daily Government Board) —which would consist of between three and five members who were to be appointed, not elected. By a subsequent ministerial regulation (8/59) which filled in some of the details of Edict 6, appointments (and dismissals) were to be made by the Minister for first-level BPH's and by the *kepala daerah* of each first-level region for the second-level BPH's below him. Edict 6 provided that appointments were to be made "as far as possible" from candidates nominated by the DPRD, either from its own membership or from outside. But the government could reject those nominations and make its own appointments if it chose. The members of these executive boards were to be free from party affiliations, and they were no longer to be the executive servants of the DPRD. Rather, they were to be regarded as assistants to the *kepala daerah* in matters falling within the field of autonomy, just as Ministers of State were assistants to the President and not responsible to Parliament. Their tasks were to be assigned by the *kepala daerah*, and they were to be accountable to the DPRD only through him. The status of these executive boards was in itself a clear indication of the way in which executive power was now to be concentrated in the hands

[9] Edict 6 and Ministerial Regulation 7/59 concerning the form of words to be used in the oath for regional heads and members of the regional executive council.

of the *kepala daerah* alone. Edict 6 replaced the wording of Law 1/57—"The regional government is composed of the Regional Representative Council and the Regional Executive Council"—by the words "The regional government is composed of the *kepala daerah* and the Regional Representative Council."

It will be seen that this was a fundamental change in the whole local government plan. It was also quite unheralded by earlier controversy. Edict 6, it is true, contained some echoes of the old Law 22/48. The idea of appointment of the regional head from a list of candidates nominated by the DPRD had a familiar ring, though the ability of the centre to ignore the wishes of the DPRD was now regarded as a permanent possibility rather than as a temporary deviation during a transitional phase. But the provision that the *kepala daerah* was now to be personally responsible for the execution even of matters falling within the field of autonomy represented a considerable strengthening of the office, and in fact it amounted to a practical fusion of central and local functions. Law 22 in operation under its escape clause, had combined central tasks and the chairmanship of the local executive in the one hand, but it had attempted, at least in theory, to preserve the distinction between the two aspects. Presidential Edict 6 also made the theoretical distinction between the *kepala daerah* as a central organ and as a regional organ. Nonetheless, the change in the character of the DPD and the concentration of the executive power of local governments in the hands of the regional head himself almost obliterated any practical distinction. Since the regional executive was now made responsible to the regional head, rather than to the regional representative council, it was not likely to matter a great deal whether the regional head was acting, at any moment, in his capacity as a central official or as a local official. This may be seen most clearly, perhaps, with respect to the implementation of Law 6/59.

Law 6/59, it will be remembered, concerned the transfer to the regions of the "general government" powers of the *pamong pradja,* with the exception of the fields of maintenance of peace and order, the co-ordination of the work of central agencies with each other and with the work of regional agencies, and the supervision of local governments. This law had not been implemented before the presidential decree of July 5, 1959, and the proclamation of Edict 6 clearly altered the whole environment in which implementation would take place. A ministerial instruction of September 29, 1959, stated specifically that the execution of Law 6/59 would have to be adjusted to fit the terms (*disesuaikan*) of the presidential edict. In other words, since the *kepala daerah* had become the repository of regional executive power, the functions transferred to the DPD by Law 6/59 were now to be transferred to the *kepala daerah* alone. Thus, whatever precise form the proposed transfer of *pamong pradja* powers to regions might have taken had it been carried out within the general framework of Law 1, the effect of Edict 6 was clearly to render such a transfer of no practical effect. The field of general government would continue in practice to be reserved from political control at the regional level.

INITIAL APPLICATION

At the time of writing it is still too early to predict with confidence the precise way in which Edict 6 will be implemented or the degree of acceptance which it will find in the regions themselves.

One question of considerable importance concerns the character of the persons who may be appointed to the office of regional head. The *kepala daerah,* new style, was to be an official of the centre with supervisory and co-ordinating powers, and he was to be, once more, a link in the *pamong pradja* chain. This was made quite clear in the explanatory appendix; and according to a subsequent presidential regulation [10] he was to use the *pamong pradja* title of rank—Governor for first-level regions and *bupati* for second-level regions. But he was not necessarily to be selected himself from the ranks of the *pamong pradja.*[11] In the first place, the provision that candidates for the office were to be nominated by the local representative councils necessarily opened the possibility for appointment from beyond the service. The centre had preserved a wide loophole by which it could ignore the wishes of councils, but in addition it was free to appoint such individuals as it pleased. In fact it did so. Appointments were made from the ranks of the armed services, senior police officials, and private individuals, as well as from the ranks of the administrative service. Local wishes were ignored

[10] Presidential Regulation 5/59.

[11] Nor was he actually to become *pamong pradja* merely by virtue of his appointment. A distinction is made between national civil servants (*pegawai negeri*) and state servants (*pegawai negara*). The former category included all those whose salaries and conditions of service were regulated by the normal civil service regulation—the PGPN (*Peraturan Gadji Pegawai Negeri*). The latter category included the President and Ministers. Members of the *pamong pradja* were *pegawai negeri.* Regional heads were to be *pegawai negara.* A *kepala daerah,* Level II, though using the title *bupati,* was not actually to be a *bupati.*

in a number of cases.[12] This was particularly the case with first-level appointments. Of the first twenty-two of these appointments only eleven were of people trained in the *pamong pradja* (Central and East Java, West, Central, and East Kalimantan, Irian, North Sumatra, Atjeh, Bali, Nusa Tenggara East, and Nusa Tenggara West). Of the remainder five were soldiers (Djakarta, West Java, South Sulawesi, Riau, and Djambi) and one was police (South Sumatra).

In the case of second-level appointments the situation was a little different. The way in which the vacant positions were gradually filled suggested that the Minister was prompted by two criteria in exercising his power to appoint—a desire to appoint the administrative servants of the Ministry and a desire to respect local wishes as far as possible. An early analysis of appointments within the first-level region of East Java, where the replacement of existing *kepala daerah* went rapidly, gave an indication of a trend which was to be confirmed elsewhere. Of the first twenty-six appointments twenty-one were members of the *pamong pradja* who had been included in the lists of nominees sent forward by representative councils. In these cases there was no conflict between the two criteria. In two cases where no member of the *pamong*

[12] In Greater Djakarta, for example, council nominees, including a former Minister of Home Affairs who had been supported by PNI, Masjumi, NU, Parkindo (*Partai Kristen Indonesia*), and other smaller groups, were passed over in favor of a military appointment. In West Java the DPRD nominees included both the existing Governor and the existing *kepala daerah,* but both were rejected, again in favor of a soldier. In Central Java the existing *kepala daerah,* formerly a member of the *pamong pradja,* was also rejected, though in this case in favor of another member of the *pamong pradja.*

pradja was included in the list of nominees, the Minister showed himself willing to take notice of the strength of local support for particular candidates. And in two further cases where local feeling was strongly in favor of a particular candidate the Minister accepted that choice, even though it meant the rejection of *pamong pradja* members who had also been nominated.[13]

By the end of 1960, when almost all vacancies had been filled, the over-all picture showed that out of 238 appointments made 150, or 63 per cent, were from the *pamong pradja*. But this figure obscures the real significance, for the future of the service, of the return to the principle of appointment. If account is taken of traditional differences between various regions, the tendency to draw regional heads from within the *pamong pradja* may be seen to be much greater. In East Java 25 out of 35 appointments were made from this source. In Central Java the figure was 32 out of 34. In West Java, where Darul Islam presented a complicating factor, only 8 members of the *pamong pradja* were appointed as *kepala daerah*. Outside the island of Java, where the pattern of administration under Dutch rule had been varied, only 81 second-level appointments out of 141 had been *pamong pradja* appointments.

To generalize from these figures, it would appear that, in second-level regions where a tradition of *pamong pradja* government existed, *pamong pradja* appointments

[13] In Kabupaten Madiun and Kota Surabaja, the existing *kepala daerah* (both PKI) were reappointed, though in the latter case a member of the *pamong pradja* had been nominated also. In Kota Madiun and Kabupaten Magetan also, PKI candidates were appointed, and in the latter case also the PKI nominee was preferred over a *pamong pradja* candidate.

were preferred if local wishes allowed it. For first-level regions, on the other hand, the important thing from the point of view of the President was the individual acceptability of candidates, rather than their character as formed by past training and by the common experience of service in the administrative corps. And even at the second level it was possible, under Edict no. 6, that regional government could become more subject to arbitrary influence from above than was the case formerly when central authority, though it had been firmly exercised, had been exerted in an institutionalized form.

Since, by virtue of their appointments, regional heads became state civil servants, they came under the existing rule prohibiting civil servants in the higher grades from possessing a party affiliation. Where individuals were already known to have played an active party role, their mere resignation from their parties could not be expected to change their sympathies. The prohibition could, however, have an important long-term effect. The tendency of many members of the *pamong pradja* to join parties, particularly the PNI, in the hope of safeguarding their future advancement has already been noticed. The new measure, combined, of course, with the general decline in the political importance of the parties, removed that incentive. Whether this would restore the service to a position of greater political neutrality was more dubious.[14]

[14] Early appointments to the position of *kepala daerah* of first-level regions were accompanied by appointments of deputy regional heads (*wakil kepala daerah*), an office for which no legal provision had as yet been made. These appointments would seem to indicate a clear recognition of party affiliation. In Greater Djakarta, West Java, and Central Java these appointments were drawn from the ranks of the PKI or its close supporters. At the same time former

A second major question concerns the use which the centre is likely to make of its new power to appoint the members of regional executives. The initial implementation of Edict 6 in this field in fact produced less change than the edict itself permitted. Ministerial Regulation 8/59, which filled in details concerning actual methods of appointment, provided that appointments to (and dismissals from) the *Badan Pemerintah Harian* were to be made by the Minister for first-level regions and by the *kepala daerah* of each first-level region for the second-level regions below him. A number of qualifications for membership were listed, similar to those already laid down by the President for regional heads: in addition to the requirements in Law 1 for DPRD membership (residence in the region concerned, freedom from any convictions for a criminal offense, not deprived of voting rights, not an undischarged bankrupt, and so on), members were to have reached a certain educational level—higher secondary school for members of first-level executive bodies and lower secondary school for members of second-level executive bodies. But in the first instance, members of existing DPD's who were ready to accept appointment and who were willing to be sworn according to the new prescribed oath would be appointed as members of the new BPH's. In fact, almost all existing DPD members were willing to continue in office on these terms. (This was not

ties with the PNI appeared to be a disqualification for appointment. This pattern appeared to reflect the President's manipulation of the current balance of political forces. Subsequently, formal provision was made (Presidential Regulation 2/60) for the *wakil kepala daerah* for first-level regions. The deputy was to be appointed in the same manner as the *kepala daerah,* and he was to assist the *kepala daerah* in the performance of his duties.

surprising, since nearly all DPRD members had already agreed to accept the new oath of loyalty to the 1945 Constitution and to continue in office, in spite of the opposition which had been expressed by party leaders in Parliament to the whole character of Edict 6.)

There were certain consequences of this conversion of DPD's into BPH's. Members of a *Badan Pemerintah Harian* were to be free from party affiliation.[15] Since members of existing DPD's were normally party men, their decision to accept reappointment involved them in resignation from their parties. And they were no longer to be members of the DPRD, so that their reappointment thereby caused vacancies which had to be filled by normal procedures.

In spite of the continuity of membership which was achieved by the ministerial regulation, the change in the character of the regional executive clearly altered the whole environment in which party organization and activity had developed at the regional level. It is difficult to assess the precise effect of the change, for, though the parties had so far been the vehicles for local self-government, the rural population might not be so deeply touched by the decline in party power. That population still possessed its own form of self-government where it counted most—at the level of the village. And there party may be less important than traditional patterns of authority. It is possible, however, that the new dispensation may have important effects for the relative strength of existing parties. In reducing the incentives for active party life in the regions it may tell particularly against

[15] Presidential Regulation 3/59 amending Presidential Regulation 2/59 dealing with state service and party membership.

the PNI, and it might leave a freer field of operations for the PKI which, in some areas, has shown skill in developing its organization and mobilizing support for itself even at the village level. These two parties were, in effect, the main competitors for the support of the same group of voters, the non-Moslem or only nominally Moslem *abangan* element. But this is to speculate.

In January 1960 a further restriction was imposed on parties as a result of the President's Regulation no. 7 of December 31, 1959. Regulation 7, designed to "simplify" parties, laid down certain conditions to which parties had to conform. In a statement of basic principles, parties had to state clearly their acceptance of the 1945 Constitution and of the Pantja Sila—the five principles underlying the state: nationalism, popular sovereignty, humanity, social justice, and belief in God. Parties were required to follow only peaceful and democratic methods. Party membership was to be limited to Indonesian citizens, and, except with government permission, acceptance of foreign aid was forbidden. In addition to these requirements action against small parties was foreshadowed. It was provided that a party must possess branches in at least a quarter of the first-level regions of Indonesia and branches also in at least a quarter of the second-level regions throughout the country. (It was argued in some quarters that this would encourage small parties to form a number of branches containing a mere handful of members each and that it was a less reliable guide to the stature of a party than was total membership.) The President was empowered to ban or dissolve any parties which failed to meet these conditions. A further clause was added also. Parties could be banned if their leaders had taken part in, or given assistance to, revolts against the government, unless the party concerned officially expelled the offenders. This provision appeared to be directed specifically against Masjumi and PSI, which had not condemned those of their members who had been associated with the Revolutionary Republic of Indonesia. In July 1960 the President called on the two parties to show that they had complied with the regulation in this respect. In August, no such evidence having been given, he ordered their dissolution under the regulation.

Finally reference must be made briefly to the most recent development, taking place almost at the time of writing, which represents a further attempt to restrict the field of party activity and to bring regional government still more closely into line with developments at the central level. In March 1960, by presidential decree, Parliament was "suspended," and the President subsequently announced his intention to replace it by a new "mutual help" (*gotong rojong*) parliament. The new parliament, installed in June, was composed of 130 representatives of political parties and 153 representatives of the armed forces and functional groups. In September 1960 Presidential Edict 5/60 proposed to extend this type of arrangement to the regional representative assemblies which had been left unchanged by Edict 6/59. Existing DPRD's were now to be replaced by *gotong rojong* assemblies—DPRD-GR. Under the new edict only 50 per cent of the membership of each DPRD was to consist of party representatives. The remaining 50 per cent was to be composed of representatives of functional groups. Representatives of both classes were to be appointed. In the case of first-level councils appointment was to be made by the

Minister from a list of nominees submitted by the *kepala daerah* of each first-level region. The number of nominees submitted was to be equal to twice the number of seats available. In the case of second-level regions appointment was to be made by the *kepala daerah* of the first-level region from a similar list of nominees submitted by each second-level *kepala daerah*. It was further provided that the appointing authority in each case was only to appoint as council members persons who were considered to be in agreement with the general aims of the government, embodied in the two now generally used abbreviations, USDEK and Manipol. The word USDEK derives from the initial letters of the five concepts—the 1945 Constitution (*Undang-undang Dasar, 1945*), Indonesian socialism (*Sosialisme Indonesia*), guided democracy (*Demokrasi Terpimpin*), guided economy (*Ekomoni Terpimpin*), and Indonesian individuality or identity (*Kepribadian Indonesia*). "Manipol" refers to the Political Manifesto of the President of August 17, 1959.

In some respects this edict, and the subsequent ministerial instruction concerned with its implementation, left fairly vague the precise procedure for appointment of council members and allowed for a wide range of discretion on the part of the *kepala daerah*. One question not decided by the edict and the instruction was whether the representatives of functional groups might have party affiliations. Was it possible for parties in this way to increase their strength beyond their allotted 50 per cent? In practice different answers have already been given to this question. In East Java candidates with party affiliations were not accepted as representatives of functional groups. In Jogjakarta, by contrast, the representatives of functional groups (other than army and police) were actually chosen by the parties. A further important change introduced by the new edict was that, instead of the DPRD having its own separate chairman, the *kepala daerah* himself would perform this role. His central position in the regional government system arising from the vesting in him of executive power under Edict 6/59 was thus considerably strengthened. This was said to be in line with the "Indonesian identity."

The powers of the *kepala daerah* may be extended even further. One question not yet clarified concerns the procedural rules for the conduct of meetings. It appears to be intended that all decisions of representative assemblies must be unanimous and that, failing unanimity, unresolved questions are to be referred to the *kepala daerah* for decision. In this way the principle of consensus would actually be written into the system.

The implications of Edict 5/60 are still to be worked out in practice. It can merely be said that this latest institutional change followed naturally from those already embodied in the earlier edict and that the further limitation which it imposed on party power was a logical consequence of the measures designed to control party activity at the central level.

At this point it is possible to record only a cautious judgment on the radical change of direction which has been given to local government planning within the framework of guided democracy. The return to the principle of appointment of regional heads and the change in the character of the executive were not necessarily permanent solutions, of course. The official proclamation of Edict 6/59 naturally produced great opposition from political party spokesmen and from the party press. This was not surprising, since Law 1 was the parties' own work. Resentment was sufficiently vocal to persuade the President to announce that the measure would operate in the first instance for an experimental period of only one year. The enactment of Edict 5/60 at the end of that first year, however, showed a further tightening of central control, and it would seem unlikely that a complete return to Law 1 would be made at any foreseeable date in the near future. One idea behind the two measures—the idea of combining responsibility for representing the centre and responsibility for the execution of local tasks in the one pair of hands—was deeply rooted in the Indonesian governmental system. The advantages of a firm central control in Indonesia's present circumstances do not need to be stressed further here, though the details of any particular compromise between central needs and local autonomy may always be the subject of dispute. It may be wondered, however, whether the return to the principle of an appointed regional head also required such a drastic change in the nature of the regional executive and representative councils. Edict 6, in fact, effectively ended the implementation of Law I and constituted a very drastic blow to the whole local government system established by that law. In particular, the removal of executive responsibility to the regional legislature was clearly designed to confine regional initiative within very narrow bounds.

Unfortunately, the change did not really appear to be dictated by considerations relating to the efficiency of regional governments. The motive behind the edict and its successor would seem, rather, to have been a doctrinaire one: that they represented the application to the regional sphere of what were held to be the principles of guided democracy. Uniformity in central and local patterns might appear tidier and more conducive to the elaboration of a coherent "conception," but the regions might well feel that the contemplation of a conception was not enough. At the very least the new arrangements could become a symbol toward which local resentment might be directed in the future.

10

Local Government and Regional Feeling

IT was suggested in the opening pages of this essay that plans for the development of local government in Indonesia were intended to serve simultaneously two distinct ends, the satisfaction of regional feeling and the provision of an efficient territorial administration for a population of which a large proportion was politically unsophisticated. Thus far, in the attention given to the forms of local government as outlined in legislation and established in practice, we have taken for granted the relevance of the general decentralization plan for the first of these goals. The reasons for the central government's emphasis on the second goal have been discussed at some length, but the character of regional feeling itself still requires critical analysis. The whole assumption underlying the preparation of the local government scheme (it also underlay the federal proposals of the Dutch) is that the regional problem as such is the sort of problem which can be solved in principle by the concession of sufficiently large doses of autonomy. This assumption may at least be questioned.

Obviously the assumption is not entirely mistaken. If

the concept of regionalism denotes a common outlook and sense of identity shared by the inhabitants of a particular area and perhaps reinforced by a distinctness of customs and habits, then it is certainly an important factor in the Indonesian situation. The very motto of the Republic, "Unity in Diversity," recognizes the reality of the strength of regional awareness, and the presence of such distinct societies as those of Minangkabau or Batak, Balinese or Dyak, cannot be ignored. Differences of language alone would be sufficient to mark off one area and people from another. Local patriotism finds expression in a variety of ways ranging from a determination to preserve the elements of local culture from the leveling influence of a broader Indonesian nationalism to resentment over such apparently trivial matters as the honoring of other than local heroes in the naming of streets or public institutions. The cry of a Minangkabau girl in Djakarta when the central government resorted to military action against the "Revolutionary Government of the Republic of Indonesia" in February 1958 crystallizes the whole outlook—"They have bombed my country." The fact that these sentiments are difficult to measure does not make them less real or less important.

At least as important as the ethnic factor in explaining local patriotism is the presence of economic differences from area to area, in particular the fact that the major exporting areas of Indonesia are to be found concentrated in parts of Sumatra, Borneo, and Sulawesi. These areas, in consequence, feel that they contribute to the over-all economy of the country out of all proportion to the benefits they receive. Again, there is the type of regional feeling which arises from the uneven distribution of population throughout the islands. Since the island of Java possesses approximately 58 million of the 90-odd million people of Indonesia, it is hardly surprising that the inhabitants of the more sparsely populated areas should fear its political domination. "Javanese imperialism" is a concept often referred to in the outer islands. It is to the ethnic Javanese that hostility is particularly directed, though the Sundanese whose home is to be found in the western third of the island of Java are not always exempt. And suspicion prompted by mere numerical superiority is accentuated by the traditional association of the Javanese with government. It is commonly believed, for example, that the Javanese enjoy a privileged position in the administration services of the central government and that even outside Java they occupy important posts to the exclusion of local men. It is not always possible to test such beliefs, but investigation in several areas suggested that popular beliefs as to the dominance of Javanese personnel in local branches of central government departments were often not well founded.

It would seem obvious that where regional feeling is based either on ethnic or cultural groupings or on fears of Javanese predominance the idea of receiving substantial powers of self-government might reasonably be expected to go a long way toward softening a local sense of grievance. Autonomy (whether under a federal or a unitary system) should provide an adequate field for the exercise of initiative and a means of balancing the position of Java. But other factors are present which are rather different in character. It may be argued that a good deal of what is called regional feeling is more exactly sectional feeling (sometimes party feeling) which happens to coincide with broad geographical divisions, but which is directed against the policies pursued by the central government rather than against the existing distribution of functions between centre and regions.

The variation from place to place in the strength of national political parties does represent a complicating feature of the situation. All of the four major political parties—PNI, Masjumi, NU, and PKI—have been significantly represented in the island of Java, but two of these, PNI and PKI, are primarily Java-based parties, whereas Masjumi's strength has been much more widely spread. Some of its main centres (in terms of relative not absolute strength) have been found outside Java, particularly in West Sumatra and South Sulawesi.[1]

For this reason ordinary party rivalry at the national level has tended to acquire a regional flavor. Or perhaps it would be more precise to say that the party alignments were in fact symptomatic of the regional differences. Whichever way it is stated and whatever the social pattern underlying the distribution of political strength, the regional separatism which has been brought into the open since 1956 has been roughly associated with party oppositions. Against the background of mounting opposition to the second Ali Sastroamidjojo government, the military coup in Central Sumatra in December 1956 might be interpreted not simply as a reflection of the peculiar disabilities of the province, but partly as a tactical move

[1] In the general elections of 1955 Masjumi secured 50 per cent of the total votes in Central Sumatra, 40 per cent of the total in South and Southeast Sulawesi. These percentages were significantly higher than those obtained by any other single party in any other single region, except for NU in South Kalimantan (48.6 per cent). See Feith, *The Indonesian Elections of 1955*, p. 78.

designed to bring about the fall of the government, even though that government was based, at the time, on a PNI-Masjumi-NU coalition. The coup was quickly followed by the withdrawal of Masjumi's five Ministers from the Cabinet, and the party remained in opposition both to the government and to its successor, the Djuanda government, formed in the following April. Similarly, the formation of a military government in Sulawesi in February 1957 sprang immediately from Soekarno's proposed inclusion of the PKI within a "four-legged" government. The Sumatran situation deteriorated further during the remainder of the year, and the leading figures in the formation, in Padang, of the Revolutionary Government of Indonesia in February 1958 were again leading Masjumi members of the Natsir wing of the party. On all these occasions the separatism of West Sumatra and North Sulawesi did not necessarily point to a desire for greater independence from the centre. That element was present. But more important was dissatisfaction with the government as a government.

Also worth noting is the presence of an ethnic element in this division along party lines. The PNI has tended to attract civil servant support, especially from the ranks of the *pamong pradja,* and reflects, perhaps, the traditional interest of the Javanese in government rather than in other spheres of national life. Masjumi's main ties were not with the bureaucracy, but with commercial circles of towns and villages.[2] In Java, its major strength lay in West Java, i.e., within the area of the Sundanese, not the Javanese, ethnic group; it was inevitable that the develop-

[2] See Feith, *The Wilopo Cabinet, 1952–1953,* pp. 39 ff., for an analysis of the social bases of support for the two parties.

ment of Masjumi's political opposition to the central government should contain an admixture of anti-Javanese feeling.

But it would be a gross oversimplification to place too much emphasis on the party overtones to the regional problem. A more significant ingredient in the development of regional hostility to Djakarta is to be found in the presence of economic grievances. Broadly, the obvious difference between the export-producing outer islands, principally Sumatra, on the one hand and Java, a net importer, on the other has provided the ground for the general complaint that the former areas—the earners of Indonesia's foreign exchange and the source of her prosperity—do not receive attention from the central government in proportion to their economic importance and that, on the contrary, they are battened on by Java. Although this grievance has loomed large in the great debate between centre and regions, it has rarely been stated with precision, and it will be found that it contains elements of myth as well as of fact. It is important, of course, that the grievances should be felt to exist whether or not they are genuine. But an attempt must be made to discover precisely what it is that is being said when the complaints are made.

The argument has tended to take two main forms.

(1) It has been said that government spending is not fairly divided between Java and the rest of Indonesia—that the outer islands, which as exporters make a substantial contribution to revenue through customs duties, are entitled to a greater share of expenditure on public works than would be justified on a population basis. In particular, as an especially sore point, Java's network of

roads and railways is contrasted with the scanty communications of the other islands.

(2) It is said that foreign exchange, earned primarily by Sumatra, is not fairly distributed—that, in its import control policy and its distribution of import licenses, the central government discriminates unfairly against the outer islands. Because of the record of discrimination it is argued that the regions should be entitled to control a proportion of the foreign currency that they earn.

The two points are closely connected, of course. The desired expansion of government spending embraces also the demand for imported capital goods for public works, and for that foreign currency is required. When the Djuanda government came into power in April 1957, it was faced with regional demands for actual control of 70 per cent of the foreign exchange which they earned. The government countered this demand with a promise to introduce an intensified public works program outside Java. However, having distinguished the two types of complaint, it will be convenient to deal with them separately as far as is possible.

(1) It is very difficult to determine in principle how a proper balance should be struck in the matter of government spending between areas and people—in the Indonesian case, between the needs of the most populous island and those of the more sparsely populated but economically important islands. And, indeed, regional complaints have not usually been based on any careful analyses of figures of distribution of government spending. Although it is clear that Java could not survive without the rest of Indonesia, at least without a drastic tightening of

the belt, could the rest of Indonesia survive effectively as a political unit, or a series of units, without Java? If it is held that there are mutual political advantages in unity, there may still be wide differences as to the basis on which essential public works and public services should be provided.

It is an odd feature of the situation which has faced the central government since 1956 that the very regions which were loudest in their complaints of neglect and which showed most disaffection—West Sumatra and North Sulawesi—were not the major contributors either to government revenue (through company tax and customs duties) or to the country's reservoir of foreign currency. For example, in 1956 Padang, the main port of West Sumatra, exported to the value of Rp.187,300,000. This was a small proportion of the country's total export figure of Rp.10,208,900,000.[3] The figure may be compared with the exports of the really important areas—North and South Sumatra—which between them accounted for over half the country's total exports.[4] During 1957, in spite of the fact that West Sumatra was technically cut off from central control, it continued to receive from the centre its grant-in-aid of the provincial government, together with funds for the maintenance of central government services

[3] The figure for Sulawesi in the same year was approximately Rp.240,000,000. This did not include copra exported illegally. Even if the widest allowance is made for smuggling, the total would still be small compared with the figures for North and South Sumatra.

[4] North Sumatra's exports in 1956 reached Rp.2,090,000,000, and South Sumatra's exports were Rp.3,324,000,000. Two ports, Belawan (the port of Medan) and Palembang, accounted for Rp.1,827,800,000 and Rp.2,243,900,000 respectively.

in the area. The amount involved was approximately Rp.400,000,000. It is most unlikely that West Sumatra could have raised an equivalent revenue from its own sources.

It does not follow from this that government expenditure for developmental purposes is already distributed on a fair basis. In the West Sumatra case it would merely appear that the argument that the area did not receive central assistance in proportion to its value is in itself insufficient to explain the defection of the province. Judgments about what are the reasonable needs of an area are, in any case, bound to contain a strong subjective element, but it is obvious that regions which are as yet economically underdeveloped cannot immediately expect to be provided with governmental services or communications on a scale equivalent to that of the main centres of population or production. At the same time, the mere fact that the disability is felt is the politically important fact—hence the decision of the Djuanda government to move as rapidly as possible in the direction of implementing the Nasroen recommendations. The Financial Equilibrium Act, as already noted, was intended to remove this particular source of discontent by providing a clear minimum of financial assistance for the poorer regions and by transferring central taxes to the regions themselves. An important feature of the change was the intention of making the regions responsible for the collection of at least a part of their own revenue so that, if they were to benefit from increased resources, they would also have to accept the less popular aspect too.

(2) The question of local revenue for the poorer areas was important, but the complaints arising from the centre's

control of foreign exchange were just as frequent in the chorus of regional complaints and were possibly a more important issue. Until June 1957 the government, as part of its general financial policy, had maintained a system of import licensing linked with the existence of an official exchange rate pegged at a highly artificial level. (Except for a period following the official introduction of what was practically a floating rate in 1957, the unofficial value of the rupiah in terms of other currencies has been approximately one-third of its official value.) These controls, it was held, operated unfairly against the outer islands, which lacked access to foreign exchange holdings. It was not always made clear exactly where the unfairness lay. Was it a demand for more foreign currency to be available for private importers, or for more foreign currency to be available for regional governments, or for the allocation of imported capital goods to the task of regional development whether carried out by central or regional governments? All three demands were probably present, but the most usual form was the second, the complaint that regional governments lacked the exchange to enable them to initiate adequate public works programs. Closely connected with this sense of injustice, however, was a more individual grievance—that of the actual producer of export crops, who was paid in rupiahs calculated at the official rate of exchange and who naturally felt that he was robbed of two-thirds of his earnings. The wide gap between the two rates of exchange constituted for the producer and for the exporter a constant temptation to bypass the centre altogether, a temptation shared by regional governments which looked to direct trade with the outside world to supply their needs. In fact, barter trade was carried on with the more or less open approval, and sometimes direct participation, of local civil and military authorities. In certain areas, notably Sumatra and Sulawesi, such trade was actually carried on under direct army control on the grounds that this was the only way to secure equipment for both military and civil needs. The trade was not haphazard: a variety of regulations, differing slightly from area to area,[5] was issued under the authority of local military commanders and provided for the supervision of trade virtually on an official basis, and the inability of either the central government or its high command to prevent the practice led almost to the tacit acceptance of this semiofficial smuggling, at least until January 1958 when all trade regulations of local military commanders were declared illegal.

Although compelled, up to a point, to accept what it could not prevent, the central government reacted in a variety of ways in its attempt to prevent the growth of what amounted to the establishment of separate currency areas. In the case of copra exports, an attempt was made to improve existing marketing arrangements. The marketing of copra in Sulawesi and Maluku—the main copra areas—had been conducted through an official agency, the

[5] Note, for example, the difference between Atjeh, where exports took place on the basis of counterimports up to 70 per cent of the value of exports; Riau, where the central government itself by government regulation permitted foreign currency to pass; and Padang, after the coup of December 1956, where 20 per cent of the gross revenue from foreign trade was to be paid in free-rate rupiahs to a development fund for local purposes and 80 per cent of the remainder was to go to counterimports under conditions: 25 per cent for prescribed essentials and 75 per cent available for free import.

Copra Foundation (*Jajasan Kopra*), established during the existence of the State of East Indonesia. The Foundation bought copra from the producer at a fixed price and disposed of it either within Indonesia or on the external market. The operation of this agency evoked serious complaints on a number of grounds: that profits were not devoted to developmental works within the areas concerned, but were invested elsewhere (e.g., in housing projects in Kebajoran, Djakarta); that the price paid to the producer, though it bore a reasonable relation to the world market price if converted at the official rate, was too low in view of the much higher illegal rate of exchange; and that the Foundation was corrupt, entering in its books only a proportion of the copra that it received and disposing illegally of the remainder. In view of these complaints, it was hardly surprising that a flourishing barter trade should have developed in the area. In 1956 the central government was compelled to intervene. It liquidated the Foundation and announced its intention to replace it by a co-operative marketing agency (*Induk Koperasi Kopra Indonesia*—IKKI) to conduct its operations under a more direct supervision by the Ministry for Economic Affairs. The situation was altered, of course, by the events of 1957 which removed North Sulawesi from central government control. Before this happened, an alternative marketing arrangement had been developed in one part of the area, namely, Minahasa. A local agency was established there —the *Jajasan Kelapa Minahasa* (JKM)—which was eventually given official permission to operate. The JKM, like the Copra Foundation, bought compulsorily from the grower at a fixed price. Its rupiah profits, however, were retained for local government and other purposes within the regions.[6]

This type of arrangement could go some distance toward meeting the complaint that the profits of government trading agencies were not spent in the regions where they were made, but it did not affect the more important regional complaint concerning access to foreign exchange. One attempt to meet this complaint was the establishment in certain areas (e.g., in Tapanuli in 1957) of local foreign exchange bureaus (BDP—*Biro Devisen Perdagangan*). This enabled regions to acquire import licenses without going through Djakarta. However, the centre still controlled the over-all allocation, and such a method could not serve as a general solution unless there could be evolved an agreed formula about how foreign exchange receipts should be divided between centre and regions. The surrender of control over exchange could, in effect, amount to a division of the country into a series of distinct currency areas.

A more drastic reaction, though only of temporary effect, was the virtual devaluation of the rupiah which took place in 1957. In June 1957 new regulations provided that exporters would receive an export certificate (*bukti ekspor*—BE) which represented a claim to the foreign currency earned by the export. (A tax of 20 per cent was levied on the BE, but this was taken in rupiahs.) The claim was

[6] The JKM paid the government of Daerah Minahasa a subvention of Rp.60 per ton of copra handled by it, and this went into the general revenue of the region, being, in fact, the largest single item in the budget. Over and above this contribution the government of the *daerah* might request special assistance (*bantuan*) for particular projects, e.g., reafforestation. And the JKM itself could give direct aid to worthy causes within the region.

salable on the open market, and importers had to present the certificate in order to obtain foreign exchange. In effect, the BE amounted to a departure from the fixed rate of exchange and the adoption of a floating rate subject to ordinary market fluctuations. The exporter, in consequence, could convert his foreign currency into rupiahs at a market rate. The broad result of the move was thus of advantage to exporters and to producers of export produce at the expense of consumers—in other words, of advantage to particular interest groups wherever they might be rather than to particular regions as such. Producers had had a genuine ground for discontent in the past, and it happened that their voice was particularly strong in the outer islands.

The fact that this was so is important for an understanding of a large part of the regional problem. Although the demand of regional governments for a greater share of imported goods was a serious demand, it was the grievance of the individual producer of export produce which gave the real edge to the more general sense of regional injustice. The fact that he could get approximately three times as much for his produce by direct trade made him unable to resist the feeling that he was actually being robbed of the difference by the central government. This was a misleading picture. The artificially fixed official rate had been merely a part of a general control policy. But it was inevitable that the disparity between the legal and the black-market rates should add a personal grievance to the complaints about bad roads and bridges. Unfortunately, the adoption of a floating rate was not a long-term remedy. It was inflationary in tendency, and the succeeding months saw a rise in the price of basic foodstuffs. And though the floating rate should have reduced the temptation to engage in smuggling, in fact barter trade continued, since the outer islands preferred, possibly for political reasons, to retain their degree of *de facto* independence from the centre in the field of foreign trade. During early 1958 the value of the rupiah continued to fall, and the government eventually decided to peg it once more in April of that year. With this decision the currency situation in effect was returned to the position which had obtained before the BE was introduced, though at a new level. Once again the gap between the official exchange rate and the free market rate, never entirely removed even under the BE system, began to widen. The BE system was abolished finally in August 1959.

Thus, while the exchange policy of the central government had imposed disabilities upon the producer, it was not easy to find a remedy. Currency control was a central feature of general economic policy. So was the accompanying policy of import restrictions. Together they were a response to the economic situation in which the country found itself. The falling value of the rupiah was, after all, a reflection of a general economic situation, and many of the disabilities of which the regions complained arose from that situation. There is no way of redressing these grievances without a fundamental improvement in the country's total financial position.

For this sort of problem the development of a system of local autonomy does not provide an answer. The field of fiscal and commercial policy is a matter of central control whatever the form of the state and whatever the degree of decentralization within it. Even a federal Indonesia would need to make this field one of federal rather than of state concern, unless it was prepared to see the virtual growth of separate currency areas within the state, in which case the federal tie would be a very loose one indeed. As it is, the regions may have objected to many aspects of central economic policy, but so far they have not demanded so radical a solution as that. In this setting autonomy might certainly have ameliorated many important aspects of what is called regionalism; but the satisfaction of local desire for the exercise of a greater degree of initiative in the handling of local matters was still likely to leave unresolved difficulties which would continue to express themselves in local resistance to the policies of Djakarta.

APPENDIX A

Seats Held by the Four Main Parties in the "Transitional" Councils (1956) and the Elected Councils (1957) of Second-Level Regions in Java

THE 1956 transitional councils were formed by the allocation of council seats to parties in proportion to the votes cast for those parties in each region in the 1955 general election. The 1957 councils were directly elected in the regional elections of that year. The figures for the two sets of councils are not strictly comparable because of an increase in the size of councils under Law 1 of 1957, but they give an indication, nonetheless, of changes in the order of party strengths. The regions are *kabupatens* except where stated otherwise.

		PNI	Masjumi	NU	PKI	Size of council
			West Java			
Bandung (*kota*)	1956	6	4	2	6	25
	1957	7	5	2	11	35
Bogor (*kota*)	1956	3	4	3	1	15
	1957	3	4	2	2	15

		PNI	Masjumi	NU	PKI	Size of council
West Java (cont.)						
Sukabumi (*kota*)	1956	3	3	1	1	10
	1957	4	4	1	3	15
Tjirebon (*kota*)	1956	3	2	2	4	15
	1957	3	2	2	5	15
Bandung	1956	6	8	2	5	30
	1957	6	9	2	8	35
Bekasi	1956	8	8	5	—	30
	1957	3	8	3	4	35
Bogor	1956	5	12	3	2	30
	1957	5	13	3	4	35
Garut	1956	4	11	2	3	30
	1957	6	12	2	6	35
Indramaju	1956	5	8	4	4	30
	1957	5	10	4	8	35
Krawang	1956	6	3	3	2	20
	1957	10	4	3	5	35
Kuningan	1956	9	6	1	2	24
	1957	9	8	1	6	35
Lebak	1956	5	7	2	—	20
	1957	9	9	2	3	35
Madjalengka	1956	12	9	—	3	25
	1957	10	11	1	8	35
Pandegolang	1956	5	8	3	1	20
	1957	9	13	5	1	35

		PNI	Masjumi	NU	PKI	Size of council
West Java (cont.)						
Serang	1956	3	11	5	1	30
	1957	4	13	6	1	35
Subang-Purwakarta	1956	6	4	1	3	20
	1957	8	7	3	9	35
Sukabumi	1956	8	8	2	2	25
	1957	10	11	2	6	35
Sumedang	1956	4	3	1	2	21
	1957	7	4	2	7	35
Tanggerang	1956	5	11	1	2	28
	1957	6	12	1	3	35
Tasikmalaja	1956	6	10	6	3	30
	1957	6	11	7	6	35
Tjiamis	1956	10	7	2	7	30
	1957	10	9	2	11	35
Tjiandjur	1956	9	9	3	2	30
	1957	12	10	3	4	35
Tjirebon	1956	5	4	8	5	30
	1957	4	4	9	10	35
Central Java						
Magelang (*kota*)	1956	2	1	1	6	13
	1957	3	1	1	7	15
Pekalongan (*kota*)	1956	7	2	4	1	15
	1957	5	2	5	2	15

		PNI	Masjumi	NU	PKI	Size of council
Central Java (cont.)						
Salatiga (*kota*)	1956	1	—	1	6	10
	1957	2	—	—	9	15
Semarang (*kota*)	1956	3	1	3	14	25
	1957	5	2	4	20	35
Surakarta (*kota*)	1956	5	2	—	11	21
	1957	6	3	—	17	30
Tegal (*kota*)	1956	5	3	2	3	15
	1957	4	3	2	5	15
Bandjarnegara	1956	11	4	2	1	22
	1957	15	6	4	4	35
Banjumas	1956	16	4	6	3	30
	1957	15	4	7	7	35
Blora	1956	10	2	4	10	28
	1957	10	2	6	16	35
Bojolali	1956	4	4	3	12	23
	1957	5	5	4	20	35
Brebes	1956	12	4	7	4	30
	1957	12	4	8	8	35
Demak	1956	5	1	13	5	24
	1957	6	1	20	8	35
Djepara	1956	5	1	12	2	21
	1957	7	2	19	6	35
Grobogan	1956	7	2	7	13	30
	1957	6	2	7	18	35

		PNI	Masjumi	NU	PKI	Size of council
Central Java (cont.)						
Karanganjar	1956	9	2	—	6	20
	1957	11	2	—	16	35
Kebumen	1956	10	4	8	6	30
	1957	10	5	10	9	35
Kendal	1956	8	4	8	7	27
	1957	9	4	11	10	35
Klaten	1956	8	5	—	16	30
	1957	8	5	1	19	35
Kudus	1956	6	1	8	4	20
	1957	7	2	12	9	32
Magelang	1956	6	4	12	6	30
	1957	7	4	14	8	35
Pati	1956	11	2	6	9	30
	1957	9	2	7	14	35
Pekalongan	1956	16	2	10	2	30
	1957	16	2	13	4	35
Pemalang	1956	15	—	7	8	30
	1957	13	1	10	9	35
Purbolinggo	1956	13	6	6	1	26
	1957	15	7	8	4	35
Purworedjo	1956	19	1	6	3	29
	1957	19	1	8	5	35
Rembang	1956	8	2	6	4	20
	1957	8	2	8	7	26

		PNI	Masjumi	NU	PKI	Size of council
Central Java (cont.)						
Semarang	1956	3	1	9	16	30
	1957	3	1	12	18	35
Sragen	1956	12	4	—	3	20
	1957	16	7	—	10	35
Sukohardjo	1956	6	2	—	11	20
	1957	9	3	—	21	35
Tegal	1956	13	5	8	3	30
	1957	13	6	9	6	35
Temanggung	1956	4	3	5	8	20
	1957	5	4	9	15	33
Tjilatjap	1956	8	3	4	13	30
	1957	7	3	5	18	35
Wonogiri	1956	14	2	1	12	30
	1957	14	3	—	16	35
Wonosobo	1956	10	1	8	2	21
	1957	16	—	13	5	35
East Java						
Blitar (*kota*)	1956	2	—	2	6	10
	1957	2	—	2	10	15
Kediri (*kota*)	1956	4	1	3	6	15
	1957	3	1	3	6	15
Madiun (*kota*)	1956	4	1	1	8	15
	1957	4	1	1	8	15

		PNI	Masjumi	NU	PKI	Size of council
East Java (cont.)						
Malang (*kota*)	1956	4	1	5	7	20
	1957	4	2	7	12	27
Modjokerto (*kota*)	1956	2	1	3	3	10
	1957	2	1	4	6	15
Pasuruan (*kota*)	1956	2	1	6	1	10
	1957	3	1	8	3	15
Probolinggo (*kota*)	1956	1	1	4	3	10
	1957	2	1	5	5	15
Surabaja (*kota*)	1956	4	1	5	11	25
	1957	4	2	8	17	35
Bangkalan	1956	5	4	20	1	30
	1957	6	4	21	1	35
Banjuwangi	1956	6	2	11	9	30
	1957	6	2	11	13	35
Blitar	1956	5	1	8	14	30
	1957	5	1	9	19	35
Bodjonegoro	1956	5	8	5	11	30
	1957	5	9	6	15	35
Bondowoso	1956	7	3	11	1	23
	1957	10	5	17	2	35
Djember	1956	7	3	14	4	30
	1957	8	4	14	6	35
Djombang	1956	9	3	12	5	30
	1957	9	3	14	8	35

		PNI	Masjumi	NU	PKI	Size of council
East Java (cont.)						
Kediri	1956	7	4	7	10	30
	1957	7	4	8	14	35
Lamongan	1956	4	13	6	7	30
	1957	5	14	7	9	35
Lumadjang	1956	11	2	8	4	25
	1957	14	3	10	7	35
Madiun	1956	6	2	5	10	25
	1957	7	3	5	18	35
Magetan	1956	6	2	3	10	22
	1957	9	3	4	18	35
Malang	1956	9	1	10	7	30
	1957	9	1	11	10	35
Modjokerto	1956	8	3	8	4	25
	1957	10	3	11	8	35
Ngandjuk	1956	14	2	6	7	30
	1957	13	2	7	11	35
Ngawi	1956	6	3	2	11	24
	1957	8	4	3	19	35
Pamekasan	1956	2	2	11	—	20
	1957	3	4	17	—	34
Panarukan	1956	6	2	11	1	20
	1957	9	3	19	3	35
Pasuruan	1956	7	2	18	3	30
	1957	8	2	21	4	35

		PNI	Masjumi	NU	PKI	Size of council
East Java (cont.)						
Patjitan	1956	6	6	—	8	20
	1957	9	9	1	16	35
Ponorogo	1956	7	3	4	13	30
	1957	7	3	5	18	35
Probolinggo	1956	7	2	16	2	30
	1957	8	1	19	3	35
Sampang	1956	1	2	16	—	20
	1957	2	3	26	—	35
Sidoardjo	1956	5	3	12	6	27
	1957	5	4	15	11	35
Sumenep	1956	3	7	19	—	30
	1957	4	7	18	1	35
Surabaja	1956	3	5	12	9	30
	1957	3	5	15	11	35
Trenggalek	1956	8	4	4	3	20
	1957	10	6	6	11	35
Tuban	1956	7	4	8	9	30
	1957	7	5	8	13	35
Tulungagung	1956	9	2	9	7	29
	1957	7	3	10	12	35

APPENDIX B

Extracts from Law 22 of 1948 Relating to the Position of Kepala Daerah

Article 18

(1) The Regional Head of a province is appointed by the President from at least two, and at the most four, candidates nominated by the provincial Representative Council.

(2) The Regional Head of a *kabupaten* (or large municipality) is appointed by the Minister of Home Affairs from at least two, and at the most four, candidates nominated by the Representative Council of the *kabupaten* (or large municipality).

(3) The Regional Head of a *desa* (or small municipality) is appointed by the Regional Head of the province from at least two, and at the most four, candidates nominated by the Representative Council of the *desa* (or small municipality).

(4) The Regional Head may be dismissed by the proper authority at the request of the Regional Representative Council concerned.

(5) The Regional Head of a Special Region is appointed by the President from the descendants of the family which exercised power in the region in the period before the Republic of Indonesia and which still rules the region, having regard to the conditions of ability,

honesty, and loyalty and remembering the customary procedures of the region.

(6) For a Special Region a Deputy Regional Head may be appointed by the President, having regard to the conditions set out in par. (5). The Deputy Head of a Special Region is a member of the Regional Executive Council.

Article 28

(6) Regional regulations are considered operative after being signed by the Regional Head and proclaimed according to a method determined by the Regional Representative Council.

Article 36

(1) The Regional Head supervises the work of the Regional Representative Council and the Regional Executive Council and has the right to delay the operation of decisions of the Regional Representative Council and the Regional Executive Council when, in his opinion, such decisions conflict with the general interest or with laws or Government Regulations or regulations of higher regional governments, when these decisions are taken by a Regional Representative Council below the province.

(2) The delay referred to in par. (1) must be reported within seven days to the Regional Representative Council or Regional Executive Council in question and also to the President in the case of provinces and to the next highest Regional Executive Council in the case of other regions.

(3) If, within three months, the President or the Regional Executive Council referred to in par. (2) has made no decision, the postponed decision comes into effect immediately.

Extracts from Law 1 of 1957

CHAPTER II: THE DIVISION OF INDONESIA INTO SELF-GOVERNING REGIONS

Article 2

(1) The area comprising the Republic of Indonesia is divided into large and small regions which possess the right of managing their own "household affairs" and which are arranged at the most in three levels, in descending order as follows:
 (a) First-level regions, including Djakarta Raya;
 (b) Second-level regions, including municipalities; and
 (c) Third-level regions.

(2) Principalities, according to their importance and level of social development at the present time, may be established as Special Regions, Level I, II, or III, or as ordinary self-governing regions, Level I, II, or III, with the right of managing their own household affairs.

CHAPTER III: THE FORMATION AND ORGANIZATION OF REGIONAL GOVERNMENTS

Section 1—General

Article 5

The regional government is composed of the Regional Representative Council and the Regional Executive Council.

Article 6

(1) The Regional Head, by virtue of his office, is Chair-

man and a member of the Regional Executive Council (DPD).

(2) The Chairman and Vice-Chairman of the Regional Representative Council (DPRD) are chosen by and from the members of the Regional Representative Council.

Section 2—The Regional Representative Council (DPRD)

Article 7

(1) For each region the number of DPRD members is to be determined by the establishing law, on the basis of the number of inhabitants who should have one representative in the Council and with regard to the minimum and maximum numbers of members for each region, as follows:

  (a) For first-level regions there should be one representative for every 200,000 inhabitants, with a minimum of 30 representatives and a maximum of 75.

  (b) For second-level regions there should be one representative for every 10,000 inhabitants, with a minimum of 15 and a maximum of 35.

  (c) For each third-level region there should be one representative for every 2,000 inhabitants, with a minimum of 10 and a maximum of 20.

(2) Alterations in DPRD membership total as laid down in (1a), (b), and (c) are determined by the Minister of Home Affairs.

(3) Membership of the DPRD is for a four-year term.

(4) Members of the DPRD who are appointed to fill a vacancy hold their seats only for the remainder of that four-year term.

(5) As an exception to the provision of par. (3) above, the first members of a DPRD will lay down their member-

ship together at a time determined in the establishing law.

(6) The election and replacement of members of the DPRD will be arranged by law.

Article 8

The membership of Regional Representative Councils is open to Indonesian citizens who

(a) have reached the age of 21 years;

(b) have been domiciled in the area concerned for at least six months;

(c) can read and write the Indonesian language in Latin characters;

(d) have not lost control of their property as a result of a judicial decision which is still current;

(e) have not been deprived of their right to vote or their right to be elected by a judicial decision which is still current;

(f) are not of unsound mind.

[There follow clauses concerning the other qualifications of members—remuneration, the oath, and so on—and, in Section 3, concerning the mode of calling meetings and the rules of meetings.]

Section 4—The Regional Executive Council

Article 19

(1) The members of the Regional Executive Council are chosen by and from the members of the Regional Representative Council, according to the method of proportional representation.

(2) The Chairman and Vice-Chairman of the Regional Representative Council cannot become members of the Regional Executive Council.

Section 5—The Regional Head

Article 23

(1) The Regional Head is chosen according to arrangements to be determined by law.

(2) The method of appointment and dismissal of the Regional Head is to be fixed by law.

Article 24

(1) Until the legislation referred to in 23 (1) is passed, the Regional Head for the time being is to be chosen by the Regional Representative Council, having regard to the qualities of knowledge and ability necessary for the office and in accordance with the conditions set out in pars. (2) to (7).

(2) The result of the election of Regional Head as referred to in par. (1) must be approved by (a) the President in the case of first-level Regional Heads and (b) the Minister of Home Affairs or an authority designated by him for second- and third-level Regional Heads.

(3) The Regional Head is chosen for one electoral term of the Regional Representative Council or, if he is elected during a term to fill a vacancy in the office, for the remainder of that term.

(4) The qualifications of ability and knowledge referred to in par. (1) and the method of election and confirmation will be defined in a Government Regulation.

(5) The office of Regional Head shall become vacant because of (a) death, (b) the completion of an electoral term as indicated in (3), (c) resignation, (d) a decision of the Regional Representative Council removing him from membership of that Council.

(6) Without lessening the effect of par. (5) above, the Regional Head shall cease to hold office as a result of a decision of the Regional Representative Council (a)

removing him from his position as Regional Head, (b) removing from office the Executive Council.

(7) The resignation or dismissal of Regional Head under par. (5c) or (d) and par. (6) requires the approval of the appropriate authority, as indicated in par. (2) above.

Article 25

(1) The Head of a Special Region is appointed from candidates nominated by the Regional Representative Council from the descendants of the family which exercised power in the region before the establishment of the Republic of Indonesia and which still rules the region, having regard to the qualifications of ability, uprightness, and loyalty and to the customs of the region, and his appointment or dismissal is made by (a) the President for Special Regions of the first level, (b) the Minister of Home Affairs or an authority designated by him for Special Regions of the second and third levels.

(2) For a Special Region there may be appointed from candidates nominated by the Regional Representative Council a Deputy Regional Head, and his appointment or dismissal is made by the authority who appoints/dismisses the Regional Head, having regard to the conditions set out in par. (1).

(3) The Head and Deputy Head of a Special Region are, by virtue of their positions, Chairman and Vice-Chairman respectively, as well as members of the Regional Executive Council.

CHAPTER IV: REGIONAL POWERS AND OBLIGATIONS

Section 1—Regional Representative Council

Article 31

(1) The Regional Representative Council regulates and controls the household affairs of the region except for those matters which, by this law, are assigned to another authority.

(2) Without lessening the effect of (1), the establishing regulation may define matters which fall within the competence of the Regional Representative Council from the time of its establishment.

(3) Powers referred to in par. (2) may, from time to time, be extended by Government Regulation, having regard to the resources and the ability of each region, and at the request of the Representative Council concerned, and, in the case of second- and third-level regions, after obtaining the opinion of the next highest Executive Council.

(4) Provided it does not contradict the decisions of this law, the Regional Representative Council, by Regional Regulation, may surrender to the region below it power to deal with matters within its own competence; before coming into effect such a regulation must be approved first by the Minister of Home Affairs for first-level regions and by the next highest Regional Executive Council for other regions.

Article 36

(1) The Regional Representative Council may, in the interests of the region or in the interests of the matters referred to in Chapter IV, Article 31, make regulations termed "Regional Regulation" with the name of the region added. Regional Regulations must be signed by

the Chairman of the Regional Representative Council.

(2) A Government Regulation may determine the form of Regional Regulations.

Article 38

(1) Regional Regulations may not conflict with higher legislation or with the general interest. . . .

Article 42

(1) The governments of several regions may co-operate in dealing with matters of common interest.

(2) Joint decisions concerning matters referred to in par. (1), together with amendments or repeals, must be approved first by the Minister of Home Affairs in the case of first-level regions and by the next highest Executive Council in the case of other regions.

Section 2—Regional Executive Council

Article 44

(1) The Regional Executive Council executes decisions of the Regional Representative Council.

(2) The Regional Executive Council is responsible for the day-to-day running of the regional government.

Article 45

By Regional Regulation the Regional Executive Council may be given the task of issuing implementing regulations under that Regional Regulation.

Article 46

Decisions of the Regional Executive Council are signed by the Chairman of the Council.

Article 47

The Regional Executive Council prepares as thoroughly as possible all matters which must be considered by the Regional Representative Council and which are subject to decision by it, unless the Regional Representative Council delegates such preparatory work to another body.

Article 48

In executing their tasks as set out in Articles 44 and 45 the members of the Regional Executive Council are collectively responsible to the Regional Representative Council and must give an account of their work when asked to do so by the Regional Representative Council. [The clarificatory appendix to the law remarks, concerning Article 48: "This Article determines the responsibility of the Regional Executive Council toward the Regional Representative Council in the execution of its tasks. Following from Law 22 of 1948 it is here decided that the Executive Council shall be collectively responsible to the Regional Representative Council.

"The Regional Executive Council may divide its work among its members, and with regard to this work each member is responsible to the Regional Executive Council itself (as a college). Members of the Regional Executive Council certainly have an individual responsibility, i.e., to the Regional Executive Council concerning the tasks allotted to each, but with regard to the Regional Representative Council the whole Regional Executive Council is together collectively responsible."]

Article 50

(1) If the Regional Representative Council is clearly negligent in its management of regional matters so as to cause harm to the region or to the State, the Government, by Government Regulation, may determine the manner in which the region must be managed and prescribe changes from the arrangements set out in Article 31.

. . . . .

(4) If the situation referred to in (1) occurs, the Regional Head, pending the issue of a Government Regulation as laid down in par. (1), will, for the time being, take over the rights, duties, and obligations of the regional government.

CHAPTER V: THE REGIONAL SECRETARY AND REGIONAL OFFICIALS

Article 51

All regional civil servants, together with national civil servants and servants of other regions seconded to the region, are under the control of the Regional Executive Council.

Article 52

(1) The Secretary of the region is a regional civil servant who is appointed and dismissed by the Regional Representative Council on the request of the Regional Executive Council, having regard to the conditions set out in Article 53, par. (1).

(2) The Secretary of the region is the Secretary of the Regional Representative Council and the Regional Executive Council.

(3) If the Secretary of the region is unable to perform his duties, or if his office falls vacant, the Regional Executive Council may appoint another regional official to act for him.

Article 53

(1) Conditions governing the appointment, dismissal, suspension, salary, pension, deferred pay, and other matters concerning the legal position of regional civil servants are laid down in a Regional Regulation which, as far as possible, must be in accordance with the regulations made by the government for national civil servants.

(2) The Regional Regulation referred to in par. (1) must be approved by the Minister of Home Affairs for first-level regions and by the next highest Regional Executive Council in the case of other regions before it comes into effect.

Article 54

(1) The conditions governing the work of a national official who is seconded to a region are determined by Government Regulation or, for regional servants seconded from another region, by a Regional Regulation of the region which seconds the official.

(2) National officials, or regional officials seconded to a region, are paid from the finances of the region to which they are seconded unless the Government Regulation referred to in par. (1) determines otherwise.

CHAPTER VI: FINANCE

Article 56

(1) The Regional Representative Council has the right to levy regional taxes and charges.

(2) A general regulation concerning regional taxes and charges is to be determined by law.

(3) Regional regulations which establish, alter, or abolish regional taxes and charges require the prior approval of an authority determined in the law referred to in par. (2) and according to a method laid down in that law, before they can come into effect.

Article 57

National taxes may be surrendered to regions by means of a law.

Article 58

(1) To the regions may be given (a) the receipts of national taxes in part or in whole and (b) payments, subsidies, and grants-in-aid.

(2) The giving of these funds shall be ordered by law.

Article 61

(1) On the first occasion regional budgets shall be determined by law for first- and second-level regions and by Government Regulation for third-level regions.

(2) After that, regional budgets shall be determined by the Regional Representative Councils.

(3) Regional budgets as referred to in par. (2) shall not come into effect until first approved by the Minister in the case of first-level regions and by the next highest Regional Executive Council in the case of other regions.

CHAPTER VII: SUPERVISION

Article 62

By law or Government Regulation it may be determined that regional decisions concerning certain subjects will not come into effect unless first approved by (a) the Minister of Home Affairs for decisions of first-level regions, (b) the first-level Regional Executive Council for decisions of second-level regions, (c) the second-level Regional Executive Council for descisions of third-level regions.

Article 63

(1) When a Regional Representative Council decision is required by this law to await the prior approval of the Minister of Home Affairs in the case of first-level regions and of the next highest Regional Executive Council for other levels, the decision may be executed if, after three months from the date on which it was forwarded for approval, the Minister or the appropriate Regional Executive Council has not made a determination.

(2) The three-month period may be extended for, at the most, a further three months by the Minister or the appropriate Regional Executive Council, and its decision must be conveyed to the Regional Representative Council in question.

(3) When a Regional Representative Council decision under the terms of par. (1) is not approved, the Minister or the appropriate Executive Council must give a suffi-

cient explanation to the Representative Council in question.

(4) In the case of such a rejection the Legislative Council in question may, within a month from the receipt of information concerning the rejection, appeal to the Executive Council above the Executive Council which rejected the decision. If the rejection was made by a first-level Executive Council, the appeal may be made to the Minister, and if the rejection was made by the Minister, the appeal may be made to the President.

Article 64

The decision of the Regional Representative Council or the Regional Executive Council may, if it conflicts with the general interest, a law, a Government Regulation, or a Regional Regulation of a higher level, be delayed or revoked by the Minister or an authority designated by him in the case of first-level regions and by the next highest Regional Executive Council in the case of other regions.

Article 65

(1) The Minister or an authority designated by him may delay or revoke decisions of a Regional Representative Council or of a Regional Executive Council of Levels II and III if they conflict with higher legislation or with the general interest, if it is clear that the first-level Executive Council empowered to take such action under Article 64 has failed to do so.

(2) A revocation as provided in par. (1) is made after hearing from the Executive Council which was empowered to take the action.

Article 69

(1) The government supervises the execution of regional government, the method of supervision to be laid down by Government Regulation.

APPENDIX D

Extracts from Presidential Edict No. 6 of 1959 (as "perfected" in November 1959)

Article 1

The regional government is composed of the Regional Head and the Regional Representative Council.

Article 2

In executing his tasks the Regional Head is assisted by a Daily Government Board.

Article 3

The term Regional Head includes the Regional Head of the Special Region of Jogjakarta, except where otherwise stated.

Article 4

(1) The Regional Head is appointed and dismissed by (a) the President for first-level regions and (b) the Minister of Home Affairs and Regional Autonomy, with the agreement of the President, for second-level regions.

(2) A first-level Regional Head is appointed by the President from candidates nominated by the Regional Representative Council concerned. In cases where this nomination does not include any candidate who fulfills the conditions for appointment as Regional Head, the Regional Representative Council in question is

asked by the Minister of Home Affairs and Regional Autonomy in the name of the President to nominate a second list of candidates. If the second list of candidates also fails to include a candidate who fulfills the conditions, the President will appoint the Regional Head from outside those candidates.

(3) The Regional Head of a second-level region is appointed by the Minister of Home Affairs and Regional Autonomy, with the agreement of the President, from candidates nominated by the Regional Representative Council in question. In cases where this nomination does not include any candidate who fulfills the conditions for appointment as Regional Head, the Regional Representative Council in question is asked by the Minister of Home Affairs and Regional Autonomy, with the agreement of the President, to nominate a second list of candidates. If the second list of candidates also fails to include a candidate who fulfills the conditions, the President will appoint the Regional Head from outside the list of candidates.

(4) The appointment of Regional Head, as set down in pars. (2) and (3) of this Article, will operate having regard to conditions of education, ability, and governmental experience which will be determined in a Presidential Regulation.

(5) The Regional Head is a state civil servant whose office and title, position, and remuneration will be determined subsequently in a Presidential Regulation.

(6) The Regional Head is appointed for one term of office equal to the term of office of the Regional Representative Council concerned, but may be reappointed at the end of that term.

(7) The Regional Head cannot be dismissed as a result of a decision of the Regional Representative Council.

Article 9

The Daily Government Board is composed of at least three, and at the most five, members, except in circumstances set down in Article 19.

Article 10

(1) Members of the Daily Government Board are appointed and dismissed according to regulations which will be issued by the Minister of Home Affairs and Regional Autonomy.

(2) Members of the Daily Government Board referred to in par. (1) will be appointed as far as possible from candidates nominated by the Regional Representative Council in question from the membership of that Council or from beyond it.

Article 13

For the time being the establishment of Regional Representative Councils will be ordered on the basis of existing legislation.

Article 14

(1) The Regional Head is (a) an instrument of the central government, (b) an instrument of the regional government.

(2) As an instrument of the central government the Regional Head

(a) controls the order and general security of the region;

(b) carries out co-ordination between central government offices in the region and between those offices and the regional government;

(c) supervises the execution of regional government;

(d) exercises other general powers belonging to the sphere of central government.

From (a) to (d) include matters which, under existing legislation and regulation, are executed up to the present time by the Governor for first-level regions and by the *bupati*/mayor for second-level regions.

(3) As an instrument of regional government the Regional Head is responsible to the Regional Representative Council, both in the sphere of regional household affairs and in that of assistance in government [*medebewind*], with the understanding that the Regional Head may not be dismissed by a decision of the Regional Representative Council.

Article 15

(1) The Head of a first-level region possesses the power to delay decisions of the first-level Regional Representative Council and decisions of second-level regional governments when, in his opinion, they conflict with the main lines of state policy, the general interest, or legislation of a higher level.

(2) A second-level Regional Head possesses the power to delay a decision of the Regional Representative Council, Level II, when in his opinion it conflicts with the main lines of state policy, the general interest, or legislation of a higher level.

(3) Without lessening the power to delay or veto decisions of first- and second-level regional governments which, in his view, are considered to conflict with the main lines of state policy, the general interest, or higher legislation, the Minister of Home Affairs and Regional Autonomy may make a decision concerning decisions which are delayed under pars. (1) and (2) of this Article.

Article 16

(1) Members of the Daily Government Board are assistants to the Regional Head in matters within the field of regional household affairs (autonomy) and in that of assistance in government [*medebewind*].

(2) Members of the Daily Government Board (a) give advice to the Regional Head, whether solicited or not, (b) execute specified duties assigned to them by the Regional Head, and concerning these are responsible to the Regional Head.

(3) When he considers it necessary, the Regional Head may instruct a member of the Daily Government Board to give, in his name, information to the Regional Representative Council concerning the work which falls within its field.

Article 18

(1) The existing Regional Representative Councils will become Regional Representative Councils under this Presidential Edict subject to the decision that members will take an oath or affirmation before the Minister of Home Affairs and Regional Autonomy or his deputy.

Article 19

Existing Regional Executive Councils are abolished and the ex-members thereof may be appointed as members of Daily Government Boards except where they indicate that they are not prepared to be so appointed.

Article 21

The management of regional government in the field of autonomy and of assistance in government will remain in force on the basis of the arrangements laid down by Law 1/57, except where they conflict with a decision of this Presidential Edict.

Article 22

Conditions which arise as a result of the execution of this Presidential Edict will be settled by the Minister of Home Affairs and Regional Autonomy.

Glossary of Indonesian Terms

abangan, element in Javanese society which is merely nominally Moslem and which adheres rather to pre-Moslem Javanese beliefs. (From *abang,* elder brother.)

Badan Pemerintah Harian, Daily Executive Board.

berimbang, in proportion, balanced.

Biro Devisen Perdagangan (BDP), Foreign Exchange Bureau.

bukti ekspor (BE), certificate representing a claim to foreign currency earned by an export. (Lit. "proof of export.")

bupati, regent, chief administrative officer of a *kabupaten* (formerly regency).

daerah, region. The term was also used to denote a specific type of regional division created within the State of East Indonesia, 1946–1950.

daerah istimewa, special region.

desa, village complex in Java and Bali.

dewan, council.

Dewan Nasional, National Council (created 1947).

Dewan Pemerintah Daerah (DPD), Regional Executive Council.

Dewan Pertimbangan Agung, Supreme Advisory Council—organ provided for in the 1945 Constitution.

Dewan Perwakilan Rakjat (DPR), People's Representative Council, i.e., Parliament.

Dewan Perwakilan Rakjat Daerah (DPRD), Regional Representative Council.

fraksi, group in Parliament or in local councils which acts together. A *fraksi* may be a party or a group of parties or of individuals.

gotong rojong, mutual help.

gubernur, governor.

jajasan, institution, enterprise.

Jajasan Kopra, Copra Foundation.

Jajasan Kelapa Minahasa, Minahasa Coconut Foundation.

kabupaten, administrative subdivision of a Residency and itself divided into districts; formerly regency. (Administrative official—*bupati.*)

kelurahan, village complex in Java (in some cases coincident with *desa*) which elects its own administrative officer, the *lurah.*

kementerian, ministry. (From *menteri,* minister.)

Kementerian Dalam Negeri, Ministry of Home Affairs.

kepala daerah, regional head.

keresidenan, residency.

ketjamatan, subdistrict—territorial division embracing a number of villages. (Administrative official—*tjamat* or assistant *wedana.*)

kewedanaan, district—territorial division of a *kabupaten* and itself composed of a group of *ketjamatan.* (Administrative official—*wedana.*)

komisaris, commissioner.

kota, town, city, municipality.

kota besar, large municipality.

kota ketjil, small municipality.

kotapradja, municipality.

lurah, administrative officer of the Javanese or Sundanese *desa* or *kelurahan,* elected by the village itself.

Madjelis Permusjawaratan Rakjat, People's Deliberative Assembly. Under the 1945 Constitution it embodied popular sovereignty.

marga, the regional community of South Sumatra.

medebewind, the power of a local government to perform duties delegated to it by the central government or by a higher level of local government.

mufakat, the practice of reaching decisions by discussion and consensus.

negara, state.

Negara Indonesia Timur (NIT), State of East Indonesia. This entity was established by the Dutch in 1946 and eventually was constituted as a state of the Republic of the United States of Indonesia, 1949–1950. It was absorbed into the unitary Republic of Indonesia in August 1950.

negeri, country; also the village community of Minangkabau.

otonomi, autonomy.

padjak, tax.

pamong pradja, territorial administrative service of the central government.

Paruman Agung, (1) council of Balinese rulers established in 1938; (2) council established in Daerah Bali in 1947 consisting of representatives from each *swapradja.*

Paruman Negara, advisory council established in each of the Balinese principalities in 1938.

patih, chief secretarial official of a *kabupaten,* next in rank under the *bupati.*

pedukuhan, hamlet, a part of a Javanese *desa.*

pegawai, civil servant.

pemerintah, government.

penetapan, decision, edict.

Peperda, abbreviation for *Pe*nguasa *Per*ang *Da*erah—Regional Military Authority.

peralihan, transitional.

peraturan, regulation.

peraturan pemerintah, government regulation.

prijaji, member of Javanese aristocracy.

rumah tangga, household.

sementara, for the time being, provisional.

serikat, bound together, united.
suku bangsa, a people, ethnic group.
swapradja, self-governing principality.
swatantra, self-governing unit.
tingkat, level, grade.
tjamat, subdistrict officer, in charge of a *ketjamatan*.
wali kota, mayor, official in charge of a municipality.
wedana, district officer, in charge of a *kewedanaan*.

Bibliography

LEGISLATION

Basic Laws

Basic law concerning regional government: RI Law 22 of 1948.

Basic law concerning regional government in the State of East Indonesia: NIT Law 44 of 1950.

Law concerning the bases of regional government: Law 1 of 1957.

Law concerning the election of members of the regional representative councils of provinces and the regions within them: Law 7 of 1950.

Law concerning the election of members of regional representative councils: Law 19 of 1956.

Law concerning the financial equilibrium between the state and the self-governing regions: Law 32 of 1956.

Establishing Legislation

FIRST-LEVEL REGIONS

North Sumatra: Government Regulation in place of law, 5/1950.

Central Sumatra: Government Regulation in place of law, 4/1950.

South Sumatra: Government Regulation in place of law, 3/1950.

Atjeh: Law 24/1956.

Djambi, Riau, West Sumatra: Emergency Law 19/1957

Djakarta Raya: Republic of the United States of Indonesia, Presidential Decision 125/1950, and RUSI, Emergency Law 20/1950.

West Java: Law 11/1950.

Central Java: Law 10/1950.

East Java: Law 2/1950.

Jogjakarta: Law 3/1950.

Kalimantan: Emergency Law 2/1953.

West Kalimantan, South Kalimantan, East Kalimantan: Law 25/1956.

Central Kalimantan: Emergency Law 10/1957.

Maluku: Emergency Law 22/1957.

East Nusa Tenggara, West Nusa Tenggara, Bali: Law 14/1958.

West Irian: Emergency Law 20/1957.

North Sulawesi, South Sulawesi: Government Regulation in place of law, 47/60.

SECOND-LEVEL REGIONS

Kabupatens in West Java: Law 14/1950.

Kabupatens in Central Java: Law 13/1950.

Kabupatens in East Java: Law 12/1950.

Kabupatens in Jogjakarta: Law 15/1950.

Large municipalities in West, Central, and East Java and Jogjakarta: Law 16/1950.

Small municipalities in West, Central, and East Java: Law 17/1950.

Kabupatens and large municipalities in Kalimantan: Emergency Law 3/1953.

Kabupatens in South Sumatra: Emergency Law 4/1956.

Large municipalities in South Sumatra: Emergency Law 5/1956.

Small municipalities in South Sumatra: Emergency Law 6/1956.

Kabupatens in North Sumatra and Atjeh: Emergency Law 7/1956.

Large municipalities in North Sumatra and Atjeh: Emergency Law 8/1956.

Small municipalities in North Sumatra and Atjeh: Emergency Law 9/1956.

Kabupatens in Central Sumatra: Law 12/1956.

Large municipalities in Central Sumatra: Law 8/1956.

Small municipalities in Central Sumatra: Law 9/1956.

Second-level regions in Maluku: Law 23/1957.

Second-level regions in West Nusa Tenggara, East Nusa Tenggara, and Bali: Law 69/1958.

Second-level regions in North Sulawesi and South Sulawesi: Law 29/59.

SELECTED LIST OF BOOKS, PAMPHLETS, AND ARTICLES

Amrah Muslimin. "Otonomi Daerah dalam Negara Kesatuan Republik Indonesia sedjak 17/8/1950 hingga 18/1/1957," *Swatantra*, Nov. 1957.

Amrah Muslimin. *Pemerintahan Daerah menurut Perundangan Terachir* (*Tahun 1957*). Djakarta, 1957.

Badri, J. *Otonomi Daerah Masalah dan Beberapa Perbandingan.* Djakarta.

Bruine, J. de. "Istilah² dalam Undang² perimbangan keuangan antara pemerintah pusat dan daerah²," *Ekonomi dan Keuangan Indonesia,* March 1954.

Bruine, J. de. "Pembajaran², subsidi², dan tundjangan² kepada daerah dalam lingkungan hubungan keuangan," *Ekonomi dan Keuangan Indonesia,* Feb. 1954.

Djody Gondokusumo. *Tatahukum Daerah Otonom.* Jogjakarta, 1950.

Dris, M. D. "Taxation in Indonesia," *Ekonomi dan Keuangan Indonesia,* Aug.–Sept. 1958.

Feith, H. *The Indonesian Elections of 1955.* (Cornell Modern Indonesia Project, Interim Reports Series.) Ithaca, 1957.

Feith, H. *The Wilopo Cabinet, 1952–53.* (Cornell Modern Indonesia Project, Monograph Series.) Ithaca, 1958.

Finkelstein, Laurence S. "The Indonesian Federal Problem," *Pacific Affairs,* XXX, no. 3 (Sept. 1957).

Fryer, D. W. "Economic Aspects of Indonesian Unity," *Pacific Affairs,* XXX, no. 3 (Sept. 1957).

Geertz, Clifford. "Religious Belief and Economic Behavior in a Central Javanese Town: Some Preliminary Considerations," *Economic Development and Cultural Change,* Jan. 1956.

Haar, B. ter. *Adat Law in Indonesia.* New York, 1948.

Jaquet, L. G. M. "The Indonesian Federal Problem Reconsidered," *Pacific Affairs,* XXV, no. 2 (June 1952), 170.

Jay, Robert R. "Local Government in Rural Central Java," *Far Eastern Quarterly,* XV, no. 2 (Feb. 1956).

Kat Angelino, A. D. A. de. *Colonial Policy.* Abbr. trans. by G. J. Renier in collaboration with the author. The Hague, 1931.

Kongres Desentralisasi Daerah² Otonom Selurah Indonesia ke I. *Menudju Otonomi jang Sempurna.* Bandung, 1955.

Legge, J. D. "Central Supervision and Local Government in Indonesia," *Australian Journal of Politics and History,* III, no. 1 (Nov. 1957).

Legge, J. D. *Problems of Regional Autonomy in Contemporary Indonesia.* (Cornell Modern Indonesia Project, Interim Reports Series.) Ithaca, 1957.

Maryanov, Gerald S. *Decentralization in Indonesia: Legislative Aspects.* (Cornell Modern Indonesia Project, Interim Reports Series.) Ithaca, 1957.

Maryanov, Gerald S. *Decentralization in Indonesia as a Po-*

litical Problem. (Cornell Modern Indonesia Project, Interim Reports Series.) Ithaca, 1958.

Middendorp, W. "The Administration of the Outer Provinces of the Netherlands Indies," in B. Schrieke, ed., *The Effect of Western Influence on Native Civilisations in the Malay Archipelago.* Batavia, 1929.

Nasroen, M. *Daerah Otonomi Tingkat Terbawah.* Djakarta, 1956.

Nungtjik, A. R., *et al. Menudju Otonomi Daerah seluas-luasnja.* Vol. I, A. R. Nungtjik; vol. II, R. Pardede; vol. III, Hutomo Supardan Harjowisastro and J. Piry. Djakarta, 1958.

Otonomi dan Daerah Otonoom. Djakarta, 1953.

Paauw, Douglas S. *Financing Economic Development: The Indonesian Case.* (For Massachusetts Institute of Technology.) Illinois, 1960.

Paauw, Douglas S. "The Role of Local Finance in Indonesian Economic Development," *Ekonomi dan Keuangan Indonesia,* Jan. 1955.

Pauker, Guy J. "The Role of Political Organizations in Indonesia," *Far Eastern Survey,* Sept. 1958.

Samadikoen, R. *Decentralisatie dan Pelaksanaannja.* Surabaja, 1958.

Schiller, A. Arthur. *The Formation of Federal Indonesia, 1945–1949.* The Hague and Bandung, 1955.

Schrieke, B. *Indonesian Sociological Studies: Selected Writings of B. Schrieke.* 2 vols. The Hague and Bandung, 1955–1957.

Skinner, G. William, ed. *Local, Ethnic, and National Loyalties in Village Indonesia.* (Yale University, Cultural Report Series, Southeast Asia Studies.) New Haven, 1959.

Soedjatmoko. "The Role of Political Parties in Indonesia," in P. W. Thayer, ed., *Nationalism and Progress in Free Asia.* Baltimore, 1956.

Soempono Djojowadono. *Demokrasi dalam Masa Pembangunan di Indonesia.* Jogjakarta, 1958.

Soenarjo Dipodiningrat. *Pembentukan Daerah Otonom Tingkat ke III.* Jogjakarta, 1956.

Soenarjo Dipodiningrat. *Proces Demokratiseering dan Otonomiseering Pemerintahan di Daerah Istimewa Jocjakarta.* Jogjakarta, 1954.

Soepardi. *Anggaran Keuangan Daerah.* Djakarta, 1955.

Swatantra: Madjalah Bulanan Balai Pembangunan Daerah. Djakarta, 1957.

Ulinski, John A. *Some Aspects of Local Government in Indonesia.* Mimeograph. Sept. 1954.

Usep Ranawidjaja. *Swapradja: Sekarang dan Dihari Kemudian.* Djakarta, 1955.

Widaja Soeriadiradja. *Himpunan Peraturan-Peraturan mengenai Pemerintahan Daerah Swatantra.* Djakarta, 1953.

Widjojo Nitisastro and J. E. Ismael. *The Government, Economy, and Taxes of a Central Javanese Village.* (Cornell Modern Indonesia Project, Monograph Series.) Ithaca, 1959.

Yamin, Muhammad. *Proklamasi dan Konstitusi Republik Indonesia.* Djakarta and Amsterdam, 1957.

Index